Will The REAL MEN... Please STAND UP!

A NINE STEP PLAN FOR LASTING ROMANCE AND PASSION

An empowering, compassionate and realistic guide to achieving happiness, fulfillment and inner peace in your relationships.

Ella Patterson

Author of **#1** bestseller *Will The Real Women Please Stand Up* and *1001 Reasons To Think Positive!*

Will The
REAL MEN...
Please
STAND UP!

Other books written by Ella Patterson

Will The Real Women... Please Stand Up!
1001 Reasons To Think Positive.
1001 <u>MORE</u> Reasons To Think Positive

Dedicated to my loving brothers:
Herbert Leon
Richard Renord
Miland Lamont
Vincent Orlando
Melton Ramone

and my beloved son
Martin III

Will The Real Men... Please Stand Up!

A Nine Step Plan For Lasting Romance and Passion

Ella Patterson

Knowledge Concepts Publishing, Inc.

Will The Real <u>Men</u>... Please Stand Up!,© by Ella Patterson
Published by Knowledge Concepts Publishing
P. O. Box 973   Cedar Hill, Texas 75104-0973
A division of Knowledge Concepts Educational Systems, Inc.

Copyright © June 1999 by Ella Jones-Patterson
All rights reserved. Printed in the United States of America

All stories in this book are true, but names and circumstances are been changed to protect the identities of the persons involved.

ISBN: 1-884331-11-4

All rights reserved. No part of this book may be reproduced or transmitted in any form. Nor by any means electronic or mechanical, including photocopy, recording, or by any information storage and retrieval system, without the subsequent written permission of the copyright author, or the publisher. For information address: Knowledge Concepts Educational Services, P. O. Box 973, Cedar Hill, Texas 75104

Library of Congress Cataloging in Publication Data
Ella Jones Patterson,
Will The Real <u>Men</u>...Please Stand Up!: a guide for lasting romance and passion / Ella Patterson -1st ed.
     p.   cm.
     ISBN: 1-884331-11-4

1. Romance.	2. Passion.	3. Sexuality	4. Dating	5. Relationships
6. Hygiene	7. Spirituality.	I. Patterson, Ella.		II. Title.
				95-94105
				CIP

Printed in The United States of America
This book includes an index
Quotes obtained from *1001 Reasons To Think Positive* by Ella Patterson
1999 -- First Edition
10 9 8 7 6 5 4 3 2 1

Table of Contents

		Acknowledgments	
		Introduction	1
	1.	Starting Over	6
Step 1.		**GETTING REAL**	
	2.	Get A Real Life	14
	3.	Real Men: Image or Myth	22
	4.	What Do Men Really Want From Women?	30
Step 2.		**TAKING ACTION**	
	5.	How To Take Action	35
	6.	How To Communicate Better With Women	42
	7.	How To Find The Woman You Want	46
	8.	How To Get The Woman You Want	541
	9.	40 Ways To Make Your Move On Her	59
	10.	How To Use Your Resources To Get Her	72
	11.	How To Sensuously Work A Room	76
Step 3.		**UNDERSTANDING WOMEN**	
	12.	What Real Women Really Want!	83
	13.	Women Who Scare Men Off	87
	14.	Women Who Don't Call	93
	15.	Women Who Talk Too Much	97
	16.	Promiscuous Women	100
	17.	Getting Your Way With Her	105
Step 4.		**IMPROVING YOUR RELATIONSHIPS**	
	18.	Creating Enduring Relationships	112
	19.	Making Healthier Relationship Choices	115
	20.	Relationship Boosters	122
	21.	What Drives The Sexes Crazy	128
	22.	Is She Really The Woman For You	134
	23.	Signs That Point To Ms. Wrong	138

	24.	Older Women -- Younger Men	145
Step 5.		**LEARNING TO ROMANCE**	
	25.	The Magic of Romance	152
	26.	Keeping The Mystery Alive	163
	27.	Searching For Real Good Love	166
	28.	How Men Are Attracted To Women	172
	29.	Creating Your Own Paradise	178
	30.	Finding Healthy Intimacy	
	181		
Step 6.		**PRACTICING HYGIENE & ETHICS**	
	31.	Hygiene and Personal Ethics	188
	32.	Your Sexual Ethics	193
	33.	Taking Care of Yourself	198
Step 7.		**DISCOVERING THE ARTS**	
	34.	The Art of Touching	211
	35.	The Art of Kissing	214
	36.	The Art of Relaxing Baths	223
Step 8.		**PRACTICING SPIRITUALITY**	
	37.	Healing Your Relationships Through Prayer	229
Step 9.		**CELEBRATING YOUR SEXUALITY**	
	38.	Couples and Sexual Responsibility	237
	39	Rekindle The Passion	243
	40.	Real Sexual Fears Men Have	282
	41.	Helpful Sex Tips	248
	42.	Have Condom Sense	254
		After Thought: Celebrate Your Relationships	259
		Will The Real Men Please Stand Up! DISCUSSION TOPICS	267
		About The Author	
		Index	

ACKNOWLEDGMENTS

I would like to first give honor to God. I am blessed for being allowed to continue to serve as an instrument for empowering people.

Scores of people contributed to the publication of this manual. One of the things I've found when I try to thank everyone who's helped in the smallest way is... I don't have enough room to thank them all. I would have to start at my birth and give acknowledgment to everyone who has come into my life from the very beginning. It is those wonderful memories and energies that have taught me that through God all things are possible. Here's a partial list of those who helped to make my dreams come true.

To Ken Knight and his wonderful staff at Knight Graphics -- thanks for helping me get my act together. You never complained and you gave me the freedom to work at my pace until I got it right. To Herbert Jones Jr., my brother -- thanks for keeping me grounded. Special hugs and kisses to my son, Martin III who understood my thirst for writing and gave me the biggest and the best hugs. You are special to me. To Allen *"Buster"* Wilbon III -- (odckua) you've always been my best friend...*What a man, what a man what a mighty good man.* To my friend 'then and now'-- Ms. Debra Jemison-Hollins, thanks for helping me understand why I can always feel more than I can see. To my friend Robert Corley, thanks for being there when I was aware and unaware of your presence. To Levon Harrington, my new-found friend; you served as my think tank when others laughed at my ideas. You also gave me insight and a commonsense approach when I was confused about why individuals do the things they do. My love sings out to Craig Gilliam, who taught me at an early age how to love <u>me</u> more. Samuel Brown, thanks for keeping me on track. Pat thanks for sharing the journey with me. Much gratitude to Jan Miller, my literary agent who saw my vision and let me go at it.

I also want to thank several of my teachers for nurturing my skills and the love I have for writing. Ms. Doris Massenburg, my ninth grade teacher, you always encouraged me to write. Thanks to my professors at Bishop College who are forever in my heart, they helped me unleash my hidden talents. I offer a prayer of peace and love to all my friends.

To all of those wonderful people that helped my literary dreams and goals come forth: Susan Taylor, Michelle Griffith of Essence Magazine, Bob Asahina, Tom Joyner, Doug Banks, Willis Johnson, Roland Martin, Denise McVea, Chuck Smith, Micheal Baisden, Nanette Lee, Skip Murphy, Sam Putney, The Wig, Chris Arnold, Renee McMillian, Sandra Daniels, Y-Vonne St. John, and Scott West. Thanks a bunch.

I am thankful to magazines, journals and television shows that helped me get the word out about my book: VIBE, Good Morning Texas, Good Day Dallas, Home and Family, Lezza Gibbons, Sinbad, Gladys Knight, Les Brown, Montel Williams, Ricki Lake, Essence, Upscale, Cosmopolitan, Black Elegance, Today's Black Woman, Our Texas, Onyx, Dallas Morning News, Dallas Times Herald, Dallas Observer, Ft Worth Star Telegram, and many others all over the world.

My sincere love and honor go out to thousands of individuals who purchased my self-published books and helped blast me to the best seller list. A heartfelt thanks to all the book stores for giving me shelf space when no one else would. I sincerely thank the participants of my relationship seminars who shared their stories and encouragd me to write this book. Their support and thousands of letters continue to support me in developing and validating the principles of this book. I know they are as proud of the part they have played in the development of "entrepreneurial publishing" as they are of their contributions to this work.

I give thanks to God for the opportunity to make a difference in this world and the wisdom that comes to me is presented in this book.

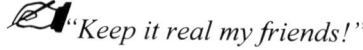*"Keep it real my friends!"*

-ella

INTRODUCTION

She wants love and passion. He wants sex and more sex. Sex seems to be more important to men while romance and passion are more important to women, but we can't understand why. Since it seems as though men and women really do think differently this book will focus on helping couples understand how to connect with each other.

In the early 90's I completed my book *Will The Real <u>Women</u>...Please Stand Up!* While working on it, I discovered that women wanted romance, passion and intimacy. Men want sex, sexuality and eroticism.

Along with these desires women wanted men to see them as intelligent and nurturing beings. Will The Real Women...Please Stand Up, was written to help women accept their sexuality in wholesome and nurturing ways. It was an attempt to inform, educate and inspire women to give him more by showing love, attention and passion.

After completing Will The Real Women, I pondered on what I should write about next. I thought it would be a great idea to write a book that would help inspire men improve their relationships with women. From these thoughts *Will The Real <u>Men</u>...Please Stand Up!* was born. I got the idea early one morning, jumped out of bed and started writing immediately. It sort of took over me. That's the same way relationships are. They take over you. Relationships have a way of overwhelming and controlling you without reason.

Couple will read this book and discover they've been doing many things wrong that they thought they were doing right. Keeping in mind all the things couples have been doing wrong has encouraged me to write this book. Men will finally realize that the best way to find the woman of their dreams is to began with themselves first. With this book couples will discover that in order to have a successful relationship they must first have a good relationship with self.

As I continued to work on *Will The Real <u>Men</u>...Please Stand Up!* I discovered that men were so busy trying to deal with their own relationship issues that they forgot about how their partner felt. Men were eager to know things like... What is a real man from a woman's point of view? How do I start over after a break-up? What calls for a separation or divorce? How do I get rid of my most devastating fears? How do I improve myself and participate in my own life? How do I go about getting the woman I want once I find her? How do I make positive moves on women? How do I create an enduring and lasting relationship? What are the signs that point to Ms. Wrong? How do I effectively practice personal ethics?, and How do I bring spirituality into my relationships?

After interviewing hundreds of couples the majority of them wanted the world to know that their primary concerns have been neglected by the people they love the most -- *their partner*. The reoccurring question I hear most from men is: "Where are all the good women?" Women are asking similiar questions as well. What couples really want-- more than anything else is support from one another.

Will The Real Men...Please Stand Up!, is designed to help men understand their intimate reltionships better. It is not the rewards of knowing what it takes to be a real man, but the process by which it comes to be known. This is the book that separates the "real men" from the "boys". This book helps men communicate with women more effectively and it gives solutions to problems men have encountered in their relationships. It answers questions that men have been afraid to ask about women.

Women may not recognize the depth of my love for men with this book, but then again these are unconventional valentines between these pages. *"His secret garden is not from Mars and hers is not from Venus!"* A man's desires might be similar to a woman's, but his needs are very different. Don't get me wrong, women and men may move their bodies in sync, and they might dance to each others rhythm, but the truth of the matter is -- men and women are different when they demonstrate love and affection. They travel the same sensuous journeys in life, but they get there on different roads.

Women don't understand men completely, at least that's what the men say and I've found that many men don't understand themselves. Men need love and support in different ways. Many times men and women do not clearly know what their needs are or how to have them met. Rather than feel frustrated all the time they just give up on their relationship. For example, women need to ask questions about their relationships in order

WILL THE REAL MEN PLEASE STAND UP

to feel the love and support she wants, whereas a man will feel annoyed and pressured if he is asked questions. When he doesn't communicate what he needs from her she feels confused, lonely, abandoned or hurt. He learns independence and self-reliance and considers them to reign supreme among all other values. He feels a need to be in control. The result of this theory causes men to grow up in our society feeling innately, internally alone. He cannot ever imagine having to go for help and considers it an option. What a shame!

The perfect way to illustrate the essence of this book is through it's simple title. *Will The Real Men...Please Stand Up!* It's written to show that men are much *more* than a failed relationship and they are definitely not a bad habit, as women have stated. They are God's creation, uniquely composed of mind, body and spirit. *Will The Real Men...Please Stand Up!* is an affirmation of all the dimensions of man.

"Everything is not for everyone, but I guarantee there is something for every one in this book." Some of the questions and answers will not be easy for you to digest. *Will The Real Men...Please Stand Up!*, was not written to make it politically correct or ask men to settle for less in women. It is not a book that seeks to pacify couples into believing you must agree with everything I say. Simply put -- this book is real and it's about real life situations and real life couples!

As you read *Will The Real Men...Please Stand Up!*, remember that it comes from a perspective of love and healing. It is an attempt to help men understand women and women understand men by incorporating better images of what positive relationships should be.

How To Share This Book With Your Partner

This an fun-filled informative book and not difficult to understand. It's an easy read with short chapters so that you can put the book down and practice the skills with your partner.

If a woman suggest to a man that he read this book, it is important that she doesn't try to force him or make him feel she wants their sex life to get better. It sounds like a cut-down to him and it makes him feel as though he's not good enough or that he needs to make improvements. He'll feel insulted if approached this way.

Instead, she should say let's read this book about love and passion. It really is informative, fun and is a really good book. Let's read it to one another. He'll respond positively if he thinks she wants to try new things instead of insisting he learns new things.

When a man approaches a woman about reading this book, he should remember not to insist she read it either. If she refuses he can read it on his own and began to practice the skills involved. As he succeeds in practicing the skills in this book she will be much more willing to read it.

If your partner resist, gracefully say OK and read the book yourself. Eventually both partners will become interested in what the other one is reading once they see it's about making their relationship better.

If your partner is not interested, place the book in strategic places in the bedroom or bathroom and they will be more willing to pick up and read it without you having to keep suggesting it.

You can either read it with or without your partner. As you read parts that you particularly like express your delight, but don't overdo it. Share the ideas that you have been avoiding for fear of sounding critical or controlling. Eventually, it will improve your communication. Reading about skills that can improve your relationship in and out of the bedroom will give both partners plenty of new approaches to practice with. The newness can assist couples in experiencing new passion.

Some of these skills or approaches may be desirable to you, but not to your partner. That's perfectly normal, and in some cases, over time your partner may change and begin to like some of the things you suggest and not like others.

Its important that you do not make demands of your partner or do something your partner doesn't like or want. Romance, passion and intimacy are precious gifts that couples give to each other when they want to express their love.

There are important factors in successful relationships that couples should began paying attention to. One of them is their mate's needs. You can do this by taking the information and use the parts you like, as if you are selecting from a menu. Remember everyone won't like the same things. You would not want to be forced to wear or eat something you don't like, so don't force your partner to do things she doesn't like.

For romance and passion to grow over time, it is important that couples not feel they are being judged or criticized for what they desire. Approach intimacy in a nonjudgemental manner.

When it comes to taste, in everything from hot dogs to architecture, one man's floor is another man's ceiling. Rather than mark this celebration of men with a collection of antidotes, this book contributes bits of wisdom that work for successful men in their relationships and how they came by this knowledge. Above all, *Will The Real Men...Please Stand Up*!, is a gift of love for couples.

These are the best of times for couples and their relationships. I offer this book as a reminder of many of the things you might already know. I have benefited from each of the ideas I present to you. I hope this book will help inform, inspire and entertain you for the rest of your days to come.

Romance and passion are gift's from God. They are a part of your blessing, and you deserve it. So come on let's get started, enjoy your journey!

"Wisdom is a continuing process."
It's similar to the human life cycle -- constantly growing, changing and improving.

1
STARTING OVER

Through change sometimes you are forced to gain a new start.

In the movie Regarding Henry, Harrison Ford plays a successful lawyer with a lucrative career, a gorgeous home, a beautiful wife and daughter. But Henry's life is not nearly as sweet as it seems. He is dedicated to his work, his marriage is a wreck and he has no relationship with his daughter. He seeks fulfillment in power, wealth, possessions, and even an adulterous affair -- but his life remains a hollow shell.

Then one day everything changes. Walking into a grocery store, Henry interrupts a robbery in progress and is shot in the head. He survives, but sustains brain damage and loses his memory.

The movie then focuses on Henry's effort to recover from his brain damage. Two people helped him the most: his young daughter, who is learning many things herself; and a physical therapist from the subculture of the inner city, the sort of person the old Henry would have held in disdain. Yet, through the help of these two people, Henry rebuilds his life. He relearns many basic skills of life -- walking, counting, reading, writing. As he learns, he begins to build a relationship with his neglected daughter. He begins to see life in a whole new way.

Henry makes a noble effort to get back to his former life of a high-powered lawyer. He makes amazing progress, but he just doesn't fit into the lifestyle anymore. Ironically, it's not his brain damage that ruins his comeback; it's the growth of his soul. What he has learned about his life prevents him from doing the unscrupulous things he used to do. He finds he cannot resume the affair with his coworker. His logic becomes simple and honest. His law firm just can't tolerate the changes so they fire Henry. As a result, he also loses a number of his high-powered friends. That sets him free to pursue a more honest relationship with those most dear to him -- his wife and daughter.

WILL THE REAL MEN PLEASE STAND UP

Through tragedy, Henry has been forced to gain a fresh start. Through that experience, in a sense, he is reborn -- reborn into a new and better life for him and his family.

Developing productive relationships will create great opportunities to help start a new life. It will help improve those things that need to be changed. Dealing productively with change is better for the man when the woman doesn't react to every situation negatively. As the relationship gets better an enormous amount of stress is released from the couple.

Change comes in many different forms. You experience change through a crisis, breaking up with a lover, getting separated or divorced from your spouse, loosing or changing jobs, or starting over and preparing to live on your own. Change that occurs through crisis is not the change made by choice. It is the type of change induced by circumstances or necessity. Most often this type of change requires a drastic lifestyle modification, resulting in an impact on you and your loved ones.

Change can also occur from the drive to improve situations. Most people refer to this as creative intellectual change. It uses proactive behavior rather than a response to circumstances. This kind of change usually occurs after realizing the present behavior has become unacceptable. This realization usually takes courage, and is considered a positive change. Physical change happens when the decision is made to improve your well-being. It's the kind of change that bolsters ego and improves general health. Internal changes foster better mental and spiritual growth that can include changing from a bad relationship to a new and better one.

Lastly, there are inevitable changes that come with time, whether we want them or not. The facts are facts. As we grow older with each new day; we experience changes in our physical appearance and our mental capacity. I remember reading a great line about this once: *"My mind and body are going in the same direction, but not at the same speed."*

When change is introduced into your life and you need to start over you must be willing to try new ideas and different methods to succeed. Change usually hits life fast and hard and is most often out of our control. Dealing with the ups and downs in life are not easy, but compound bad times with more trials and tribulations and life immediately becomes overwhelmingly intense. However, a lot of what couples learn come from enduring difficult times in their relationships

The Dating Scene

No matter what a man's age; when he finds he has to start over, reenter the work force or the dating scene, he feels very awkward, alone and anxious about what comes next in his life. This might seem like forever to him, especially when all he wants to do is get on with his life. One of his biggest concerns is: how will he reenter the dating scene.

Dating someone new will be scary at first and worrying about almost everything is normal. It's an active part of reshaping to start over. Some of the relationship stresses men find themselves encountered with when starting over are:

* How do I meet new women?
* How much of myself should I reveal to her?
* How do I know if she's right for me?
* Will I still be attractive to the opposite sex?
* Is my age a factor to her?
* Am I still desirable.
* Am I going to ever be comfortable enough to love again?
* Will I ever feel loved again?
* Will this pain ever go away?

These are the same issues you encountered as an eighteen year old, but don't worry you will get through it. Well-intended friends will offer to set you up with dates who they think are right for you, and while these dates may be very nice, available and well mannered, don't get to the point that you feel you are interviewing your potential life mates. One of the biggest mistakes men make when meeting new people is they try to discover a person's attributes, or evaluate them for qualities that they believe they should have. Doesn't sound very romantic does it?

The best thing to do is relax and enjoy single life and before long the spontaneity and adrenaline rush of meeting a new person will develop naturally, without the pressure of forcing it to work. There are times when a man can enter into a new relationship with someone too soon after ending one; such as the loss or divorce of a spouse. This rush to start over can be damaging to an otherwise healthy feeling of security. Take the time to select the right person and the time spent with her will be more enjoyable. It will be fun, unpretentious and caring. Don't try to assign a definition to a new relationship. Just letting it naturally progress is best.

In a new and positive relationship try to develop a safe haven that will help you examine and understand your emotions better. Dating can then become more exciting. This helps you feel free to try new things, share your feelings and get to know the person you're involved with more leisurely.

Entering into a new relationship with preconceived expectations will only set you up to fail. You'll sabotage yourself if you're too busy judging, and not allowing the opportunity to get to know one another honestly. Don't trip yourself up. Try not to strike out on a hunt for your life partner. Enjoy your life instead.

Getting back out there in the dating force can be intimidating, but when you really take a look at your options, you'll only be risking a little to gain a lot. Remind yourself that: every person you meet does not have to be a potential partner. Try to lighten up and have yourself some fun. It might take some time, but your life will come together again.

A Fresh Start

Stuart met Debra in a church singles group, and they quickly became friends. Both were in their early thirties, divorced and emotionally needy. As she talked freely about some recent business failure, he appreciated her openness and vulnerability. Here was a woman he wanted to take care of.

After a lengthy friendship, a romance blossomed, and marriage and children soon followed. Though Debra lacked a formal college education, she had street smarts. With

WILL THE REAL MEN PLEASE STAND UP

Stuart polishing her rough edges, Debra was able to turn her business failures into successes, doing quite well financially. Still, she felt she had more to prove.

Obsessed with her business, Debra began spending more and more time at work and less time at home. When she got home she crashed -- no time for the kind of conversation that had originally brought Debra and Stuart together. She did manage, to have some time for shopping, a hobby she took up with excessive ardor. She would spend all day Saturday shopping, then be "too tired" to go out with Stuart that night.

When Stuart complained, Debra would get defensive. She worked hard to support him and the kids, she said, so she earned her time off.

At first in denial, Stuart bought her explanations. This is just a phase, he figured, but the phase was lasting too long. Grasping for a solution, he tried working with Debra, helping out in the business, but this just added more stress to their marriage. He quit, went back to school, and earned an MBA. Then the anger hit. How dare she! She had sold herself to him as a sensitive, caring woman who would open up about anything and everything in her life, but now she was a stone -- cold, uncaring. How could she neglect their children like that? How could she go off on shopping sprees instead of going with him on a family vacations? How could she keep the family on a poverty-level budget while she spent lavishly on her business and clothing.

Stuart's anger just made her defensive and pushed her further away. He sank into depression, loosing weight and sleep. What was the use? His relationship would never be all he hoped it would be.

When he finished mourning his comatose marriage, Stuart decided to get on with his life. For all practical reasons Debra had deserted her family and there was nothing he could do about it. Yet he still felt divorce was *not* an option. He had committed himself for better or worse, though this was definitely "worse." Still he didn't need to pine away for the marriage he never had. If his wife was going to act like a single person, so would he. Oh, he would remain faithful to her, but he would get a good job to support himself and would make his own social plans. When he threw parties at their home he would invite her to be a part of them, but she usually said no, which didn't surprise him.

WILL THE REAL MEN PLEASE STAND UP

Still Stuart decided he would get a fresh start for him and her kids. If Debra didn't want to participate he would play his own game. She was always welcome to participate, but he wasn't going to wait around on her. As a result he is carving out a reasonably healthy life for himself.

And as you began to practice what you've learned you will find it reinforces your own journey toward a fresh start. Here are some surefire tips that will help you start over.

1. Look for ways to improve yourself.
Ask questions and get additional training or information. Don't rely only on what you've learned from the past. Get in the habit of working continuously to improve your relationship with self and others.

2. Ask for help if you need it.
Don't be afraid to seek help that will move you in the right direction. People are more willing than you think.

3. Avoid being negative or treating others negatively.
Send positive messages to others by having a spirited attitude.

4. Believe in yourself as well as others.
See the good in people by affirming their worth as well as your own.

5. Balance your life between work and home.
Don't be too busy to find ways to improve yourself. Discover the new you.

6. See life as an adventure.
See each other in a new way. Do exciting things with your lover on a regular basis.

7. Value difference.
Understand that your way is not always the best way or the only way.

8.   Take care of yourself.

Exercise daily. Remain healthy mentally by praying and or meditating daily.

9.   Leave a positive impression.

Give good news last. End your conversations on a good note.

10.   Don't gossip to others about your mate.

Men shouldn't. Love who you are and you'll be able to give love to others.

Carve out a reasonably healthy life for yourself.

Step 1:

Getting Real

2
GET A REAL LIFE

The best way to break a bad habit is to drop it.

It's about 6:00 p.m. on Friday and you realize you just put in another fifty hour work week. You grab a six pack of beer on your way home, plop down on your couch with the remote control in one hand and your junk mail in the other. While shuffling through the mail you see another sweepstakes offer that says you've won for the 100th time when you suddenly notice a letter from your partner. You wonder why you've been sent a letter, after all you've dated for more than a year and you've never received a letter.

You tear the letter open and began to frantically read it. The words, "It's over, I've found someone else," causes your heart to skip a few beats and your legs began to feel like jelly. You tell yourself, "This couldn't be true," but it feels like an explosion has just went off in your brain, so it has to be true. You've never felt like this before. It's not like your lover to tell you something of this magnitude in a letter. You've always been able to discuss problems or bad news face to face. You sit back down and you realize the person you've invested all your time, energy, and emotions into has just ended your relationship. It was something you hoped would last forever. After you think for a moment and try to get over the initial shock, you check your call notes to see if there's any messages telling you to disregard the letter. Surely there has to be something about reconsidering or at least something she said to soften the blow. But there's nothing. You feel hurt, rejected and alone.

Several weeks pass, and for some strange reason things aren't getting any better. In fact you still feel emotionally torn, just like you did the day you got the letter. As you fight to work through the pain, you reminisce about your relationship over and over again. You began to talk to yourself. You ask yourself, "What happened?" "What did I do?" "Why didn't I see it coming?" "Why did it have to happen this way?"

WILL THE REAL MEN PLEASE STAND UP

Finally the truth begins to emerge and you realized why your relationship with this person fizzled: you simply did not have a life. This person was your life. Your entire life style was wrapped up in someone else. You see now that all the time you were dating, your life was on hold. Any free time you had was spent with your lover. Your career, your interests, your friends, and even your relationship with God was on hold. Since your relationship has ended you have nothing to sustain you. Without her you have no life.

Sadly I have witnessed far too many scenarios like this one. Thousands of people are trapped in their relationships or never even began them in the first place because they ignore the most important rule: Get a Real Life!

One of the most important things a person can learn from being dumped is -- you have to always maintain a level of life outside of your relationships. A real life! When you invest all of your energy and self-worth in trying to get and keep a mate or simply have just a relationship you don't have a life.

People with full lives are not waiting around to be swept off their feet by some magical person. They have more going for themselves. People with lives do not have to always be in a relationship or on a date to feel good about themselves. People with lives are not church-hopping, bar-hopping, or consulting phone psychics in hopes of finding 'The Right One.' Relationships and ultimately marriages are great goals, but keeping them in perspective is best. Allowing romantic relationships to become the soul purpose in life will definitely cause problems.

If you don't have a life of your own, you won't be happy even if you date, fall in love, and get married. Why? Because you will have nothing to give to the relationship, and you will drain your dating partner completely dry. Inevitably, you will put extraordinary expectations on your mate to fulfill you, complete you, entertain you, and soothe you. No one can perform up to those outlandish expectations.

Before you met your mate, plenty was probably happening in your life. At least for most people it usually is. Have you given up all the things you enjoy doing because you're doing so much for your partner? Do you find yourself waiting by the telephone? Has your life really become your partners life? Once a person gets into a heavy relationship they are consumed and get caught up in their mates agenda. A man might even forget his friends and family until he's caught on the short end of the relationship and his partner decides to move on. This doesn't have to happen. He can show his love and still have a life of his own. Before saying "I do," follow these simple steps. They detail ways to keep your agenda as full as possible when a new person enters your life.

1.   Become More Interesting.
A person will become immediately attracted to you if you carry yourself in an interesting way. Anyone you're interested in will soon recognize after going out with you a few times whether your life is good or bad. If you don't know about anything but your own neighborhood they'll know you're not well versed in taking them to exciting places. If you eat at the little restaurant down the street all the time your date will think you lack skills in different foods or restaurants. If you appear to be boring she'll try other things to remain excited, maybe even other dates. Women are attracted to men whose existence already seem textured and rich. Your date will be delighted because you'll come across as a pretty full package. In other words you have a life -- A Real Life!

2.   Don't Make Yourself Too Available.
Most people love a challenge. When you aren't so accessible it makes your date want you more. When you receive a call to get a date, be sure to let your date know that you'll have to check your calendar. Mutter not so quietly... dinner with Carla, meeting with Bobbie, workout with Alberta, and drinks with Georgia. Be incredibly sweet while your speaking to her though. The trick is to *always* act as if you want to go out again, but you don't know when you can fit it in your schedule. *"Don't just do your date, do other things too."*

3.   Show Your Independence.
Independence is great for romance. The busier you are, the better it is for the both of you. When you show your independence, you're also able to show that you can really take care of yourself. Don't whine or act insecure. No one wants to feel they're at the bottom of your list either. Don't insist on filling up all of your mates time. It's a turn-off.

Having your own life makes you less resentful of your mate. Besides your independence won't allow you worry about the amount of time that's *not* spent with you. What a relief to know that you won't make a big deal out of it.

4.   Let Your Mate Know That Your Life Has Value.
If you are comfortable with your life you won't mind weeding out prospects you don't want. Being unmatched is no big deal for you. You can make dates with the friends you value most and besides it's better than hanging out with people you find a bore, inconsiderate or awful. If you allow yourself to feel empty when your mate is not around it's time to reevaluate your life. If your mate treats you bad when you're dating, imagine what the treatment will be like if you decide to get married. By having more going on for yourself you'll eliminate the problems of non-value and mistreatment.

5.   Pace Yourself.
You have a right to expect your mate to call you on a regular basis, but it's best not to make heavy demands. Wouldn't you feel just a little more suspicious if someone fell desperately in love with you right away?

It's important to go slowly to see if you are a good match. You don't have to turn every encounter into a relationship. Even the most promising relationships need time to develop. You'll feel less rushed and more in control if you slowly slip into romance. After a few weeks you can pick up the pace of the relationship, because you will have given yourself enough time to enjoy your moments together.

6.   Don't Freak Out Because Someone Calls You At The Last Minute.
If you decide to accept a last minute call to have dinner do it only if you don't mind being asked out. If the lack of consideration leaves you upset for the rest of the evening don't go along for the ride no matter how open your schedule is. Otherwise you're likely to let the smallest thing upset you. And that's not the best way to began or end a date.

Many time people have no idea that they're putting you at an inconvenience when they call you at the last minute. They don't recognize it as being rude. Spontaneity is a way of life for many women and they think men like it. If your mate offers little or no notice it's probably a test to see how far they can go. Showing that you won't be put in a position to make hasty decisions will earn your respect. She'll love you more because you know what you want.

7. Make Your Demand For Respect Known.

If you're dating someone who has no regard for time or you the best thing to do at the onset is make an unspoken stand for your respect. A person whose suppose to meet you at six and doesn't show up until eight is not thinking of you or your time. If your mate calls and acts as if it's no big deal and says they're on their way over, here's what you can do. Run an errand, get out of the house and let your mate have to wait on you. Stay away for at least an hour or so. When you get back maybe she'll understand the position you've been put through because she's gone through the same thing. With this simple approach you can back it up by a solid withdrawal -- you've set calm and clear limits. You'll also take back your share of control in the relationship.

8. Pretend To Move At Your Mate's Speed.

Maybe your mate is not misbehaving; just showing less enthusiasm than you'd like to see. When it comes to love, people move at different speeds, so until each of you feel as committed to one another -- which may or may not happen -- you can protect yourself. By matching your mate's level of affection you can move at the same pace. With all the things going on in our lives we can't always keep up with one another. Some people fall in love quicker than others.

By laying back a little and slowing the pace of the relationship you get a better perspective of how serious your relationship might really be. By moving at your partner's pace you won't feel rejected when the response is not what you want. We all need our space from time to time so try your best to respect your partners.

9. **Keep Your Insecurities To Yourself.**

Whatever you do, don't broadcast to the world that the wild things are over. Those anxieties can really take over when you don't get the phone calls as soon as you'd like to, or when your partner decides not to see you again. You've got to get a grip. You don't have to share everything nor do you have be perfect day in and day out. When all is said and done, revealing your insecurity to a new acquaintance will only drive them in the other direction.

10. **Avoid The Frank Discussions.**

Frank discussions don't really mean much if you're going to change your mind by the next day. Having a little uncertainty isn't all that bad. It's exciting. If you analyze everything to the smallest detail you take the fun out of the relationship. Sometimes you just have to go with the flow. Even though this is the opposite of saying no, to last minute callers, you might want to do some things at the last minute. If you find yourself asking questions over and over until you've exhausted your date you won't be a date for long.

11. **Don't Share Every Detail of Your Life.**

Keep your life a little mysterious. It makes you more interesting. If a person knows everything about you too soon, they'll become bored and uninterested. Keeping your mate on her toes adds more allure to the relationship. Certain subjects aren't needed or wanted, at least in the beginning of the relationship.

Benefits of Getting A Real Life

When you have a real life of your own, you are attractive to others. People who exude confidence, stability, and a passion for living draw others like a magnet. This is simply a natural by-product of getting a real life. Getting a real like will make you want to:

1. Gain confidence and enter a relationship that will greatly increase the odds of it being healthy and rewarding. Your capacity for intimacy will be enhanced, and

your ability to handle the challenges that come with relationships will be strengthened.
2. Ensure you don't need your partner to meet your emotional needs and complete you. This frees you to be yourself.
3. Feel content, happy and have inner peace. Become passionate about life. You know who you are, you have a support system, you have direction, and you are seeking to serve others.

Satisfying Your Needs

Just because you're in a relationship, doesn't mean you have to stop taking care of your own needs. Many times your need to be independent within your relationship is not recognized by your partner. Your partner might be a little over protective though. If you receive calls on your job, you get checked up on when you're out with your friends or your partner follows you around, her insecurities might be showing.

It's difficult being in a relationship with a person who can't seem to understand the fact that not only did you have a life before you met, but you also plan on having a life while dating. Couples are realizing more that they need to have separate relationships outside of their romantic relationship. In a relationship everyone should be able to feel that they are still in control of their lives. If your partner doesn't respect your need to maintain friendships outside of your relationship with her you will soon began to feel stifled.

Mutual respect is very important in any relationship. It's the foundation that trust is built upon. If you don't respect each other you won't trust one another. Many people have stated that when their mate doesn't trust them it hinders their independence which causes major problems in the long run.

If you need to spend time by yourself do it, but try your best not to isolate yourself. Spending time with your mate is good, but find time to do things with your family and friends also, like shopping, going to a movie, eating out or club hopping. It simply means you still have a life outside of your romantic relationship. It's important to spend time with other people. This reassures them nothing has changed with their

WILL THE REAL MEN PLEASE STAND UP

friendships or you since you started dating. Many couples also feel that spending time with other people is therapeutic. The time you spend with others also helps fill emotional needs. It helps you keep from becoming totally submersed in a relationship too quickly. In a healthy relationship, it's okay for a couple to have mutual needs that they can fulfill together, but it's always smart to have separate needs. Here's a simple quiz designed to help you recognize if you are headed for problems in the relationship.

1. Do you often cancel previous plans because she said she would call you?
2. Do you rush off the phone just because she's suppose to call?
3. Do you go on a diets because she likes men more fit and trim than you?
4. Do you avoid your friends because she says she doesn't like them?
5. Do you miss doing things with your friends because you're missing out on doing something with her?
6. Do you wear only the clothes that she says she likes to see you in?
7. Do you spend the entire weekend at home just because she's out of town?
8. Do you get rid of your favorite pet just because she doesn't like the way it looks?
9. Does she decide she's going to relocate to a better paying job in another state and when she asks you to come along do you start packing right away?
10. Have you ever caught her having an affair and you blame the person you caught her with?

If you feel that your answer should be yes to these questions you have unwisely placed yourself at your mate's beck and call by having your life revolve around their life. Begin self-appreciation by setting your own individual goals. Find out more about yourself and what you want out of life apart from your mate. Pursue your own interests. Don't erode your self-esteem by giving your power away. Your mate may not even be asking you to do this, but when you think and do things only as a couple you are becoming the dependent party in the relationship. Your mate will value, respect and appreciate you more if you continue to have a life. A Real Life!

Learn to love yourself first, before trying to find a mate.

3
REAL MEN: IMAGE OR MYTH

To have power you must be clear on what you want.

He was dancing with a woman he'd just met at a party, and they seemed to be hitting it off, well until she started trying to lead. First he thought she was making a suggestion -- Let's move toward that corner" or "Why not change the step?"- so he promenaded her across the floor while trying to regain his control. Pretty soon they were in a fierce struggle. Finally, "You're a hard person to lead," he said.

"Why do you have to lead?" she snapped, and she wasn't smiling. I couldn't believe what I was hearing! Why did I have to lead? Why do I pee standing up! All my dancing life, I've prided myself on my ability to take charge and guide without missing a beat. I know nothing about following and am happy in my ignorance. For me to be the passive partner is the weirdest feeling in the world, like signing my name up-side down or going to work in a skirt.

True, many women are no longer dainty things for whom doors must be opened, chairs pulled out, heavy packages lugged. They're capable of carrying their full weight in the workplace, on the dating front (including asking men out), and in the bedroom. The new "millennium woman" even makes explicit demands about the way sex should be performed, but many men still find these behaviors threatening.

Men have reacted to the invasion of the strong woman by falling apart. More men are in therapy today than twenty-five years ago, when feminism first gave women permission to be tough. Others have joined the "men's movement" backlash; they head for the woods, beat drums and revel in their masculinity. Then there are guys who assume typical macho posturing - strong and silent-which ceases to impress when the self-proclaimed brutes experience premature ejaculation. They need to do something a little kinky, like receive a spanking, before they can become aroused. Finally, there are those

WILL THE REAL MEN PLEASE STAND UP

who resent having to do housework, deal with women as colleagues or superiors and worry about politically correct forms of etiquette on a date.

Once secure in their dominance, men these days are disoriented. Asked to abandon their gallant, manly ways, men feel as if the world is a dance floor on which pushy broads are telling them they're no longer allowed to lead.

Myths About Men

"Men!" women can be heard to exclaim in Manhattan cafe's and in the power corridors of Washington. Most of all, "Men!" is an invitation for women to launch into a litany: He's unfaithful and unfeeling, work-crazed and breast-obsessed, can't commit and won't communicate, shuns romance and stints on foreplay. AHD, but what can you expect? We hold these truths to be self-evident-that all men are created equally incapable of sensitivity and fidelity....

Or are they? Actually, modern men are a lot more caring, more commitment-friendly, and more *vulnerable* than their reputations might suggest. Here, then, is the scientific skinny on the most common but misguided myths about today's male.

Myth 1.   Men are afraid to commit.
Any single woman will tell you, "while dating commitment still retains some of its magic." Black magic that is. Most women think the typical bachelor is a Hooding of Heartache, a practiced escape artist who will vanish into thin air at the slightest suggestion that a relationship is taking on any element of expectation.

But, the experts say, these now-you-see-'em, now-you-don't types are fairly *un*typical. Men, in fact, seek marriage in greater numbers than do women, and very few remain lifelong bachelors. Moreover, once a man tries marriage, he's hooked. When psychologist Lillian B. Rubin asked married men and women whether they would want to marry again if something were to happen to their spouse, almost every husband, without hesitation, responded yes. Nearly half the wives, however, said they wouldn't opt for a second stroll down the aisle.

WILL THE REAL MEN PLEASE STAND UP

Myth 2.   Men are breast-obsessed.

The bigger a woman's bust, the stronger a man's lust. True? Not really. "I think there is a huge interest in breasts," but I don't think it's necessarily an interest in large breasts. It's more the shape and stance of the breast."

Other evidence suggests that while flaunting ample cleavage may encourage leers and whistles, it may also discourage more meaningful attention. Researchers at Louisiana State University Medical Center asked men to rate female models-who were dressed in clothing of varying tightness and skimpiness-on their appeal as dating, sexual, and marital partners. Accentuating the body, the researchers discovered, it enhanced a woman's appeal as a sexual partner but decreased her appeal as a potential wife.

Myth 3.   Men are incapable of monogamy.

Fidelity is more important to a good marriage than is a satisfying sexual relationship, financial security, or having children from a man's point of view, no doubt? Not quite. More than three-quarters of the one thousand men surveyed in the Virginia Slims American Women's Opinion Poll agreed with the above statement. Only 11 percent said they'd pursue this "fantasy." The majority of the single men surveyed by sex researcher Shere Hite said they plan to be monogamous in their marriages.

Some highly credible research indicates that there are many more Loyal Larry's out these than Philandering Phil's. The Gallop Poll uncovered a virtual epidemic of fidelity: Eighty-nine percent of husbands stayed true to their wives. In the *American Couples* study, sociologists Philip Blumstein and Pepper Schwartz reported that only 15 percent of husbands married two years or less have strayed; among men who have been wed a decade or more, not even one in three has done the "wild thing" with a woman other than his wife since declaring "I do." Finally, when a man swears that he's never been faithful even after he's been discovered chances are he's telling you the truth, sort of. "Men don't think of sex as a betrayal of a relationship the way women do. They're much more capable of having sex as a recreational activity and having it mean very little."

WILL THE REAL MEN PLEASE STAND UP

Myth 4. Men care less about their looks than women do.

Women agonize over extra pounds and fret over frown lines, while men-even the balding, potbellied, and triple-chinned among them-strut about, confident of their staggering sex appeal. Wrong. Wrong. Wrong. Men suffer just as much as women do. Would you believe that 94 percent of men would like to change some aspect of their physical appearance? So much for seeing themselves as paragons of physical perfection.

What is the male ideal? According to an overwhelming majority of men, it's what's known in medical parlance as, the muscle-man physique. A survey of *Psychology Today* readers found that a man's ego is directly tied to having a muscular upper body.

Men also have appearance worries that women don't have. Height, for instance. More than one in three American men report that they'd like to be taller. Many also would like to have more hair. Yet more evidence of male vanity is the growing number of men going under the surgeon's scalpel for nips and tucks: According to the American Society of Plastic and Reconstructive Surgeons, cosmetic surgeons are seeing more male patients eager to improve their appearance than they were a decade ago.

Myth 5. Men bounce back from breakups more easily than women do.

It may appear that women recovers faster from a failed romance, but that's only because "men don't understand how women emote. "Women feel the pain, but in a very different way. Part of her compulsive dating is, in fact, an emotional scream for validation. Men don't cry so easily after a breakup, but they do get impotent a lot, suffer gastrointestinal disorders, drink more, and have automobile accidents." Men are also three times as likely as women to commit suicide over a failed love affair.

"The question isn't 'Who feels the pain of a breakup more deeply?'" says William Becker, a professor of religion at Bucknell University, and who has the resources to deal with these painful feelings?' Men feel the pain more. One man said that one of the loneliest and most bitter experiences of his life was when he was going through a divorce and realized that his wife could call any one of four female friends to talk about what she was feeling, while he had no one left to call because his wife was the only person who had been that kind of friend.

Myth 6.   Men never get lonely.

In researching *Alone in America*, a writer and COSMO contributor Louise Bernikow found men were loath to admit needing anyone. To them, loneliness is weak, shameful and unmanly. Just because men don't talk about loneliness, doesn't mean they're not lonely. Relying on self-evaluation, women more frequently admitted to being lonely than men did, but the scores showed males typically had higher loneliness scores.

The researchers also discovered just why men are so reluctant to reveal feelings of loneliness: Doing so exposes them to strong social disapproval.

Myth 7.   Work is more important to men than love is.

A man can have six business presentations to make in four days and do it, but he can't manage to find time for dinner and a movie with her. The evidence against men seems incontrovertible: In a showdown between love and work, love always loses. Or does it?

Asked which factors contribute most to a happy, satisfied life, the nearly two thousand men participating in the *Playboy Report on American Men* ranked love second only to health. Work placed an unimpressive fifth. Similarly, *USA Today* reports that in survey after survey in which men were asked to rank the most satisfying aspects of their lives, "husband" and "father" always appeared at the top of the list, far ahead of "job."

A man expresses his love by providing for his family. Interestingly, the *American Couples* study reveals that married men enjoy their work much more then single men do, even though the husbands and fathers are likely to face far greater financial pressures.

Myth 8.   Men are less romantic than women.

If either gender can be labeled romance junkies, it's men. They fall in love faster. Researchers recording the "romance measurements" of hundreds of young men and women-all of whom were in love or recovering from a recent romance-found that more than a quarter of the men had fallen deeply in love before their fourth date, while only 15 percent of the women had. In fact, even after twenty dates man subsequently decided they were in love. Half the women still did not feel they were in love.

Also uncovered were more would-be Romeo's than Juliet wanna-be's. "When it comes to romantic beliefs, and study after studies have found that men are more likely to believe that true love lasts forever and true love can overcome all obstacles."

Myth 9.   To men, sex equals intercourse.
When it comes to preferences in the bedroom, the *American Couples* study confirmed one major difference between couples-the importance placed on intercourse as an essential part of lovemaking. Predictable, right? Maybe not. It turns out that women are the ones who place the greater importance on intercourse. "The stereotype of a man pressuring his partner for intercourse, and the woman, in turn, de-emphasizing it, may be misleading," write the authors. "Intercourse is just one sexual act among others that men enjoy-but it's a central ingredient in women's happiness." Better communication can lead to more-pleasurable meetings between the sheets.

Myth 10.   Men are less sensitive than women.
A woman is having a problem with an unreasonably demanding boss. Over lunch, she complains to her best friend, who confides a similar problem. "I know just how you feel," the friend says. "It can really make you doubt your own abilities." At home later that day, the woman repeats her complaint to her husband. His response: "Don't worry about it. The guy's way off base. You know you're good at what you do. Anyway, you'd get another job in a minute." The woman breaks into tears. "I can't talk to you about anything," she sobs. "You never understand."

Myth 11.   Men only care about their own pleasure in bed.
One thousand men suggest that pleasing their partner was the number one sex need for over 90 percent of them. Men measure their sexual prowess mainly in terms of the female orgasm. If they don't give her at least one orgasm, they don't feel like good lovers-and their own pleasure is diminished significantly.

WILL THE REAL MEN PLEASE STAND UP

Myth 12.   Men can't fake orgasm.
In increasing numbers men report faking orgasm. They do it for the same reasons women do: to end the sex, to avoid hurting their partner's feelings, to quell any discussion of why the sex didn't work. Typically, a man will simulate the throes of orgasm as he feels himself losing an erection during intercourse.

Myth 13.   A lack or loss of erection indicates lack of desire.
Not according to sex therapists, including Marty Klein, author of *Ask Me Anything; A Sex Therapist Answers the Most Important Questions for the '90s,* who says that anger, sadness, fear, and stress can make an erection for away. In new relationships, the flagging erection most often indicates performance anxiety; in established ones, an unresolved intimacy or communication problem. There may be physical causes, including drug or alcohol use, or health problems, such as high blood pressure or diabetes.

Myth 14.   Men want sex more than women do.
Society has given men more permission to be sexual. Masters and Johnson established that the capacity for orgasm is actually greater in the female than the male. And, as we age and shed our inhibitions, women become more able to separate love and sex-while men become more focused on emotions.

Myth 15.   Men don't need foreplay.
They may not "need" much of it to become aroused when they're young but repeatedly men of all ages tell sex surveyors they want more kissing, caressing, and touching from their partners. Bernie Zilbergeld, Ph.D., author of *The New Male Sexuality*, says that as men age they need more physical caressing to become erect and stay that way.

Myth 16.   Only "sick" men are turned on by pornography.
The majority of men, and many women, are aroused by sexually explicit material. Studies reported by The Quinsy Institute have measured increased heartbeat and

respiration in both women an men (as well as increased lubrication in women) viewing such material-even when they report not being excited. Men are, in fact, "erotic visualizes," aroused by what they see more than women. Although women do get aroused by what they see, the erotic-visual connections are not as strong.

Myth 18.   Men are threatened by women who take their own pleasure in bed.
Men are excited by sexually assertive women. The number one complaint I received from the men I interviewed was that their partners are too passive sexually. They want women to take more responsibility for initiating sex-and for their own orgasms.

Myth 19.   Men are more sexually confident then women.
Because society expects it of them, men are good at projecting a sexual bravado they don't necessarily feel. Men are obsessed with their size, with most believing their own size isn't big or hard, enough. Their confidence is as easily shattered by a bad sexual experience as a women's.

Myth 20.   Men don't enjoy performing cunnilingus as often as women like.
Men believe cunnilingus is the surest path to female orgasm. Many are also very aroused while doing it. Some men complain that their partners don't want to engage in this sex act as often as men want to. Men who report they don't like performing cunnilingus most often also say they fear they don't "do it right."

Myths keep couples stuck in sexual ruts-and letting go of them can enhance your relationship and enliven lovemaking. Often what "they say" and what "everybody knows" are painfully wrong-particularly when the subject is sex. So stop believing everything you hear and start believing in yourself. What makes you (and your partner) feel good is probably the best way to go.

4

WHAT DO MEN REALLY WANT FROM WOMEN

Many relationships are difficult before they get easy, so keep at it.

There are men with doctorate degrees in communication, but women find that these same men can't communicate. What about those men with Master's Degrees in sociology but their social lives are in a mess. For years many of my male friends have complained about this woman or that woman and they seem to have a great deal of trouble finding the woman they want. They complain about the caliber of women they associate with or the type of woman they get stuck with. It goes on and on, never ending in any great degree of true happiness and satisfaction with any woman. Oh, they do find happiness and gratification, but it doesn't get any deeper than that.

I remain a little puzzled as I ponder on it more. I wanted to understand why men are so difficult to please. Why do men feel that in order to find the right woman, the best woman, the woman of his life, he had to get involved with inferior women. I wish I had some nice neat explanation but I don't. I can only express myself through my male friends dilemma's.

After my Superbowl party three of my male friends stayed around to help move furniture back in it's rightful place. Afterwards Pantrone Tequila flowed in shot glasses. My husband had stepped next door to throw darts with my neighbors and I suddenly found myself in that all too rare situation for most women: in the company of four men talking freely. I kept myself busy in the kitchen washing dishes and wiping counters as I kept the Tequila pouring. I stood there listening to four intelligent men discussing not solutions to the world problems, but the shortcomings of women.

The Girls locker room talk in my book *Will The Real Women Please Stand Up!* is G-rated in comparison. One thing started to emerge from all the explicit talk. They had a profile for women - a picture of what they were really looking for in a woman. As I searched my cabinet drawer for paper and pen I began to take notes on what they felt The Ideal Women should be. She has to:

* Have a good job, but is not so attached to it that she can't find time for her man.
* Be secure with herself, but is still able to communicate her emotions.
* Be decisive, and still able to share decisions with her mate.
* Be strong but not overbearing. She can still show tender loving care.
* Be able to accept his career moves, and needs.
* Have a good sense of humor.
* Look reasonably well.
* Be full-figured, but not over weight.
* Be sexy, but not sleazy
* Be able to swallow sperm in a single gulp.
* Be able to take a man's entire penis in her mouth with out nipping with her teeth.
* Make a man feel like he's the only man on this earth.
* Indulge in sex and not feel it's dirty or too vulgar
* Discuss sex freely and without reserve
* Be assertive and not be intimidated by other women.

Men Wants

Sam's wife had the sensitivity of a football, he exclaimed. He put her down in public and he had her believing that she was incompetent. He laughed the whole time he discussed her. All of a sudden he blurted out, "Man women sure can fool you when they're trying to hook you." Sam felt cheated because he didn't know many things about his wife until after they were married.

Carl's ex wife had left him because she had accepted her current job in another part of the country. She was moving up and didn't want him to hold her back. She didn't even clear the move with him first, she packed up and left. It didn't seem to matter to him at first, but the more he talked the more the pain shined through. He said it was the job she had been waiting for all her life. It didn't seem to him he had made the same kind of career decision at least three times without consulting her.

Lee was a pilot for a major airline. He had a reputation of being not just a fine body, but also an intellectual in the best sense of that word: He uses his intellect. He's witty, charming, insightful and a pleasure to be with. He said his girlfriend treated him like a prized possession. She like to show him off to all her girlfriends. She didn't want him to do or say anything, but just be there in case she needed him to be shown off.

James, whose a security guard at one of the local department stores intimidated the store employees so much until they would confess their crimes. Everyone in the store is afraid of him because of his "I'll get my man attitude". But I was even more surprised when he appeared on our doorstep one night bruised and scratched all over by the women he lives with. He doesn't know how to leave her he exclaimed.

I sat there looking at these four men and suddenly began to think of their dilemmas. Why do men get involved with inferior women. Why do they keep talking about what they really want and end up with something completely different? My heart goes out to each of them.

After many years of research I've listened closely to men complain about women, and I don't have a neat explanation why they can't find a women who can give them what they want. All I know is it's up to men to seek and find, live and let live. There are women out there with the qualities these men are looking for but they pass them up or look over them. It has been three years since my Super Bowl party and I know, you can't allow assertive women to intimidate. An assertive woman usually wants an assertive man. Don't get assertive and overbearing confused though.

Maybe these men are asking for too little or too less in a woman, who knows. Who will ever know what a man really wants from a woman. They're all so different. A man thinks that everything he does is wonderful; a woman has doubts.

WILL THE REAL MEN PLEASE STAND UP

The Male Ego

Recently, my husband and I were in an elevator, waiting to ascend from the depths of Parking Level Five and after a few moments, I had a revelation. "Honey," I said, "we're not moving."

"Sure we are," Martin said with more certainty that I ever feel about anything.

We waited a little longer; there wasn't the slightest sensation of motion. Yet he insisted that everything was under control because, he explained, "I pushed the button."

I hate to argue with a man who has pushed the button (men frequently take it personally when a machine disobeys their commands), but I was getting claustrophobic. So I pushed the button, and immediately-noticed-the elevator began to rise. Martin was unabashed. "there must be something wrong with that button!" he exclaimed.

I don't know one woman who would have come to that same conclusion. I certainly would have assumed I'd made a mistake. That's why I want a male ego. Men rarely seem to assume they've made a mistake.

"There should be a theme park based on the male ego," says my daughter T'Juanna, "only there's not enough land." I wonder if men could have an ego-change surgery or get a male-ego transplant, my friend jokes. One useful side effect would be that I'd no longer feel the compulsion to straighten up the house. The next time I get lost, instead of asking for directions, I'd drive around in circles, clenching my teeth, trying to read the map while I was going forty miles an hour. And if I happened to run into an abusive, frothing maniac, I could get into a nose-to nose shrieking confrontation instead of discreetly slipping away. On second thought, maybe the house isn't big enough for two male egos.

Know that real love cannot be bought, it can only be found.

Step 2:

Taking Action

5

HOW TO TAKE ACTION

The best man is the man who knows what he wants in life.

Most men are serious about improving their lives. They demonstrate this by their commitment to incorporate self-improvement skills into their everyday routines. If you want to improve your life by having more positive relationships, then you must learn to take the proper action. You can immediately experience the benefits of self-improvement in your relationships by actively working to improve all areas of your life. The first step is for you is to **Get started!**

Even though some of these suggestions may be familiar to you, the goal is to create rich, fulfilling and helpful options that vary from simple to involved ways to take action. You can't wait for the spirit to move you. You don't have to wait until you feel perfect. You need to get going.

You can work on improving your relationships the same way you work on improving your muscles. The more you work on them the more your performance improves. The more you leave them alone, the more out of shape you get. Indeed we can create magic in our lives simply by believing the phase "I am responsible for improving my life." That is about as much magic as you will need to make the formula work. Until you believe you alone are capable of improving your life - until you believe in yourself -- then everything else you try is going to be nothing more than a psychological Band-Aid.

You can follow your own script or you can follow the one handed to you. Either you direct the action, or someone else decides who will be on stage with you. And that's not all. You have the opportunity to judge your own performance. You can take complete responsibility to improve your life and all that happens in it. That's right. If you want to rearrange your life or replace the bad things or the bad people in your life you have the power to do it. You have the power to change the direction of your life. You can also find new ways to take action by talking to friends and sharing some of the techniques they use and have found to be successful too.

Putting Your Best Self Out Front

Do you want to fill your life with women who can bring you joy? Do you want to increase your happiness and pursue your dreams? If so, what's stopping you from meeting women and pursing your dream of happiness with her?

The way you present yourself physically is important in terms of attracting a woman from the start but if you want to attract really great people in your life you'll have to use a lot more than your looks. The next time you're in a movie line, the grocery store, or your favorite restaurant here are some important qualities to keep in mind that are also important ingredients of self-improvement. They are clear cut methods for taking action now and getting the most out of improving your life. If you need to make changes and are ready to take action, here's what you can do:

1. Take a look at yourself.

It all starts with you. No one else can make you happy, whole, or complete. You must be solid and complete all by yourself. Do you know who you are? Do you feel good about yourself? Do you have a solid sense of worth and value? If you answered no, plan to take deliberate action now! Do something about it. It's that simple. Make it your number one goal to solidify your identity, and deal with this once and for all. Whether you do this through pastoral counseling, professional counseling, or some other avenue for growth. Start from within and then make it happen today.

2. Take responsibility for your relationships.

If you are the type who constantly finds yourself in unhealthy relationships, it is time to identify your patterns and resolve to change them. You don't have to be a victim of bad luck" anymore. It's time to take responsibility for poor dating habits. Quit blaming others, and learn to avoid certain patterns and unhealthy partners. It's your choice.

3.   Take back what you lost.

It's easy to go too fast when you are excited about someone. At one time or another we have been guilty of putting too much emphasis on the romantic/passionate aspect of a relationship (i.e., failed to use our brain). Most of us can relate to the regrets associated with sexual indiscretion. We have all fallen in one of these crucial areas. Perhaps you have lost your confidence, dignity, or self-respect. Well, it's time to take back what you may have lost. Take things a little slower and start the process of healing through acknowledgments, confession and renewal.

4.   Take a look around.

Almost certainly, there are those reading this book who have a sparse dating life. You have either questioned yourself, or given up hope altogether. You may be wondering, "Where do I find women these days?" (see chapter 7) Or you might have even concluded that, "All the good ones are already taken." Not so. More than likely Ms. Right is someone you already know. The vast majority of happy, successful couples meet their partners in ordinary places as they go about their routine of everyday living. It's quite possible that your future spouse is right under your nose.

5.   Take time out.

Whenever you find yourself in a serious relationship, take time out to consider the fruit of your relationship -- especially when you have questions about the relationship. Above all else, determine whether or not your relationship has potential. One simple question is: Do you feel encouraged, affirmed, inspired, and challenged to grow and to be a better person when you are with my mate? That's it. If the answer is no, then it is time to take time out.

6.   Take these objectives seriously.

These objectives are only recommendations and suggestions. Ignore them and you pay the consequences. Conversely, seek to follow these objectives and you will experience positive results -- blessings. Relationships don't have to be complicated and mysterious as people sometimes make them.

7. **Speak better and attract better people.**

Whenever you speak, try to be conscious and mindful of what you are saying - and how you saying. Avoid the use of fillers -- such as "like," "Um," "You Know." It is very discouraging and unattractive to constantly hear someone use fillers after every other word. It can give others the wrong impression of you. Learn to be conversant. To some men using fillers is a way to be cool, but once they learn that lacking conversation isn't cool, they quickly try to correct this lingo. To help you with this: take in a breath of air through your mouth for a second, hold it, and then begin to speak.

8. **Get rid of the nasal whine.**

Women love to talk to men who have masculine voices. Unless you are internationally famous for your nasal whine or have a beneficial reason for whining then get rid of it. Work to make your voice more appealing to women. Open your jaws when you speak in order to avoid sounding nasal..

9. **Walk with confidence.**

Your body has a way of speaking to you as you walk. The way you walk, stand, and how you sit sends body gesture signals. People are making decisions about your every movement. Some people have aggressive walks, happy walks, energized walks, and others have wimpy walks, or tentative walks. Some have a bouncy walk while others shuffle, waddle, trot, or simply drag themselves along. In order to present yourself as someone who is self-confident, you'll have to practice being more confident as you walk.

Stand as if there is string holding the crown of your head up. Feel that string running from the crown of your head to the base of your spine. Look straight ahead with your eyes gazing forward. Tighten your buttocks. Roll your shoulders back slightly. Keep your arms relaxed at your sides. Apply the standing exercise steps to your walk. Keep your walking gait at a steady pace -- not too slow or too fast. Allow your arms to swing freely and naturally. Carry yourself as a natural and confident moving man to attract women like magnets.

10.   Don't hoard yourself.
Men who are uncomfortable with themselves sends negative signs and signals that women immediately pick up. People who aren't shy are usually more concerned about the other person. Shy people think more about how they are doing and how they might appear to others. To get over the epidemic of shyness you have to get the focus off of yourself and shift it to others.

Practice this in private, before going to parties or other social engagements. to help combat shyness. Take a small sip of air into your mouth. Hold it in a few seconds. Now, blow the air out in a steady stream until you run out of air. Repeat this until you feel your nervousness subside. Once you have calmed yourself down you can get out of your own way and confidently meet and greet people.

11.   Learn to embellish today.
The idea of actually making an appointment with yourself might be unheard of to you. Sometimes men are so busy seeing to the needs of their family, children, co-workers, spouses and other loved ones that they may never have a moment to themselves. To help overcome the need to always have something to do, here are gentle reminders to help you overcome your compulsives:

* Take time to be friendly to yourself, it's your guide to happiness.
* Take time to dream, it will help you reach your goals.
* Take time to laugh at least eight times a day, it will help you keep your sanity.
* Take time to be loved and give love, it is the privilege God has given you.
* Take time to share, the days are too short to be selfish.
* Take time to nurture yourself, it is the fountain of youth.

12. Actively participate in your own life.

Men use lots of energy trying to find passion and remain active in life. Part of this continuous effort is by staying fit mentally, emotionally, spiritually, physically and financially. Learn to recapture the part of your childhood that you felt your best. Learn to embrace and embellish what you are most passionate about. Allow yourself the opportunity to enjoy the thrill and excitement of life. Take up hobbies that will provide you with a way to unwind and have some much needed good old fashion fun.

13. Strive to be happier.

Finding reasons to be happy is easier than you might think. It's the process of enjoying each moment to it's fullest. What is it that you think about that puts a smile on your face each time you think about it? Who do you enjoy being with? What are the small things that make you smile or laugh? Find those moments in your life. Plan a good time for yourself on a regular basis. Enjoy a great meal, listen to your favorite music, do those things that bring a smile to your face and do your best to create personal happiness in your own life first.

14. Remain true to yourself.

Understand that you are good and your personal best can always use improving. Learn to feel good about your accomplishments -- the large and the small.

15. Don't allow material possessions to control you.

Don't measure your self-worth by material obsessions or possessions. Be able to give to this world your love and help in ways other than material.

16. Create success in your life.

Be able to put yourself in high gear when you are feeling low. There should be something good in your life to reflect on to raise your spirits in down times. Believe you are successful and you shall become successful.

WILL THE REAL MEN PLEASE STAND UP

17. Review your personal successes.

It may be a small or large success, but relish in the fact that there are things you can pull out in times of need. Bring personal happiness into your life.

18. Keep a positive outlook on life.

Don't allow bad thing that happen to you to create a bad mood that you can't get over. This is the best time to remember all the things that make you happy. Think of all the things in your life that have made you feel worthwhile. That medal you won, your first special thing, your happiest times, the things that make you laugh or smile. Summons the power to forge ahead.

19. Take the proper action.

By working each day to achieve the goals that you have set, you are taking the proper action. Your ego will help to improve when you are taking action to improve who you are.

20. Maintain good health habits.

Don't let negative images of yourself cause you to neglect your health and well-being. Feeling good does not always mean that you are healthy, so get regular check-ups, eat healthy, and exercise daily.

21. Meditate daily or as often as needed.

Think peaceful thoughts. Bring inner peace into your life by thinking positive and pleasurable thoughts. Love yourself, respect your self, believe in yourself and think of good ways to make this world a better place.

Take complete responsibility: improve your life and all that happens in it.

6

HOW TO COMMUNICATE WITH WOMEN

Don't borrow from tomorrow, live for today.

I have a friend -- I'll call her Jan -- who is a true Southern Belle. She was born and raised in Memphis Tennessee. She is vivacious and generous. And she's got the greatest Southern drawl I've ever heard.

While drinking orange juice and eating bagels at a friends picnic recently, Jan and I got to talking about men, women and marriage. She waited until our husbands wandered back to the concession stand for some nachos. And then she told me this story.

When she met and fell in love with her husband Joseph, they hailed from two different worlds. At twenty five Jan had lived a protected life. She still lived with her parents. She was a virgin. She was wide-eyed with idealism and naiveté and anticipation. Joseph, on the other hand, was a thirty-five-year-old Military man who had just recently came to know the Lord. He had three children from a previous marriage, and a working knowledge of worldly living.

During their engagement, the couple received the standard pre-marital counseling session at the church they were attending. This included a personality test that Jan and Joseph were asked to take separately, reviewing their answers together later.

After the test, Jan and Joseph sat together in the pastor's office and compared their answers. They were thrilled to see that more often than not, their answers complimented one another. That is until they hit question number fifty one. The question was: "Do you consider yourself sexually inhibited?"

Joseph's answer was yes.

Jan's answer was no.

Amazed and shocked, Joseph turned to his virgin wife-to-be. "What do you mean you're not inhibited? What are we talking about here? Handcuffs? Threesomes? Animals?"

WILL THE REAL MEN PLEASE STAND UP

Jan almost fainted. Holding her chest, she managed to blurt out very calmly, "Well darlin', no! I just meant I'd be willing to do it with the lights on!"

Candidly speaking there are many couples out there just like Jan and Joseph who date for months and even years and never understand what the other means when they are asked the same questions. Experts agree that good relationships thrive on a foundation of good communication. Sometimes good communication may mean not doing any talking at all. Communicating with our loved ones can sometimes mean just listening or simply being there for them. What follows are *eight helpful ways* couples can set the stage for building the best communication framework possible.

1.   Find a special place and time to talk.

Find a special place and get away from it all. Discuss your problems and your plans with your mate. It will make you feel as though you're meeting for a date.

Make your times together more exciting and fun filled. Share thoughts of the future, your likes, dislikes and soon you'll find yourself discussing those things that caused the breakdown in your relationship. Discussions about how to improve in communication can open doors for you to enjoy each other once again. It might be a phone call just to say hello, a card or note to say I'm thinking of you. Communicating can come in many forms if you just use your creativity and enthusiasm with your partner.

2.   Schedule regular time together.

Plan at least one night a week out together. Your one night together can be your oasis. Set up neutral times that are easy for the both of you to keep. Don't be haphazard, sloppy or casual about your meetings with one another. Demonstrating commitment, growth, time together and it's importance are sacred to your relationship. Making excuses, delays, being forgetful or missing dates are signs of self-sabotage.

3.   Know when you should stop talking.

There are times when communication shouldn't take place. When a topic has lead to an argument or has been exhausted or you have reached an impasse, it's best to come to a mutual agreement that you have discussed the topic as far as it can go. Simply agree to think things over and pick up the discussion at a later time, or simply accept the fact that there are some things you and your partner will not always agree upon.

4.   Agree not to hurl personal insults during a disagreement.

Developing trust between two people is a hard won victory. Personal confidences revealed in private should never be whipped out to wave like a red flag in front of your partners face. Even if you and your partner settle your disagreement, rest assured that a measure of trust will have been lost from the relationship if you hurl personal insults.

5.   Do not make snap decisions during emotional disputes.

In the heat of the moment, we are sometimes tempted to spit out vicious words to hurt one another. In addition, we are sometimes tempted to throw in our cards and leave the table, opting to walk out of our mate's life forever, only to regret it later. Snap decisions hurt relationships in the long run. Make sure that after an argument, you calm yourself before making any life altering decisions.

6.   Understand that things cannot change overnight.

Relationships are ongoing exercises in mutual growth. Accordingly, problems will not be solved overnight. If your partner doesn't show commitment to you or if you're not use to showing it, it probably won't be done overnight. Don't nag about it; with time it will happen naturally. She may not be saying all the things you want to hear, but that doesn't mean she doesn't care deeply about you. With patience time will eventually bring about the necessary change.

7.   Draw boundaries to keep outside forces to a minimum.

Married couples are usually the most vulnerable to having their private disputes discussed by family and friends. Well meaning as they may be can create more problems between you and your mate. This is not to say that a trusted family member or friend should not be relied upon for emotional support, but boundaries must be drawn so that the individual agendas of others do not make a wreck of your relationship.

8.   Try to see the other person's point of view.

One of the most difficult relationship building blocks is, avoiding the temptation to point the finger and lay the blame. Allow your partner to have her say fully without interruption, and think before you reply. Point out that you have allowed her to speak and ask that you be given the same respect. Even if you don't agree on everything it reinforces the idea that you respect your partner's feelings and that you are willing to hear her out.

9.   Bring quiet time into your life.

Creating an environment to succeed with silent commitment is necessary to capture it's true benefits. Set aside time in your day for being completely silent. You can choose the time of day as well as the amount of time you'll want to use. Quiet times enable us to release stress and teaches us how to calm ourselves.

Brainstorm to come up with new ideas and solutions to problems.

7

HOW TO FIND THE WOMAN YOU WANT

Too many men miss their silver lining because they're expecting gold.

Warren, a single man recently turned down a guys night out because no women would be present. To Warren such a gathering seemed to be a waste of his valuable wife-hunting time. In fact, his evenings are usually kept open so that he can pursue his main goal: finding a mate. He visits malls, restaurants, sports bars and women's clubs hoping to make eye contact with an eligible female.

Yet most nights, he meets no new prospects, while conducting his search in the land of one night stands. He visits bars and clubs, but he seldom meets his dream date. Though he's invited to an occasional party the women he encounter realize that he is on a search for a wife and this is an automatic turn off to them. So far his romantic blinders have netted nothing but a string of evenings sipping wine along with a thorough knowledge of the most current pick-up lines.

Knowing you can be friends with a woman isn't enough. A man needs to be able to meet a woman with whom he can create positive, nurturing and lasting relationships.. Many men build their lives around finding the right woman.

Women are definitely attracted to men with full lives, so if you're looking for love, your first step should be to pursue activities that don't revolve around the mating game. Many times even when you find someone you're interested in it only turns out that the two of you may have nothing in common but a preference for the same bars. There are great activities and adventures you can embark on that will enrich your life and connect you with eligible women.

As a real man, you're not looking for just any woman. You're looking for a certain type of woman, a woman who will physically, emotionally, and intellectually turn

WILL THE REAL MEN PLEASE STAND UP

you on. Be realistic in this mental image you create of your ideal woman. While creating this image, picture the type of woman who will also be attracted to you.

Try your best to be honest and give yourself a critical self-evaluation. In today's society it is considered acceptable for a man to go hunting for the woman he wants, and women are entitled to succumb to men who have been attracted to them. Even though men like to be chased and seduced just as much as women, there are situations that allow men to be more aggressive in their hunt. To keep from becoming too aggressive in his pursuit, a man has to be creative before a woman will completely appreciate how much he yearns for her.

There are many men who have an extraordinary lack of self-confidence when it comes to meeting a new woman. There are women who feel they are God's gift to men, and these women usually act selfish, mean and self-centered or either they work extra hard to impress.

It takes a mature and confident man to enjoy without personal judgement a direct and caring approach from a mature and confident woman. A man should first know what he wants from a woman and what's he wants in a woman. Some men want women who can hang on their arms like trophies, while others want a woman that he can raise a family with and spend the rest of their life with. There are expensive women who will only look at a man if his paycheck is as big as her taste. There are men who want a woman who has her own money and her own agenda as long as it doesn't infringe upon his. Now a days, men are looking for the woman to bring something to the table as well. There are men who are willing to provide women with these luxuries too. Men have a right to be happy whether it's for sexual, financial or purely physical reasons.

A man should be able to provide a woman with passion and romance if he wants to land her in his heart. Men love the idea of having a woman who is sensuous, romantic, passionate and loving, even though they may not necessarily put it in this order. It's time for men to wake up, stop being hypocrites and let women know what they really want. Believe me it can be done in a way that's classy and reputable by all standards.

Men want women they can come to, talk to, be open and honest with, but they have yet to find one that is truly willing to accept him as he is, even though they say they can. If you want to meet beautiful and caring women with hopes of falling in love and living happily ever after the first thing you need to do is get out of the house. Here are twenty two effective ways to meet women.

1. Change your routine.

Discover new ways to do the things you feel most comfortable doing. Do you go to the supermarket every Friday? If so, try a Saturday, that's when women do most of their shopping. Try a Monday night and you'll see a host of new faces. If you find yourself at the Laundromat on Sunday night why not try another day or night. Try a different time you'll meet members that you've never met. Visit different malls, different car dealers, different car washes. Try a different barber, one of those with an adjoining beauty salon that serves women as well as men. You'll be surprised at the new and welcome faces.

2. Choose your own activities.

Why not take a course in book keeping or accounting or even court reporting. Sign up for judo, Kong fu or karate classes. Be adventurous and go bungi-jumping, parachuting scuba diving, mountain climbing or take a hot air balloon for a date with your favorite lady. If you're having fun, women around you will notice and want to join in.

3. Dare to make her stare.

Carry or wear a conversation piece. Wear something that makes you stand out from the crowd. Try sitting in a bar, visit a bookstore or park reading your book casually and then look around to see if the lucky lady is looking at you. If so, give her a reassuring smile that everything is okay. Help her to look your way by looking at her more often.

4. Say hello to every woman you meet.

Get in the habit of speaking just because you're happy. Don't push it by adding conversation, because some women will think you're too forward. Just say hello happily and keep walking. Greeting everyone you meet will help to boost your confidence. The next time you see someone who really attracts you have the confidence to take the first step. To get you closer to her, ask her for directions to a place you already know the directions to or ask for the time. Whatever makes you feel comfortable.

5.   Don't stay at home; decide to go out alone.

You'll feel comfortable going out alone if you go to your favorite places. After visiting your favorite places a few times you'll get to know the staff, the waiters will call you by your first name and you'll feel at ease being there. You'll also be more comfortable meeting new people. By going out more you give yourself a chance to meet more people which makes your chances of meeting someone you like greater.

6.   Act like a tourist in your own town.

On your vacation you are probably more eager to discover new places and you aren't afraid to go alone. You're also a lot more adventurous on vacations. So what better reason to take a vacation in your own home town. Discover new places to go in your home town that women will appreciate. Your discovery should include places with different price ranges, variety of foods, and a great atmosphere.

7.   Offer rewards to whomever finds you a suitable partner.

You can offer anyone who finds you your future wife a financial reward. If you can't afford it offer a dinner for two or an all expense paid weekend for two. Whatever you offer is up to you. You'll be surprised at all the dates you'll get from boni-fide recommendations.

8.   Cook up something at a local cafe.

Why not brunch it on the weekends. Most cities have cafe's that serve bargain breakfasts during the week. If you go alone, read a newspaper, but remember to look up occasionally to scan the crowd. She's probably somewhere near you just waiting to be approached by you. Some of the best dates are during impromptu meetings at local cafe's.

WILL THE REAL MEN PLEASE STAND UP

9.   Check whose checking out what.
Scout local art galleries, libraries, bookstores, video stores, and magazine stands. Sometimes you can find a magazine counter near a cafe and you can sip an expresso while reading. Offer compliments to women about their reading material. At art galleries there are built in conversation pieces. Get to know something special about the art so you'll be able to add spark to your conversation.

10.   Be unconventional: Go to trade shows.
Women are known for attending trade shows to seek out men. Why not turn the table and visit trade shows that have many women in attendance. Check your local newspaper for other events that might interest you. Trade shows that interest women are great avenues for meeting large numbers of eligible singles. Usually every city throws some type of trade shows to pull people out of their homes. They introduce new products at these functions, new singing groups and often times these events last for more than two days. It's a great gathering of people.

11.   Unleash your animal magnetism by walking your dog.
Take a walk with your dog. If you don't have a dog, borrow one. Cut, well groomed and obedient dogs attract women. You'll be surprised how many women will stop and talk to your dog. To gain more attention put a fuschia bow around his or her neck. It denotes passion and romance. That alone attracts women.

12.   During intermission go hunting.
During movie intermissions, plays, concerts or sporting activities, etc. be sure to visit the concession stand. Join others if you're at a bar in the conversation. You may end up sharing the remainder of your evening with your very own star attraction.

13. Look for desert after lunch.

Even if you bring lunch to the office go out for coffee during lunch time or desert or even just for a breath of fresh air. Stretch your legs in the park, go woman watching. Maybe you'll meet someone that wants to meet you. What a great way to end a meal.

14. Volunteer.

When choosing a cause, pick one that has some importance to you, or you'll have a hard time remaining committed to it. If you are committed to the cause instead of being committed to finding woman at the function your passion will outlast your search. Working toward a common goal brings out a the best in a person. This helps you get a chance to see the real side of a woman. In a volunteer setting the atmosphere is more relaxed and you don't feel like you're trying to pair up with any particular person.

15. Take up a sport.

Involving yourself in sports opens up doors to come in contact with dozens of women, mostly at a more relaxed setting. Conversation is never a problem because at a sports event you can always find something to discuss. Any sport can be great for matchmaking. Besides women appreciate and love athletic men. You can't blame them for being turned on by toned muscles and a fit body. Attending a sports camp is the ultimate. Golf, tennis, boating, and even running camps have just as much an advantageous male to female ratio.

16. Enroll in adult education classes.

Try enrolling in courses that traditionally appeal to women if you want to meet women. Classes designed to improve your life are great for finding women who want to improve their life, such as arts and crafts, design, cooking etc. If the women who enrolled in the classes aren't available or interested, who knows with a little conversation you might find out she has an eligible sister or coworker. This type of classroom usually provides a relaxed setting for people to easily get aquatinted. You can really get to know people when you are enrolled in a class that requires creativity. And because you get to know one another for more than dating purposes it really eases the tension when you finally do decide to go out.

17. Join a professional club.
Professional clubs usually meet several times a month and the gatherings usually consist of at least ten or more people. Each week the group meets at a different place, like a bar, club, hotel, coffeehouse. They share their ambitions, exchange business cards, ideas and the atmosphere is wonderful. Everyone has a potential contact of some kind which makes it even more exciting to meet. Many times the members will bring along new people, and these new people know someone who knows someone and so on.

    Chances are your field of profession will have club affiliations that you can invite others to or get to know more about. If you aren't familiar with these groups trade magazines and your colleagues are the best way to became familiar with these groups.

18. Join a religious organization.
By taking advantage of community church club organizations that offer group meetings such as singles, aerobics and art classes as well as the use of its pool and cocktail parties you'll meet many wonderful women. Churches and synagogues have group meetings that are geared to unmarried people. They often revolve around fund-raising for religious charities. Many of these same organizations regularly rent out restaurants for an evening, inviting everyone on their mailing list, which includes a large assortment of lawyers, real estate developers and bankers. Often these groups sponsor community action days (cleaning up parks, running for inner-city kids) where you can get to know nice women while doing good deeds. And then lets not forget the trips that these same groups go on. (Retreats, conventions, etc.)

19. Expand your circle of friends.
You can't help but open up your circle and let more people come in when you began to get more active. Feel free to speak to you, to give you compliments and to also welcome

you into their circle of friends. Try not to be afraid of people. Striking up conversations with people will keep you informed and open to new ideas. When you meet new people and have new conversation with them you increase your chances of doing new things and having a more adventurous life. Your life will becomes richer when you branch out. It helps you to break out of your bubble and strike out with enough confidence to meet more new people.

20.   Travel and see the world.
Call your favorite travel agent and began booking that fabulous trip you've been thinking about. Traveling helps you to be a kid all over again. Select vacations or places where you are likely to meet new people, especially women. Find a travel agency for listings of single resorts and cruises where you'll meet a variety of people that have your same style.

Traveling alone gives the best results because you're more likely to reach out to strangers. Most people on vacation are fairly receptive to friendly overtures.

21.   Create opportunities.
It's best to create your own opportunities, and having a partner helps more. A trusted friend can encourage you to become more daring. You won't be lucky enough to attract a woman every time you go out, but you can maximize your opportunities. To help you maximize your possibilities stick with the hang-outs that you like as well as the places you hear women talking about.

22.   Use good judgement.
The best judgement is common sense. Never go to a strangers home, stay in well lit areas, and let the guy give you his number instead of you giving out your number. Don't give out your last name either because that another unwanted invitation of privacy.

Spend quality time together when you concentrate
on the romantic side of your relationship

8

HOW TO GET THE WOMAN YOU WANT

Proven Techniques

If you desire and you act upon it, then everything stands within your reach.

The best way to land the woman of your dreams is to become so irresistible to her that she can't say no. Some of the best ways to pull this off is to be warm, enduring, generous, attractive and most of all caring. You must act and look as if the world is in your hands, even if it's only a small part of it. Ask yourself a few questions before you set out to get her.

* Does the woman of your dreams have the qualities that you feel are satisfactory to you?
* Does she carry herself as a positive, nurturing and caring individual almost all the time?
* Do other people speak of her in high regard and with integrity.
*Would she make a good mother for your children?

Women are generally generous on the whole, but if you notice she's not being generous with her love, affection and warmness you'd better think twice before you get involved. Ask yourself if the woman you are attracted to is generous enough to make you happy? Generosity depends on the woman involved. Many women who are friendly aren't necessarily generous. Some women are generous with their time, some are generous with their advice, and some are generous with their sex. The generosity that's being focused on here is *spirit.*

Generosity is the time she makes for whenever and whatever your needs. And for you to be just as generous to her is worth the giving. Knowing what you want and need as a man is great, but knowing what you want and need from a woman is even better. Be sure you know what qualities you seek in a woman and then be just as sure that the woman you select has these qualities to offer.

WILL THE REAL MEN PLEASE STAND UP

As a man there are several ways you can seek out these wonderful qualities in a woman. Whatever you consider her most important quality, be sure you take the time to find it. Expect it from her and then once you decide she has it demand that this quality be exemplified throughout the relationship. Don't cheat yourself. If you wait, hoping that one day the quality will magically surface you'll only set yourself up for major let downs. Expect the best for yourself by expecting the best from the woman you choose. This is not being selfish, it's being sure of what you want and not settling for less.

Your journey toward a happy life starts with you, and as a man your happiness is your number one priority. If you're not happy you won't be able to give her happiness. Here are some proven techniques to help you get the woman you want, need and desire.

1.   Remain attentive to her.

Focus all of your attention on the woman you want. Do not allow distractions to steer you in the wrong direction. Become so genuinely engrossed in what she's saying that everything and everyone else disappears. Be able to look into her eyes attentively. Women like this. It woos them. Give her complete conversation and attention even when she doesn't think you're paying attention. Stay alert. Making her feel that she's number one, is the key to getting her more interested in you.

2.   Learn to be a good conversationalist.

Women adore men who compliment and give them praise. It instills a high self-esteem for her, and we all know women lack self-esteem in many cases. Ask interesting, yet not prying questions. Good questions will almost always consist of questions that make her talk about herself. Focus on what makes her tick and you're on the right road to winning her over. What makes her ticks are questions that will make her think you are in awe of her. Make her feel that she is an amazing person. Ask questions about her that aren't intimidating, like what's her favorite food, country, city or hobby. Questions that make her want to talk about herself can spark an interesting conversation.

She'll love you for taking the time to listen to those things she's always wanted to tell someone but didn't think anyone wanted to listen.

3. Don't be afraid to flatter her.

Since self-esteem is listed as one of the most important qualities a woman can have it pays to build her self-esteem as much as you possibly can. Tell her that she's smart and beautiful and be sure to let her know how great she is in bed if you've already been there with her. Get in the habit of telling her that you find her irresistible and gorgeous. Most women will find this exhilarating and pleasant. Compliments to a woman are one of the best ways to get her attention for longer periods of time. Be sure to be attentive to her regularly. Flattery is best when it's truthful and from the heart.

4. Make sure she's available.

When a man plays hard to get it's usually because he's trying to prove a point of some sort. But women who play hard to get see it as virtuous. If you get interested in a woman who plays hard to get don't chase her for too long. Be supportive of her but let her know that you don't like to play games, therefore you won't be chasing her for too long a period. You're looking for a woman who has a caring spirit and one who runs, plays hard to get and keeps you hoping and hopping for too long is not caring. Trying to get her does not mean you have to be subjected to humiliation. It simply means you'll have to learn new ways of getting her if you really want her. Being available makes your partner miss you when you are not around, so why not find a partner whose tries to be available for you.

5. Continue to have fun.

Sometimes she won't be able to assist you or accommodate you when you need her to. You might even be disappointed about it, but don't fret; here's a positive solution to those times when you can't be together. Make your needs attractive to her by sharing the fun with her. By this, I mean if she has a business meeting to attend and has to cancel her lunch with you, try to plan something special for dinner with her. Take the initiative to show you care all the time, not just certain times of the day. If you want to go shopping, suggest the next time she wants to go shopping that you do it together. Make a 'double date day' of shopping. She'll spend half the day shopping and you'll spend the other half. If that's too long a day try shopping on an hourly basis, the first hour is yours the second is hers and so on. Be sure to try on crazy clothing, and laugh a lot while together. Keeping each others needs in mind can be fun.

6.   Be what she likes in man.
Being straight forward with your woman and asking her what she likes can open many doors of pleasures. If she knows you like her and you treat her more special than any other woman she'll like you more. If she knows you desire her, she'll become more desirable to you. Let her know you desire her warmth, affection and attention. Touch her often and be sure to stroke her hair, kiss her hands and hug her gently throughout the day or as often as you can. Women love affectionate touching that doesn't lead to sexual intercourse. In a woman's mind showing true affection doesn't consist of sexual intercourse. Women cherish a man who has more to offer than sex. She'll like you if she's comfortable with you too. It makes her feel safe.

7.   Be familiar with life's pleasures.
Convey a combination of happiness, security and worldliness. Being secure with your life and who you are is very appealing to women. It's provocative too. Saying what's on your mind to her without hurting her feelings will turn her on rather than off. Clear speaking, non abrasive and non vulgar men get the farthest with women. Men who are familiars with life's pleasures are usually in control of their lives. It's a great turn on. It makes her want to know more about you. When a woman is encountered by a man who knows, what he wants, needs and desires in life she feels he's not playing games. Women love men who are secure with themselves.

8.   Sex shouldn't be a condition of pleasure.
Don't ever have sex unless you want to, and don't ever try to force a woman to have sex against her will. No matter how far along the relationship has gotten no means No! If she says no and you don't stop you could suffer legally in the long run. It's just not

worth the embarrassment or humiliation. If you find a woman who uses sex to manipulate, you'd better run as fast as you can, because you'll be paying every time lovemaking gets mentioned. Women have creative ways to make a man pay one way or another. Bring more value to your relationship by not allowing a woman to manipulate you through sexual encounters.

9. Stand up for something, or else you'll fall for anything.

Don't get caught in fighting about things that you can't change or those things that don't really matter. In any relationship you'll have situations where emotions get the best of you and you'll think you're being used or mistreated. There will be times that you won't agree on the same things. A rule to always remember is stand up for what you believe in, state it and them move on to bigger and better things. Make compromises by taking turns selecting what activities you would like to do. There will be times the both of you will have to give in to one another. Do it with grace, love and affection. Having the power to compromise with her is a step in the right direction.

10. Enjoy going out alone.

Don't think that every time you go out you have to take the fellas with you. Groups of men scare women off. It keeps them at a distance too. Do you really want women to be distant? The chances of meeting someone you like is always greater when you travel alone. Going out with friends can also open up possibilities, but a woman will likely approach you or make the first move if you're alone than she would if you have an entourage.

What greater thing is there for two human souls than to find they are joined for life.

9
40 WAYS TO MAKE YOUR MOVE ON HER

The best times are times you spend with someone you really like.

She shifted her posture. Her head tilted slightly, her shoulders lifted, and she gently fluffed her auburn hair. Suddenly their eyes locked for a moment. She smiled, then slowly dropped her eyelids; tilted her head down and to the side. He felt dizzy and faint, as his legs had turned to warm lead. But he wasn't about to let this signal go unanswered. If he was reading her body language correctly -- and he was -- she was giving him the universal signal to approach her.

Without saying a word he walked toward her and reached for her hand. Every nerve ending in his fingers carried a rush of excitement to his brain. They looked at each other, only for a moment, but he could have described every contour of her face.

"Has everyone found a partner?" the voice over the loud speaker asked. Then suddenly, through the same crackling sound system, the music began to play and his pulse rushed through his veins. From there the cues were given by the caller, directing their actions. Along with twenty other awkward couples they kicked back from each other, and then pulled together again. For eight long beats they stared at each other's face. They were in gym class learning to square dance...and he was in love.

Her name was Mitzy Black, as he recalled. They never spoke a word to each other, and he couldn't tell you a thing about her life. But he still talks about that feeling as if it were yesterday. He's fifty now, and this is the girl he thought was the one for him. "The feelings were too magical!" he shouts to mean anything else.

Not much changes as we mature. Making a move still makes some people hearts pound, and their knees still turn into lead at the thought of it all. Indeed steamy starts do not promote our best thinking. Intense emotions often block us from taking a careful and

WILL THE REAL MEN PLEASE STAND UP

objective look at ourselves, the person we want and the possibility of forming a relationship.

Many men think it's okay to make the first move on a woman. They don't feel that they lose out by making the first move. Yes it's scary, but you can't sit around passively waiting to be noticed by every woman that attracts your attention. But, you shouldn't set out to make a move on a woman without some tested techniques either. If you find that after using these techniques she's still isn't interested move on to the next woman who sparks your interest. Remember that every person you're attracted to may not be meant for you to have a intimate relationship with.

Use making the first move as an opportunity to widen your social circle. If you use them as the perfect time to break bread with someone who offers good conversation, or use them to enter into a new group of friends you'll save yourself undo heartache and pain.

Suppose you're set to meet the woman you've been preparing for all week. Maybe you've made plans to have drinks after work, and unless you know the woman well you may feel like you're facing a day in court -- anxious and on the witness stand. Don't fret you probably won't be expected to behave perfectly, after all you are human. Still taking a few pointers on male charm might just boost your confidence level.

Women often lack confidence. So, if you're interested in her, you'd better send out strong enough signals to let her know, or she'll miss all of them. To ease those first date jitters, why not try something new?

1.   Smile with reassurance.
Words of reassurance and facial expressions show that you are genuine with what you say. She'll love you for this. When you talk and when you listen smile at her and make her very comfortable just being with you. Notice which type of smile is the most flattering on you and which seems sincere or overdone. Look at male models in magazines and notice what type of smiles they hold for the camera.

A smile is always a nice starter and it's an easy way to open up to a person when you're not quite sure how you should began. It also helps you to make contact with out being overbearing or too aggressive. Look into her eyes politely and hold your smile for at least five seconds. It's the best green light a man can give a woman and still remain filled with integrity. If she smiles back it's the ole-go-ahead, it's an open invitation to move forward. (But not too fast). At least when you're smiling you'll began to feel better about yourself and what you're trying to do.

2. Use your eyes.

You can definitely get a person's attention by obtaining eye contact. Stare into her eyes for at least five seconds while smiling. Your eyes are the windows of your soul; use them to get your message across.

Look at her, look away, then, look back at her. It's like playing peek-a-boo with a baby. You can break the ice by using your eyes in a positive and friendly way. It helps the woman to notice you if you're too shy to approach her. Playing pee-a-boo opens up the lines of communication. Glancing in an innocent yet alluring way is pleasant, friendly and inviting. The best way to pull this one off is to stare ever so politely, all the while pulling her more toward you with each glance. If you practice this technique you will get lots of woman to approach you. It really works!

3. Remain approachable.

Say something, anything that's genuinely polite to catch her attention and spark interest. Make it a pleasant and warm invitation for her to talk to you. Sound reassuring and confident. No cut downs, negatives or gripes. If you're too shy to talk, sit next to someone you want to meet and give a soft oooooh. It sure to get a conversation going. Try making a comment, ask a question, or give a compliment. This is a good way to break the ice.

When you began to ask questions, ask anything that requires an answer -- ask for the time, directions, opinions, or even the weather. Use compliments freely; tell her you adore her shoes, you like her hair, her smile or even the way she smells. Don't overdo it though.

4.   Use wholesome opening (pickup) lines.

Many opening lines can sound so rehearsed that they also sound boring and canned. Use opening lines that are simple, sincere and appropriate for the situation you are in. At a party notice the woman you like and use what she's doing to find a way to approach her. Try not to use conversation openers like "what's a nice girl like you doing here, just say "Hello my name is... I hardly know anyone here, so I feel a little uncomfortable." She'll be charmed by your honesty, which will help make you feel more comfortable.

5.   Let your shyness shine through.

Many men will conceal their attraction, figuring its not best to come on strong. Such thinking is wrong, playing your hand too close can only lead a woman to believe you're not impressed. A better strategy -- act flustered on occasions -- blush and then turn away your gaze every so often. Such nervousness should be natural. The worst you can do is be too practiced or too smooth. A simple introduction is always good. It's better than a cliché or a come on. Most women never regret when a man introduces himself to her. Here are few great openers to help you:

* Hi Carla! Oh, I'm sorry I thought you were someone else. You look familiar.
* My sisters birthday is on Friday, she wants a new blouse, How does the one feel?
* Would you mind if I bought you a drink. I feel as if I've met you before.
* I know this seems bold, but I would like to introduce myself to you.
* Would you like to join me for a cup of coffee?

6.   Make unexpected moves. Use more than your mouth.

Your body language is 90 percent of flirting. Show physical self-awareness. Run your fingers through your facial hair, touch your face, stroke your neck. Bite or lick your lips. This is a suggestive move without being obscene. Nod your head. Innocent physical contact is nice. Lightly tap her on the arm or hand as you talk. Watch her mouth as she talks, its sensuous.

   Some women have a real problem with picking up on subtle moves. Try attention getters that are more obvious if you want her to notice. Offer her a drink, touch her hand, ask her name, tell her she looks good or hug her gently. If you want to be more subtle but still unexpected slip her a note with your phone number, or a business card with your work number.

7. Use props.

Women will notice you, but they may be too shy to approach you. If you carry or wear something pleasing to the eyes of women it will give them a reason to talk to you. That also reduces your fear of being rejected and increases the odds that you two will meet.

Carry something in your hand, like a book about love, travel brochures, or apartment hunting. It will definitely help you to capture a woman's attention. It makes her wonder what you're up to and she will be eager to meet you. Using props and supplies are great for introductions. Your simplest accessories are woman-magnets. Use them to the fullest. They spark some of the best conversations too. Gadgets that are high tech, baseball caps, T-shirt's or computer gadgets help spark interest and conversation from women. They'll ask questions like "what is it, and what features does it have. etc."

8. Soothe her nervous.

Realize women have tremendous anxiety about being rejected by men -- that's why they're not approaching you. A good way to ease her nervousness is to act as if you've known her all your life. To feel more at ease act more animated. This techniques has been known to trick your brain into overcoming shyness. It's simple...if you already know the woman you say things like "hey how's it going or what's been happening. Treat a stranger in the same manner. You'll feel more comfortable and so will she. It's easier to talk to women in this way. It lets her know you're interested in her. If you can forget your nervousness and concentrate on your partners you'll be able to really soothe her nerves.

9. Be brave.

Try out a few bolder moves. If you're in a bar hand her a glass of wine and on the napkin inscribe your personal note. As she reads it, smile and look into her eyes when she looks at you. Little notes with positive messages loosen up women and reassures her that she still looks good. It helps to revalidate your flirting techniques. Being brave does have it's rewards. Giving a woman a little innuendo makes her feel good too.

10.   Act confident and very self-sufficient.
This is the most important characteristic of a magnetic man. In those times that you don't feel completely confident, pretend you are and no one will be the wiser. The trick is to act self-sufficient as if you don't need a woman. If you develop a balance between acting confident and friendly women will draw to you. Hold your head high enough to show your happiness. And never show signs that you want a relationship too badly that you'd do anything to get it.

11.   Dress appropriate, yet attractive.
If you're looking for long term love, not a one night stand, then save your muscle shirts and shorts for another occasion. The women who are looking for longer relationships are looking for attitude, not clothing. As long as your outfit looks neat and well put together you'll do just fine. Women are initially attracted to a man's outer self. Physical attraction is the second, most important, step of getting to know the true woman on the inside.

"Keep a wardrobe of dating clothes" Find at least two outfits that really attract women. The outfits that are solid-colored and follow your physique closely, without being too tight are best. Make sure its classy and suave. It should hang very comfortable giving the woman an idea reason to feel at ease when with you. If you don't look uptight women won't see you as uptight.

12.   Be a good listener.
The most important needs every man and woman have are for understanding and acceptance. Most people use conversation as a way to try and impress the other person.

You will win her heart if you have good listening skills. This involves basic etiquette such as looking into a persons eyes while talking to them. Give the person whose talking your undivided attention and don't interrupt too many times when she is talking.

13. Be a little hard to get.
Don't make yourself so easy for her. Women like to seek men out. They like to know that they found that special person. And she want to feel like she did the picking and choosing. Even smart married women still remain a little mysterious, or a little aloof.

A woman likes to know that a man is a constant challenge to her. It makes life more interesting to her. If you're always there at her beckoning call she soon gets bored and begins to look for more challenging relationships. It's just something about that chase.

14. Develop a personality that's so magnetic she can't keep herself from you.
Your personality matters most in attracting a woman's interest. A magnetic personality comes from within. It's a combination of projecting deep pleasure, happiness and excitement all in one. You must be able to show you're happy about life.

Find ways to renew love affairs with life by: taking a course in something they really like, such as photography, travel, writing, dance, and then practice affirmations and visualizations on a daily basis. Join sports team as recreation or start a new business. All of this gives you a new attitude which shines through in their personality. Let your self-fulfillment shine through.

15. Be genuinely agreeable without being disrespectful.
One of the worst things a man can do is treat a woman with disrespect and constantly tell her she's wrong. Don't over criticize a woman or try to force her to change her life just for you. Choose to be in a relationship with a woman who has morals and values and views that are similar to your own. It should be with someone who likes the things you like. You can always assert your opinions in a thoughtful way to her but remember to be genuine.

16. See the first date from her point of view.
Because of social and biological pressures, men see the world differently than women. On that first date, be sensitive to her nervousness and need to be reserved. Put any needs you have to prove your male powerfulness on the back burner, and let her be in control of burner, and you be in control of the first date. Remember, you can always take the control back and if things get inappropriate or out of hand. And, if she turns out to be a control freak, you don't have to go out with her again.

Do you like her and want her to call you tomorrow? Fine; then let her order the dessert and wine. It makes her feel good. (You can order dessert on the second date, when she's more relaxed.)

17. If she feels good around you, she'll call you.
We all enjoy being around others who make us feel good about ourselves. How good she feels in your company depends a lot on your own emotional readiness for a relationship Women can sense when a man is angry at her or desperate to have a relationship-and both are big turn-off's that keep women from going on the second date. Don't ruin a new relationship because of anger or desperation.

18. Consider getting dating coaching.
If you often hear, "I'll call you tomorrow," but rarely receive a call, don't despair. Sometimes men unknowingly turn women off by trying too hard to be liked. Instead of understanding that you're nervous because you like her, the woman misreads the over-anxiousness as a sign of character flaws. If that happens consistently, it may be time for some dating coaching. Get your best female friend to go on a double date with you, and ask her to gently level with you afterwards about your dating behavior. Ask her to coach you, not criticize you. This will help to keep your dating confidence up.

19. Appreciate phone opportunities.
If you are ever encountered by a woman you are dying to meet don't be afraid to strike up a conversation with her. After conversing with her for about five to ten minutes muster up

the courage to ask for her phone number. Don't worry about her saying no because most women find it flattering for a man to ask for their number. A few days after getting her number you will need to call her. Make sure what you say is interesting, direct and full of humor as well.

Give her a chance to get better aquatinted with you before you come on too strong. Be sure to make your conversation as non-threatening as possible. After a few talks with her the idea of going a date with you will become more and more appealing.

20.   Acknowledge that both of you may have the jitters.

If the atmosphere is tense, say something like, I'm a little uncomfortable when I first meet someone. By putting the words out there it will help to relax the both of you. Be mindful of how you say things. It's not what you say that matters, it's how you come across with what you say. Since both of you are probably nervous try not to be to hard on one another. Keeping one another relaxed is the key to first date success.

21.   Don't feel that you must shut up and listen.

Most women aren't only interested in the sound of their own voices. If a woman feels like she's the only one talking she'll become bored and disinterested. If she feels like you're just a bump on the log or she's talking to a wall she'll shut you out of her life and find someone who has the ability to make conversation.

22.   On the other hand don't take control of the entire conversation.

Some men don't know when to shut up. Verbal torment from men can not only drive a woman crazy it can also end the beginning of a beautiful relationship. Nervousness or over zealous attitudes can cause men to spout out going on and on never giving a woman a chance to add anything to the conversation. The anxiety of having to listen to a man whose inconsiderate and unstoppable in conversation wears a woman down therefore leaving her an out by getting out of the relationship.

23. Don't do a dog and pony show.

Many men take on the role of an entertainer when a date doesn't seem to be going well. They think it's their job to perform if the woman is too quiet. The more loquacious and frantic you get the more likely she is to clam up getting quieter and quieter until you a doing dog stunts. The best thing to do is try to calm yourself down, change your tactics, ask a few questions that are non prying and then go with the flow.

24. Don't interrogate her.

It's okay to try to draw her out of her quiet shell, but rapid fire question will only make her uncomfortable, and make you sound like a private investigator. Women feel pressured and imposed upon when too many questions are asked in succession. Asking one question after the next let's a woman know you're sizing her up, and that's okay but to get to the point of badgering her is out of the question. The best thing to do if you must ask questions is be sure they are not intimidating. Don't be so obvious when you're trying to find out if this is the woman for you. At least keep it fun.

25. Pay attention.

The worst thing a man can do is tune out his date. Acting as if you are focusing on her will only show through on the next date if not the present one. Giving lots of eye contact is great, but when your eyes wonder as soon as she begins to talk you are not focused and you'd better believe she's going to notice it. If you do ask questions you should at least be prepared to listen to the answer.

26. Don't overdo it.

By the same token it's best not to be too practiced in listening. People know when you're overdoing it. You must able to find balance in not listening or over listening. And yes you can be too focused. Not taking your eyes off of a person can be misleading. There is a big gap between what you really feel and what you actually project. It can be very unnerving. Everyone wants the center of attention, but the interest has to be sincere. Overkill can destroy the trust you are trying to establish.

27. Talk about things she likes to find out more about.

Try talking about her hobbies, her job or her favorite things in life. To do this you ask questions that aren't intimidating. Ask her what is her favorite childhood toy, or what does she like to do, or maybe even what's her favorite food. Her career is a great topic because most women like to talk about their careers. Find out who her idols are and then watch how she'll like you more for knowing so much about the people she admires. Getting a woman to open up can be tough, but if you find something they feel comfortable talking about you're already one step ahead.

28. Don't try to force her to open up.

Women don't want a psychological therapy session when they go on a date and neither do you. If you're trying to force her into an emotional hang-over the next day try to psycho-analyze her. If you do this your relationship is near doom at the onset when you try to force her to open up. If she doesn't volunteer answers, she looks uncomfortable and she doesn't want to talk, you should do the right thing by changing the subject to more suitable things. It takes a certain amount of trust for anyone to open up and be real with themselves. No one opens up completely on the first date unless they've known each other for a long time.

29. Allow her to remain neutral.

Talking about subjects that make her feel comfortable are the best way to keep a woman interested in you. Talking about her favorite things are a great way to remain neutral. If you can't talk about these things don't fake it because she'll know you're trying to bait her. Touch on politics, movies, the latest tabloid story or any subject she'll appreciate and respect you for mentioning.

30. Don't invest too heavily in the first date.

If you spend large sums of money on your clothing, hair, nails, and a jazzy outfit you may feel as if you've wasted the effort if your date turns out to be incompatible with you or you just don't think she's your type.

31. Look at your first date as if it's an interview.

Determine first if you want to go any further. Don't go all out or treat it with a sky's the limit attitude so if it doesn't work you won't have spent a small fortune preparing for the date. If you don't put your all into it you won't be setting yourself up for a fall. You can also suggest having your first date during lunch time so if things don't work out you will have an excuse to leave. If you're compatible and you find that there is hope for the future with this person you can then decide to have a dinner date for later in the week. At the very least if things don't work out you will still have had a good meal.

32. Regard your first dates as a date for enjoying food with someone.

No matter what you think, a first date is great for enjoying good food. It beats sitting at home and watching old reruns and eating by yourself. Nevertheless, don't make it obvious that you're just interested in getting a good meal. Try your best to give her a charming time with you. First dates give you the opportunity to size up the person and you'll know right away whether or not you want to see her again.

33. Give her your attention.

Give her your attention and be attentive to her. Being nice is not against the law. It's no skin off your butt to behave like the perfect gentlemen and a gentlemen is always gracious. Maintain a pleasant manner, even if you're not attracted to her. Don't act as if you're being bothered. Imagine how you would feel if you were treated in a rude manner. You never know you might not be meeting an intimate mate but a new best friend.

34. Have good conversation.
A good date is usually full of good conversation, you laugh a lot and you feel relaxed. Your conversation helps to make the evening fun. You learn new thing and feel good about answering questions. Don't lead on and don't act like a stiff. It sets the pace for future encounters.

35. Don't feel compelled to do anything that makes you feel uncomfortable.
Drinking too much, doing drugs, or being pressured to participate in things you don't like is the first sign it's a bad date. If you feel uncomfortable avoid this person like the plague. Remain strong and stick to your guns. Don't be compromised and remain a valued and respected person at all times.

37 Leave her for a short while.
Once you've said enough to keep the conversation going, tell her you need to speak to someone (go to the men's room, get another drink, or go and really speak to someone across the room or even in another room) but remember to be back in five to ten minutes. This keeps you from crowding her and more important when you return you'll return as a friend and someone with whom she's already acquainted.

Many men refuse to make a move on a woman. They think that flirting is fake, too aggressive, tacky and vulgar. The truth is, flirting is a simple way to be playful. Flirting is considered a game that almost everyone plays at one time or another. One of most successful ways an eligible man can get the attention of a woman is to flirt with her. How else will women know you're interested in them.

You can't sit around waiting to be noticed by every woman that attracts your attention.

10
HOW TO USE YOUR RESOURCES TO GET HER

If you look up and finds a woman staring at you, she might be interested in you.

When you're trying to figure out the best way to find the mate you have to get creative. There are certain things you'll have to already know if you want to get closer. Ask yourself these questions: Where are the women hanging out? What is it that most women do during their days? That's right most of them work! So if you want to find a woman, go to the places that working women hang out during the day. Looking for a few good women is not as difficult as it may seem. Women are more at ease with daylight meetings because they don't feel like they're being picked up or they are the day's special at the meat market. When you and the woman feel comfortable with meeting one another you'll plan to meet in a more romantic setting and this can often lead to something that the both of you will like. You'll be surprised at the numerous ways you can meet women. Listed are some of the most practical ways to use your resources to meet women.

1. Go To The Source.

If you admire and fantasize about being with a female police officer don't result to calling 911 with false emergencies, why not just go to the source. To help you here's a few things you should consider: Stop by and ask pertinent questions like directions, or question pertaining to their line of business and so forth. Visit several places and ask questions that will help you meet and converse with them. If you want to meet an attorney go to the law library, a courthouse, or her office. It's just that simple; you go where the women you like will spend the most time.

WILL THE REAL MEN PLEASE STAND UP

2.   Read The Papers.

It's time for you to look at the newspapers a little differently. Ask yourself what section your ideal woman would read. Scan that section keeping your eyes out for ads. Women in sales will be attracted to motivational seminars. Single mothers will read the community calendar and respond to ads promoting children's events.

Let's say you're interested in a woman who's interested in outdoor activities, turn to the appropriate section, perhaps the sports pages. Listed there are all the sports activities and clubs in your area: baseball, tennis, golf, hiking, and every other sport available. Now you know where she'll be, just waiting on you to arrive so she can meet you. Pick an activity you like and show up ready to participate. She'll have no idea you're there to meet someone just like her.

3.   Join Groups, Clubs or Organizations.

Women often join clubs that are related to their hobbies or jobs. At your library reference desk you'll find a listing of every job in existence. Women who need to work on presentations skills join organizations on public speaking. Women interested in the arts join the performing arts organizations. The lists are endless and so are your opportunities to meet the woman of your choice. Here is one approach that might just help you: Sign up for local meetings that the woman you desire has with her peers. When you call to register for the meetings try to get the person who is running the meeting. Regain your composure as you ask questions about the background requirements of it's members. On the evening the group is scheduled to meet arrive early, introduce yourself and scan the room for possible dates or even friends. After the meeting who knows you might be invited to continue your conversation on a later date.

4.   Use The Yellow Pages.

Turn to the table of contents in your local yellow pages. Find your desired woman's occupation and flip to the reference page, which list companies under that job category. Check out whether any of those businesses are near your employment or home. This type of research can reveal great amounts of information about the company and the person's status. If you find your chosen profession and you see the picture of the woman you like advertised with the ad, she'll probably be single too.

It's not easy finding a great woman so you have to do all you can to expand your dating pool. One method that has been extremely useful is meeting a good friend for lunch. Pick a restaurant near your friends workplace and arrange to meet -- early at her office. This will give you time to scope out her office mates. The trick is to see and be seen so that you can get a few quick introductions. This works if you relax and go with the flow.

5.   Use The Business Card: "Approach".

If you prefer to be more straight forward in your approach, keep a few cards from your favorite restaurant or bar handy. Choose to carry different restaurant cards. Write your name and number on the back of them and keep them readily available. Later when you meet someone give them one of the restaurant business cards and say "this is a fabulous place to enjoy a good meal. Maybe I could take you there sometimes." This way your come on is direct yet more calming and romantic to the woman.

6.   More Business Cards: "Strategies".

Suppose you're at a party flirting wildly with a woman whose attracted your attention. She's confident, witty, friendly and very sexy looking. Searching for something to write with, you discover your business card. Here's what you do: Simply hand her your business card, and say something like "I'm sorry I didn't get a chance to meet you earlier, but please take my card and if you wouldn't mind, give me a call so that we can discuss tonight's party." While she's waiting on her coat find out what she likes. You might ask, "What are some of the best places to visit here? Simple questions that might involve lengthy answers are great for breaking the ice. Ask her what are her hobbies. Talk about careers, local restaurants, and sports. You can always talk about work, but save that for the dinner date. Of course by now, both of you are aware that sightseeing, restaurants and sports are not the real motive.

7. Five Minute "Collect A Card" Tactic.

What if you see someone you'd like to meet and you're tired of giving out restaurant business cards. Give out your own. Select three or more crowded places that you enjoy going to. If you like them that means they are probably jammed with people you also like. You must visit at the peak moments and you must also be unaccompanied. Don't spend more than an hour per week in each place. Scan the room and pick out several women that keep your attention. The trick is to collect at least five business cards within the one hour limit and you're going to pass out at least 10.

Talk to each woman for about five minutes. Don't worry five minutes is long enough to introduce yourself get her name and give her a business card during your conversation. If you're a little nervous, that's okay because she's probably more nervous than you are. Set her at ease and make her feel comfortable. Don't ask for her name or number, if she gives it to you on her own that's good because that means she's interested in you too. If she doesn't offer her name or card this will help narrow down your margin of rejection and you won't be expecting her to do a mad rush for the phone when she gets home.

You can take a break to the men's room and write down what features about each person you liked or disliked to help you remember things about them so you'll be prepared when she calls. She'll think you're so thoughtful because you remembered.

Never ask a woman out more than twice when you meet her. If she can't make it the first time and you attempt to take her out a second time and she still finds a reason not to go don't worry, file it away and remember that everything is not for everyone so you haven't lost -- the chemistry just wasn't there.

These Business Card tricks do cause for a plan of action, but you can learn a lot about women this way. So instead on concentrating on the one person that rejected you , see it as a positive experience and keep having loads of fun.

The price of personal greatness is responsibility

11
HOW TO SENSUOUSLY WORK A ROOM

When you walk into a room hold your head up high.

There's no better idea than to throw your own party and work the room. The ideal of meeting new people is exciting yet scary for many people. You meet at the party and now you suddenly feel terrified. What's the problem? You need a little tutoring in the art of socializing and mixing in large and small groups. Here are a few quick tips to help you pull it off.

1. **Don't travel with an entourage.**

The worst thing a man can do is travel in packs. Women will not feel comfortable talking to you when she notices you have an entire group with you. It's intimidating to her. It's humiliating to be turned down while you're with your friends also. Even women who don't mind introducing themselves to men feel a little uncomfortable when he's surrounded by his friends.

You should go alone or find one friend to go to social gatherings with you. Be sure it' someone who has an appetite for partying just as big as yours. It has to be someone who can get along at a party without crowding you. Being a part of a more adventurous duo will motivate you to show a little more gregariousness than you probably would on your own. Supportive friendships are great, just don't overdo it by bringing too many friends with you. You don't need a entourage.

Whatever you do, don't make your duo a female friend. It doesn't matter how platonic the two of you are, a female stranger watching from a distance will not know that you are just buddies and will be hesitant to approach you. The only exception to the rule: You and your female pal are both extremely independent, in which case, you'll quickly desert each other once you've walked through the door.

WILL THE REAL MEN PLEASE STAND UP

2. Don't feel too loyal.

Is she's charming enough for you to feel relieved at not having to make small talk with any other women? Don't get too comfortable. Don't settle for the first woman you see either. Move around. Find a gracious way to get out of conversations so that one woman will not monopolize all of your time. The best way to keep from becoming loyal to one woman is to excuse yourself politely saying you'll be back later, you'd like to mingle with the other guest for a few minutes. Or you can tell her you haven't said hello to the host yet and you don't want to ignore some of your friends you've noticed that are there. When she sees you mingling with others she'll want you even more.

3. Don't turn flirting into a numbers game.

Now that you know how to limit yourself, you should know how to keep from spreading yourself too thin. When working a room you should do some sorting before you start selecting any woman. Chat a few minutes with your chosen women, then move on. Try to associate with the ones who look like good prospects. Try not to discriminate, others will notice and you'll be the one to end up left out and dissatisfied.

4. Don't communicate with women only.

A man's biggest mistake is to socialize with women only. First off, it turns the party into a hunt for women. Such determination is easily noticed and detected by others. Secondly, it's a big turn off to men and women alike. You actually deprive yourself of the possibility of making new friends with men and women when you strike out to talk to only women. And you never know what meeting men will do for helping you to get to know women who are eligible and available.

5. Look your best.

Looking your best doesn't mean you have to dress too outrageous. Wear clothing that compliments your body and will make people want to approach you in friendly ways. Clothes can be nice conversation pieces also. If your clothing has history that's even better. Don't be too stiff or stuffy about what you try on for the night. Having a playful attitude will show through and make you interesting to women.

6. **Commit to an occasional outrageous act.**
Sometimes your best icebreaker is an unexpected move. Having an appeal with a little brazen seductiveness and quick wit is appealing to women. Not everyone can pull off such behavior or will want to, so choose an outrageous act that works for you. Asking outrageous questions will set a woman's soul on fire. The spontaneity effect it has on women is sometimes just what the doctor ordered. Asking simple yet directly crazy questions from time to time will add spark to your conversation. When you have a lack of reserve it helps to open others up and loosen them enough to drop their inhibitions.

7. **Become the party's photographer.**
Taking pictures can help you to become a great socialite at major events. The power of the lens will also give you more freedom. It allows you to walk up to perfect strangers and ask whether or not you can take their pictures. Inevitably they'll be flattered. Even if you don't really want to take pictures just having the camera can help you to become aquatinted with beautiful women. Taking pictures at parties is a perfect way to approach women without being overbearing.

8. **Play the guessing game.**
Try to guess what type of profession the women at the party are involved in. Playing this game with a woman you're interested in is even more fun.

9. **Visit the most unusual places.**
The spots that are the most fun are the areas at a party where no one else hangs out. Perhaps in a well lit corner, by a bookshelf, or near a collection of fine art pieces. When other prospects see you browsing they will join you and ask what's so interesting. From there you're open to chat freely. This technique will only get you so far, so be prepared to use other strategies I've mentioned as a follow up to this one.

WILL THE REAL MEN PLEASE STAND UP

10. Have your favorite drink.
Not many drinks, just one or maybe half of one. A light beer, a martini, or your favorite mixed drink will do just fine. You'll immediately start taking things less seriously, suddenly gaining the perspective that everybody around you is most likely feeling as jittery as you. And maybe approaching that good looking girl at the end of the table won't seem terrifying.

11. Be more informed than the next person.
No matter what your profession try to be well versed in something other than what you do. It's nothing more boring than talking to a person who has nothing to talk about but one subject. Don't allow yourself to become so wrapped up in your own world that you neglect the world around you. Stay up on current events by reading the newspaper, magazines and good books. Knowledge of things that interest other people makes you a better conversationalist. Become more informed about the world and you will attract positive attention from others.

12. Act like you're having a good time.
Even if you're not feeling like a party animal on the night of the party try to have a great time. No one wants to meet a man who looks likes he's depressed and moody. And don't think because you're standing quietly looking out the window you will get rescued from woman. Women won't be interested in a man who looks as if he's carrying lots of baggage. Your best nights are those when you are already having a good time.

Throwing Your Own Party

13. Bring on the ambiance.
First off, the lightning. Scatter a few candles around. Cover floor lamps with a scarf. And don't overlook the power of a light blue bulb it softens the glow. A few strategically positioned vases of flowers also adds to the festive atmosphere.

WILL THE REAL MEN PLEASE STAND UP

Novelty themes can also help create an entertaining mood. Whether you're attending a party or throwing one you should now have the necessary meeting skills to set forth and conquer. And remember "the more you mix the better you'll be."

14. Invite everyone you know.
Go through your phone book, your rolodex and your old high school year book if you have to and find everyone you know and throw the biggest party you can afford to give. Don't forget to call all those new acquaintances you've just met, professional and otherwise if you feel there's a social rapport with them. People really do like going to parties because they also get a chance to meet new people. They'll be flattered that you thought of them. Tell each person you invite to bring along a friend, preferably singles.

15. Have a co-host.
Having co-host will help you to save money on all the food and drinks and you'll get a bigger invite list this way. When you let others co-host with you the party becomes more fun and it allows different groups of people with different tastes the opportunity to show up. To help assure the success of your co-hosted parties find a couple of friends who hang out with different crews. This will help you to come up with never-before-seen prospects. One final advantage of joint efforts; your friends can help pay for the cleanup person you'll want to hire for the next day cleaning.

16. Don't run out of drinks.
Ever notice how a party quickly thins out when the drinks runs low? Within your budget at least 70 percent of your resources should go toward beer and spirits. Keeps your drinks cold by putting them in a tub of ice or in a big plastic garbage can, but consider if you put the drinks in your tub you're going to probably have lines of people at the bathroom.

Some men like to buy a keg to save money. Having the best you can afford will liven up the bash. People walk in and see you've spent money and it builds the excitement. They feel more like they're at an event and they also feel more welcome. Make sure everyone can manage to mingle and get their drinks without hassle.

17.   Provide snacks but don't go crazy with them.

Spend your time preparing more for the party than decorating the foods because people won't notice the decorations as much as the atmosphere and the people there. People do get hungry when partying and drinking. And if they are drinking its best to keep their stomachs full.

18.   Don't have a sit down dinner.

When you have sit down dinner you don't allow your guest enough of a mix. If you confine your guest to a sit down dinner the atmosphere is usually more subdued and laid back instead of fun and outrageous. People often feel they need to be on their best behavior at sit down dinners.

Instead, have twenty or thirty friends come over assign each of them a dish to bring. This allows everyone to become a physical part of the party. Throw a few pillows on the floor and allow people to sit where they please for comfort. People don't mind sitting buffet style and you'll feel freer to socialize instead of running back and forth to serve each course.

19.   Use more than one strategy to work a room.

By combining more than one of these strategies you'll always have a back up system to lean on. Applying more than one or several of these strategies helps to add a little more life each time you use them.

Learn the art of socializing and working a room.

Step 3:

Understanding

Women

12

WHAT *REAL* WOMEN REALLY WANT!

Even though you've been hurt, keep your heart open.

While waiting on the arrival of my best friend, Denise in Dallas, Texas, I found myself interviewing several men who were also waiting on the same plane to land. As I mentioned to them the differences that arise between men and women I could see other men eavesdropping. At one point I asked the gentlemen sitting next to me, "What do you think women want from men? Before he could answer another man commented, "They want money! After a long silence, he added "any dummy knows that."

The men who were close enough to hear his comment began to give each other high five's. The females near by frowned, and as I looked at one of the women I asked, "Would you like to respond to that?"

She glanced at all the men. "Did any of you notice the S-500 Black Mercedes in the parking lot?" After a short pause she added, "It's mine... bought and paid for by me." She began to look at each man directly in their faces." "You may think women are after money, but many women don't need or want your money. "Besides not all men have money." "We do have the ability to make our own you know!"

This simple gesture prompted me to add this chapter to my book. Moving ahead I asked over five hundred men what they thought women wanted from them and 80% of said money.

Sure, some women desire men with money, but these are women who are shallow in their own development. Any man who thinks a woman is after his money would be a fool to even let a woman like that in his life. The thing women wanted more than anything else was: they wished certain men would pack a bag and check into a Room for Improvement. Women might have handled the last millennia a little differently if they'd

WILL THE REAL MEN PLEASE STAND UP

been in charge. But in general, they're very, very, very fond of men. Women think of men as the opposite, not the opposing, sex. And while some women find the differences troubling, others are worthy of a hearty ooh la, la!

If they can put a man on the moon, goes one late-twentieth-century jest, why can't they put all of them on the moon? Our answer: Because we'd sorely miss the following things about the men we like.

1. When you're dancing, the big of the hand on the small of my back.
2. That they don't take everything personally.
3. Their healthy affection for their body-as-is. We get hysterical when we don't fit into our tightest jeans. Men only start worrying when they don't fit into the car.
4. The way they get blessed out listening to a smart woman talk.
5. The open and trusting manner in which they'll point to a restaurant menu item and ask "Do I like this?"
6. French-kissing.
7. When they drape their jacket around our shoulders on a chilly evening.
8. If you ask them "Who's prettier, me or Halle Berry?" they instinctively know the correct answer. ("That pig? Compared to you? No contest!")
9. Their tendency to fall in love with some goofy aspect of you that you never noticed before: "I'm crazy about the way your ear curls like a potato chip."
10. Their refusal to take the blame when they know they don't deserve it.
11. Their buns.
12. That they aren't exactly sure when you're wearing makeup and when you're not, and can't remember whether mascara is the tube thing or the pencil thing.
13. Their knack for memorizing dialogue from *The Godfather* (as long as they don't say "I want no inquiries made....I want you to arrange a meeting of the heads of the Five Families" more than once a week).
14. The stricken/ecstatic look on their face when they're holding a friend's baby and suddenly, for the first time, they can imagine themselves doing this for real.
15. The smell of Right Guard and honest sweat battling for dominance.

WILL THE REAL MEN PLEASE STAND UP

16. They'll kill hairy insects the size of Latvia for you, even though they don't much relish he task either.
17. They're willing to let you off at the entrance, park 16 blocks and walk.
18. The graciousness with which they allow us to pick at their dessert when we've declined to order one.
19. Talking to them in the bathroom while they shave.
20. Sleeping like spoons.
21. Fighting with them after you've both gotten the hang of doing it fairly.
22. They make such fabulous brothers.
23. The way they look in well worn jeans and a white dress shirt with no tie.
24. When they tell us they'd be friends with us even if they didn't love us.
25. The way they assume we have an opinion on the designated-hitter rule.
26. When they say Pat Schroeder would make a great president, and it's not even to get us into bed really.
27. He cried at *Fried Green Tomatoes*, too.
28. Their great ways of making love.

Women Want To Pursue Men Without Guilt

To think that men are the natural aggressors in a relationship has been proven a myth. Such a belief is based on our social lives and supports the notion that only men lead and women follow. Most women are hesitant to be aggressive because they've been conditioned to assume a passive role. That's not the reality and nature of her being at all. Women have a great deal of finesse that allows them to communicate more broadly in nonverbal ways. A man restricts his communication by words, women will communicate by gestures, posturing, facial expressions, eye contact, etc.

From all indications men will continue to chase women until women catch *them*. Perhaps men will realize they will best survive within captivity of a loving woman who is willing to take the risk of attracting them to ensure they will settle down. Here's proof that men love to be pursued by women:

WILL THE REAL MEN PLEASE STAND UP

1.   It supports him.

It prevents him from taking the risk of being rejected. At least half the men today have a fear of being rejected whether they admit it or not. Even if they have tough skin and can tolerate rejection, the scars still pile up and are difficult to heal. An aggressive women reassures his ego and feeds his self-esteem because it's flattering to him.

2.   It's a role reversal.

Role reversal relives his anxiety and reduces day to day pressures on him. In society women have the notion that men must be the aggressors. There's relief from the perceived burden that he must have a hearty conversation to make contact with a woman, and also take the initiative.

3.   It stimulates him.

It allows him to engage in a positive attitude about her, because it seems to imply that she is accessible. A woman's aggressiveness transmits a message of a liberated attitude and experience in the dating game.

4.   It relieves him of being blamed for something he did not initiate.

By encouraging the come on by women a man avoids charges or accusations, that he started the encounter in case it doesn't work out. If he doesn't stick his neck out first, and waits for a positive signal from her, he can claim innocence.

5.   It promises him economic benefits.

He assumes she is willing to share the costs of dating expenses. It also gives the impression that she is economically independent.

13
WOMEN WHO SCARE MEN OFF

Be creative...your creativity is a place where no one else has been.

It's a day like any other when a seemingly normal woman walks into my office, sits down and says something like, "I don't know what I do to turn men off. Somehow and someway I push them away." Maybe I'm too demanding, or not demanding enough; I don't know. Men are so confusing."

And it could be the very same day in that very same way, in that very same chair that a seemingly normal man, unrelated to the first woman, sits down and says, "I don't get women. I must be doing something wrong or I'd have at least a semblance of a relationship with one of them." Women are so confusing."

I've seen it time and time again. Each gender trying to make contact with the other but becoming dazed and confused in the process. Like an animal who has come to close to a hot-wired electrical fence, I've seen both men and women jump back and retreat from the opposite sex because they didn't want to risk the potential pain from misunderstanding or rejection. So they keep their distance.

The barrier between the sexes is built early on in life by the fear of being teased for having a "girlfriend" or "boyfriend." Remember those days? Some people just can't seem to forget them. The male and female social universes intersect only as the adolescent years approach. It's a wonder that male-female relationship are so confusing and distant.

Now, let's begin at the beginning. I'll start with a straight-forward fact: When men and women get together there are, in effect, two worlds -- his and hers. So why then does sexually accomplished women scare men off? It depends. Sometimes intimacy can actually get in the way of developing a healthy relationship - if that's the main or sole focus. It can also be intimidating if you are sexually light years ahead of your mate.

After Laurie, 29, had been exclusively seeing Dan, 28, for a few months, she decided to make the first move. Dan was shy and hadn't dated much, but Laurie felt herself falling in love with him. One night, when Dan affectionately kissed her, Laurie "attacked him," as she put it, maneuvering him into her bedroom. "I stroked and caressed Dan, using special techniques that had pleased my other boyfriends," she says. "But this time I had so much passion built up and I came on with such intensity that Dan couldn't perform," Laurie continues. "The potentially romantic evening completely backfired. I was so overpowering-like I couldn't wait-that I think Dan felt intimidated, that he had to give a great performance in bed." Instead of having a romantic night of Passionate lovemaking, Laurie and Dan spent an awkward and frustrating six hours together. Laurie feared that this small disaster would destroy their blossoming relationship, and after Dan abruptly left that morning, she faced the dilemma of many women today: Is there such a thing as being too good in bed? Who knows, but listed are the most common reasons women scare men off.

1.   Super sexual partners.

Of course, we all want to be superb sexual partners, but is there such a thing as being overqualified in the lovemaking department and can it backfire? The answer is yes! In past generations, women's roles were clearly defined: to be naive and inexperienced lovers, led by their partners. But today, things are different. There's nothing wrong with women initiating sex or performing well in bed. "It's important to realize that sexual arousal and response for both men and women requires relaxation, or at least the relative absence of anxiety," notes Richard C. Reznichek, M.D., of a California-based medical group. "The 'too good in bed' partner may come on so strong, or assert so much control, that the other partner will be intimidated or overwhelmed. That feeling can rapidly lead to anxiety or even fear-and consequently a loss of arousal and response."

WILL THE REAL MEN PLEASE STAND UP

2. Fantasy vs. reality.

Enjoy! The idea of a woman being too good in bed! What a problem!" Most have fantastic lovers who initiate sexual intimacy. They love the idea of having the female be the initiator and the aggressor; they love the fantasy of the woman wanting them so much that she can't control herself," says Judith Stiffer, Ph.D., a certified sex therapist and host of the Better Sex Video Series. "But the reality is overwhelming, leading to fears of not measuring up. For example, the male taking the initiative and the female being receptive. All of these issues will climb into bed with them and affect their ability to communicate effectively in a sexual way. "Sadly," Seifer continues, "it is still easier for people to have sex together than it is for them to talk about it! Typically, couples don't discuss sex until after they have tried and failed, as in the case of Dan and Laurie."

3. Game playing.

"I didn't play hard to get at all," says Laurie. "I pulled out all the bedroom tricks I had, which was probably way to much, too soon! But after we discussed it, Dan had no problem at all. He didn't feel as though we were competing or that he couldn't measure up to my expectations. We had a very satisfying relationship for four years." "In a committed relationship, partners can afford to take turns being the 'too good' one. However, new lovers need to tread more lightly until they are comfortable with each other's likes and dislikes. Psychologist Deirdra Price, Ph.D., emphasizes that no matter what your sexual knowledge, honest communication is crucial. Some people are more sexually experienced and already know how to give and receive pleasure. "Testing the waters is one way to see how a new sexual partner will respond to your experience. Suggest what you would like to do and see how she reacts. If her response is negative, it's important to find out why." Price adds that "the most important aspect of sexual intimacy is being able to communicate about your body's desire. It is also important to be in a relationship with a woman who likes you and accepts all of your unique characteristics and experiences." However, extensive background in the sexual arena-or the fear of coming across as "too good in bed"- may cause some women to hold back with their partners. "Just because a woman is good in bed, doesn't mean she should be written off as a whore."

4. Too much of a good thing?

Says Karl, 33, a politician, "I was so great in bed that a couple of old girlfriends came to see me even after they were married. One single girlfriend and I never got out of bed. Ironically that was the problem. The relationship didn't grow from there; she never even introduced me to her friends, much less her family. "This didn't do much for my self ego, "Karl continues. "I had years of therapy to find out why I used sex as a Power trip. It was the one thing I felt I had control over in my life. But deep down it really wasn't satisfying. I wanted to be in a special, committed relationship with someone who loved me, but sex always ruled."

5. Quality vs. quantity.

Today, with the fear of AIDS, more and more couples are thinking in terms of commitment and love instead of no-emotional-strings-attached, one-night stands. And women want love partners who not only care deeply for them, respect their intellect and support their career choices, but who satisfy their sexual needs, too. After all, lovemaking is just one part of the relationship. "Sometimes You give up physical satisfaction to get psychological satisfaction, "says Debra, who has learned through many failed relationships to like and respect herself and has since avoided one-night stands and superficial relationships." I want men to like me for who I am as a person," she says, "not just to see me as someone to satisfy their physical needs." The man's pursuit of you is taken away if you meet him with too much passion at the very onset - it's a turn-off for many "Movies have given us a lot of misconceptions about the first time we make love with someone, showing all that built up romantic passion," Debra continues. "The relationships that last are generally those that have a slower introduction, sexually as well as on all other levels." Never lose sight of the fact that you want a physical relationship that is mutually satisfying. Whatever you can do to enhance the quality of your lovemaking should be welcomed by both of you. Such unconditional communication between two people who are in love and attracted to one another is bound to foster emotional and sexual growth, both as a couple and as individuals. It's important to remember that often it's her and the way she makes you feel that makes you so good at lovemaking. That should make any man feel great!"

6.   Women want men with an outlaw spirit.
Women may tell other women that all they want is a generous man, but men know the real truth. Women will talk until they are blue in the face about how they want a kind and gentle man, a man who every now and then opens an emotional vein, a guy who weeps without shame, a lovely fellow who is just as likely as you to suggest, during your next trip to the video store, how much fun it would be to rent a love story.

The only man whose going to buy that line is the one who's dense. Why do women insist that they prefer men of the sunny, uncomplicated variety, when their actions clearly reveal that they're most turned on by a man possessed of a brooding, outlaw spirit? Who are they trying to convince? Please! Women loved to love bad boys. They love the kind of guy who looks somewhat displaced, or sort of irresponsible or fetchingly unkempt. There's also the little boy lost who's never had an intimate relationship that lasted more than four months. You know the type. The kind that wears the silly grin and smiles all the time. He's an emotional accident waiting to happen.

Come on, give me a break. Acting like a bad boy gets men any women they want. Women have been reported as saying they notice the bad boy types much sooner than the good boy types. That's what attracts women to men. Every now and then the bad boy might do something nice, like call her collect to say hello, and she thinks he's so thoughtful for taking out time to do it.

As a matter of fact women love these bad boys more, or at least lose sleep over them. Since they know how to make women love them it makes women love them more. Not all women like to be ignored or jerked around, but women find men that are a project and hard to get simply irresistible. This isn't what she intended to happen. So when he begins to treat her bad and doesn't call or he doesn't act worried when she's sick, or he waits three days to return her calls, it makes her fall even deeper.

WILL THE REAL MEN PLEASE STAND UP

One night after being treated terribly she came to his apartment and asked if she could come up. There was now something different in her voice, not just concern for why he hadn't called but something more. She was really concerned. He immediately thought to himself he had hit pay dirt and he did; he had hooked her. He made her feel that she had pulled him away from what he was doing although he really wasn't doing anything by saying I guess I have a little time to spare. He then went for a drink with her and she paid for the drinks.

The assumption is always that men are by nature not forthcoming, that they are tough emotional nuts to crack. That's bull! Men are mostly interested in women. Bright, competitive men are observant. What most women see is bad boys and for whatever reason, they do surprisingly well with women. Monkey see, monkey do.

Horse sense equals stable knowledge.

14

WOMEN WHO DON'T CALL

It's okay to change your mind.

I'm with my friends Tina and Paula in a restaurant on the Upper East Side of Manhattan- and we're exchanging dating stories. Tina, a 32-year-old architect, indulges herself in one of her favorite pastimes: reminiscing about the ones that got away. This time her story had a slightly different twist.

"His name is Samuel, and he was hot," she says, shaking her head as she looks down into her drink. "He had long brunette hair, a great smile, and mischievous green eyes. He was handsome and quick-witted, too. And," she says, "his body was so tight that the women on his job wore spandex just to get his attention.

"I'll never forget our date. I cooked dinner at my apartment. I was in fine form: my Chicken Cordon Bleu was in a league of its own, the flaming Cherries Jubilee was never better. We went down to a jazz club in the Village, and a nightcap at the Plaza, and then it was back to my apartment, where we made love like wild passionate animals." (Tina is prone to such grandiose embellishments).

I never saw him again after that night. He told me he'd call me once he returned from his business trip. It never happened. I don't know why and I've regretted it ever since."

Paula, a 31-year-old attorney, remembers the junior editor who never called her back. She'll always remember him, because he was gorgeous, and because of the unusual aftermath. "About six months later she ran into him when she was shopping in Barney's. He saw me from across the store and started yelling at me. Wow, was it so embarrassing. "You think you can take me out, sleep with me, and never call me again?!" he yelled. "Who the hell do you think you are lady!" I tried to explain to him that I was going to call him, but I was waiting on him to call first. He didn't believe a word of it. He just lashed into me. I tried to ask him out again, right then and there, but there was just no way." Here are eight reason women say they don't call:

1. **She wasn't ready for a relationship.**

Many times when women decide to become involved they are still on the rebound from a previous relationship. My fiancee and I had broken up five or six months before. Her involvement with Art was earmarked for special delivery. It had all the makings of a fine relationship-but that meant responsibility, commitment, earnest romance...all the things she was striving to avoid in those idyllic days. She knew she wasn't ready.

2. **She would have been too good for me.**

Sometimes people prevent themselves from getting involved in relationships as a means to punish themselves. "Self-punishment is a very common mode of human behavior, for a variety of psychological reasons," says Alice Fox, a New York City psychotherapist. "Staying indoors, overworking, becoming involved in destructive relationships, and, yes, avoiding good relationships, are all forms of self-punishment. It's unfortunate, but very common."

My state of mind then was not healthy. She was into some extremely self destructive behaviors (like drinking and partying a lot and, quite honestly, sleeping her way through the Key), and in her heart of hearts, she didn't feel that the time was right for a lasting relationship or a good man.

3. **She was Geographically undesirable.**

She was living in Key West. He was living in Key Largo, 50 miles away. Not a major problem, but a nuisance. She knew that she would be leaving that part of the country at some point. Her future didn't lie in the Keys. Art, on the other hand, was involved in the local media, and his career was more firmly entrenched. She didn't want to get too comfortable, because she would be the one that had to relocate.

WILL THE REAL MEN PLEASE STAND UP

4. She met someone else.

Two days after her date, she met a diving instructor who was a Denzel Washington look-alike. It never amounted to anything more than a friendship, but many times he knocked her off her feet. She got up and went after him again. In retrospect she saw that he was a tease, neither accepting her advances nor completely rejecting them. Sadly, she was a casualty of her own unrequited lust for him.

5. It was too much too soon.

The fire of our passion was intense and consuming, all right...which was probably why it burned itself out so quickly. Every reasonably long relationship she'd ever had started off nice and slow. No phone calls every five minutes, no dating every night...and no sex, at least not in the beginning. (Her record for waiting is two months, and she probably would have gone longer if necessary.) It may sound old-fashioned, but she's not alone. She firmly believe that if they hadn't slept together the first night, they probably would have had a beautiful relationship.

6. She wanted to keep her options open.

Is she the only one? Who among us hasn't at least once kept somebody on ice while they play out their options? Some people are very cautious about loneliness, and strive to keep as many doors open as possible. The more options the less disappointments.

7. We had too much in common.

Sounds ridiculous, right? We liked diving, tennis, poetry and members of the same church. We were partial to the Pittsburgh Steelers (for different reasons) and despised the Oakland Raiders (for the same reasons). Although the norm may be to look for a mate with similar interests, in the long run I'd rather be involved with someone who has opposite interests. That way when you talk about things, you're either receiving or delivering new information. Tell me about Jamaica, tell me about advertising or banking or whatever else you do for a living, but don't tell me about the Pittsburgh Steelers, honey, because there's no way you're going to tell me something I didn't already know.

8. Calling would have been too painful.

When it comes to matters of the heart and integrity, she had nothing to say about the male species. They are all snakes. Even if she had made a conscious decision to not see him again, she doubts she would have made the call. It's just too painful. Most men would rather do 12 triathlons than face an unpleasant 2-minute conversation with a woman. Even if she had called, she probably would have made up some excuse to terminate the relationship. She would have said that I'm moving to Australia or something. And, knowing her, she probably would have said, I'll call as soon as I get back."

I guess there are dozens of reasons why a woman never calls back, but none were very concrete. There was a period there when the relationship could have gone either way. But by the time a week or two had gone by, the relationship had dissolved, silently, without a bang or a whimper.

When the moon is full and the weather is a certain way, her gaze turns to the stars, and she thinks about him. She wonders what happened to him, if he's married or divorced, if he's happy. "And I always wonder", I say to my girlfriends who are now asleep in their chairs, "I wonder why he never called me?"

The difference between smooth sailing and shipwreck in a relationship lies in what you as a couple are doing about rough weather.

15
WOMEN WHO TALK TOO MUCH

Think before you speak.

The rules of restraint don't always apply to what you ask or what you feel a need to tell. Unfortunately, not every woman knows the beauty of discretion. It's really quite sad how people can talk so profoundly about highly personal matters to perfect strangers. Some people are just open like that. So let's get to the point of the matter, What makes women talk so much about their personal matters? Here are the most common reasons:

1. She may be testing her dates.
Those women have a tendency to let their dates in on family matters or painful history, including the things that society condemns people for. Most healthy women will want to run after finding out these personal tragedies. They consider it excess baggage being brought into the relationship. You are not her therapist, so if she dumps too much to soon on you you've got to wonder.

2. She think her neediness makes her m ore desirable.
Wrong. Testing her isn't the only reason a woman tells all early on. Some confess past hurts as a way of signaling their neediness, a quality they think men find desirable. This type of care taking neediness might be attractive to some men, but do you really want to be with someone who acts you as if she's needy all the time.

3. She thinks she's expected to open up.
Easy rapport can prompt confessions -- especially if you're with someone who's already divulged their secrets. If your demeanor frequently encourages women to open up maybe you're being too sympathetic. Just because a woman tells you all of her personal history

doesn't mean you have to open up to her. By the time you get through sharing your war stories, the two of you will be so depressed that you might not be able to stand being around each other. So if you must talk about your problems be sure to keep it light at least in the beginning.

4. **Forbidden topics.**
There are some topics that shouldn't be discussed. Money, ex-boyfriends, career crisis, medical profile, astrology or the occult and family craziness are off limits when you're trying to make an impression. The following is a straight forward guide to why these subjects make men squirm.

Money. You probably hate being sized up by your income. Still, you'd be surprised how rude some women can be. Talking finances isn't just rude, it's insensitive

Ex-boyfriends. Amazing as it may seem, some women love to throw up old dates in the face of their new one. When she results to these tactics tells her you can see she hasn't gotten over the previous person yet. Suggest that she call her girlfriends or someone who wants to hear it.

* *Career Crisis.* So you've stumbled off the fast track -- or maybe you never even made it to the starting gate? That may not be the news your date wants to hear. The trick is to sell yourself, talk about what is going well in your life.

* *Your Medical Profile.* Medical history and medical problems should be off limits. Of course you should tell the truth, but you don't need to give her your life history on the first or second date. Anything even with the slightest grossness should never be mentioned unless you're trying to run her away.

* *Astrology or The Occult.* To tell a woman you've just met that you've called the psychic hotline can be detrimental to your relationship. Even though you may be very excited about your astrological future or prediction it's best not to open your self up too

WILL THE REAL MEN PLEASE STAND UP

soon. The minute a you start talking about her psychic or her astrological sign people become very uninterested and turned off.

* *Family Craziness.* Recounting family problems, hurts or pains to dates is the best way to get rid of your date. Remember that not every woman has a dysfunctional family. If a woman has no understanding of troubled family dynamics she's going to start wondering whether dating you is the smart thing to do. Try not to talk about those things that will make her feel she has to live up to the standards of your family.

* *Being a Bitch.* Some *men* have reputations for being bitches. When a woman disagrees with you don't jump all over her. Don't make bitchy remarks just because you can't have your way with her.

All of the images of men can either make or break their relationships. As one man put it "it's the little things we do."

Leaping before you look can be a big drop

16

PROMISCUOUS WOMEN

Admit the truth, at least to yourself.

Women who have sex with lots of men are considered promiscuous. Promiscuity is not as in as it used to be according to numerous sex therapists. Not the practice -- that's going along just fine, thank you - but the word itself, which they say connotes a moral judgement. The new, politically correct term for promiscuous women is a "sex addict!" Promiscuous women get a bad reputation because they wear short skirts, tight clothing, low cut blouses or dresses and they spend too much time in the back seat of cars. Sex addicts are similar, but they get to tell their stories to people like Ricki Lake and Jerry Springer. In the end, the words all mean about the same thing. Women having sex with numerous partners has always been considered a bad thing.

Men are called "studs" if they sleep around, but there just doesn't seem to be a positive word that means women-who-have sex with-lots-of-men-and-that's-just-fine. Why not? Is there such a thing as enjoyable casual sex for women? Do multiple partners and one night stands lead only to clumsy couplings, lonely mornings and low self-esteem? Many women and men would argue that sex only feels safe or fun or good when it occurs within a monogamous, long-term relationship. But what of the more free wheeling women?

Some women really do want the guy with the perfect triceps and the endearing dumb stare to take them home, lick all over them like a lollipop and disappear the minute the passion has ends. These women can enjoy sex for sex sake even when there's no romantic backdrop, no promise of love or talk of commitment. Far from feeling compelled by an addiction, such women usually put a good deal of thought into their behavior, and many are able to find sexual partners that really do satisfy them.

WILL THE REAL MEN PLEASE STAND UP

For many women, good sex doesn't only happen within a relationship, they can often go home with someone they don't know and have a lot of fun doing it. Phone calls, flowers and trips to exotic places are not what all women are looking for. Men don't realize that they are sometimes the result of too many tequila shots.

Women don't like to recall how many men they've had sex with so they often create code names to describe anything from a French kiss up to everything else, but not including intercourse. Those who've had sex with more than thirty men at any given time refuse to call themselves sex addicts. Especially if they consider some of these relationships long-term traditional relationships.

Intimacy is not a problem or a fear for women who can enjoy sex outside of the relationship. Intimacy in many women's opinion is suppose to drive sex and that's always a great feature of it, but some of the best sex in many women's lives have been with someone they've just met.

Women eventually want long term relationships, but for the time being or after a dramatic relationship they are opting to have short term sexual affairs. They feel frees them from emotional connections. They also are quoted as saying "I like sex but I like to sleep alone. If they sleep over they find that it becomes much more important than just a sexual encounter. If they go home they don't feel as though they owe the man anything. Uncommitted sex let's many women who are sexually active enjoy themselves without the complexities of a relationship that she's not ready to handle.

Casual Sex

Casual sex can offer women a kind of excitement not found within a traditional relationship. These same women prefer to try new positions and experiences with someone she doesn't know very well. With a man she just met a woman might find herself doing things she would have never done with her ex-boyfriend.

One woman describes how a man she just met asked her to spit on him and even though she didn't understand it or even think she'd like it she tried it. He asked again so she started doing it and once she started she found it to be exhilarating and fun. It was so different from what she had ever experienced, but afterwards she was content not to see him again. Some fantasies are meant to stay fantasies.

Women have urges to try new things just like men do. Women often refer to lack of excitement in a relationship as boring, but men often interpret it as she's confused. All a women really wants is new adventure, excitement and vitality in their relationship. When they don't get it they are forced to seek this passion elsewhere, thus beginning affairs that people condone them for.

Emma has handcuff's that she's never used but she wishes she could meet someone who'll encourage her to. Most guys that she's talked to are afraid of a woman and handcuffs. They express concern that the woman is going to leave them handcuffed to the bed. But these same women say they don't want a man in their bed all the time, they want their beds to themselves.

Women Who Seduce Men

There's a hidden group of women who prefer exploring new things with men they are in deep relationships with. These are the women who enjoy seducing men because it creates a different type of excitement for them. Seducing men helps some women feel more in control of themselves and their relationships. Sex can be quite thrilling for this group of women because the less they know about the person the more turned on they are. Seductive women like having sex with many men because each encounter makes them feel more in control. It starts with the first glance, the smile, the gaze, and as he smiles back these women find a reason to walk to another area just to strut their stuff. Once she has his attention she asks him if he needs some air and when he walks her to get some she pats herself on the back It's all a game to seductive women, sort of like "attract and conquer." These women use sex to assert power.

The manipulation is to get him to follow her home. Seductive women continue this type of control all through the night. It's exciting to them. They prolong sexual experiences for four to five hours, directing the course of orgasms. Far from feeling used, she experiences a thrilling sensation of power.

WILL THE REAL MEN PLEASE STAND UP

Often women with many partners reserve intercourse for men with whom they have established some kind of relationship. Sex may not come with love, monogamy or even on a date to see a movie, but some level of friendship is very common.

For the most part, women who indulge their libidos don't leave their common sense behind. Women who are at the height of their sexuality use good sense, condoms, birth control pills, and spermicides during each encounter. Such caution isn't true across the board, however many women use birth control pills but don't use condoms. They confess condoms burn, they hurt, and they feel unnatural in many cases. Some women are just very sensitive in their vaginal areas.

Latex and spermicides cannot guard against every danger though. No matter how much one tries to separate physical pleasure from emotional pleasure it's difficult to do. However confident the woman, she can still suffer blows to her self-esteem as a result of having sex outside of a trusting, committed relationship. Once intercourse is over, the feelings of connection often ends too. Without the bond of intimacy that usually occurs in a steady relationship, women often feel disappointed after the orgasm fades.

Perhaps they think sex will provide them with love, affection and attention and when it fails to achieve the results they want, they feel worst than they did before. Some women notice early in the game when they are in trouble and they work to change their sexual behavior or their expectations about casual sex. Others need the help of friends and good therapy while still others find their sexual behavior to be so compulsive that their sexuality interferes with the rest of their lives. In extreme instances, the sex addict may need therapy and support groups may be needed to get these women's lives back on a positive track.

Yet overall, it's hard to believe that every woman who sleeps with multiple partners has an addiction or even much of a problem at all. Comfortable with their own choices such women have usually found their peers just as accepting. None of them to the best of their knowledge, has ever had what their mothers would term as a "bad reputation."

The men who these groups of women have had sex with not only didn't inscribe their names in the dirt on the locker room wall they didn't even mention them. Despite the notion that women who sleep around are destined to be known as sluts, loose women or promiscuous these same women have successfully dodged societies bad labels. Part of this simply reflects a shift in modern attitudes. For a woman armed with such an attitude, sex shops, sex stops and sex-pots have appealed to them because it means she can get something done to her and she can do what she like to do during sex.

More importantly, these women aren't just getting picked up by anyone who comes along; they're actively choosing men with whom they wish to get naked and entwined, and they tend to seek out men who accept and appreciate their sexuality, not condemn it. Quite possibly, their reputations don't suffer because their friends and lovers don't view women's sexual appetites as objectionable, controversial or remarkable in any way.

Have a goal or end up working for someone who does.

17

GETTING YOUR WAY WITH HER

The secret of men who win is persistence.

Leslie's voice is barely controlled as she disagrees with her future mother-in-law for the tenth time that day. "Leslie, your invitations will not be white. I picked pink," Leslie says icily, thinking, that will show her who's really in charge here.

Lulu's roommate insists she smoke outside, which she absolutely agrees with-in principle. But when her roommate isn't there, Lulu sometimes lights up right in her roommate's bedroom, just because she hates being told what to do.

Ben craves air-conditioning, but Alex freezes easily. Every night, they go through the same routine. He turns it up, she turns it down, repeatedly. They are unable to compromise, each determined to get their own way and prove the other person is enamored enough to give in and sleep uncomfortably.

But air-conditioning is far from this couple's only problem. The roasting pan could fester in the sink before neither Alex or Ben gives in and washes it. And determining whose turn it is to choose which video to rent quickly escalates into a screaming match.

Leslie, Lulu, Ben and Alex (and perhaps even you) are among the many people who have adopted Frank Sinatra's "My Way" as a personal anthem. Nothing is too petty to dismiss as an opportunity to get their way. It makes life so exhausting it can zap the love right out of a relationship-with every friend, lover, mate, sibling, boss, or coworker. The question is eventually raised: Who's going to get his of her way here? And inevitably, a voice inside you will be shouting, Me! Me! Me!"

The problem is not that we all want things to go our way but that some of us need them to-all the time, even at the expense of someone else's feelings. We're unable to tolerate a situation that requires compromise. And when the need to win becomes too important, what you get instead of love is one long power struggle.

Whether this describes you (and it probably describes all of us more often than we'd like to admit) or whether you are closely involved with a person who has this problem, it helps to understand the dynamics.

Control Is Seductive, Captivate and Alluring

You are on an airplane, seated next to a woman whose arm is draped comfortably over the armrest. Consequently, your own arms are folded awkwardly in your lap. You realize you'd like half the armrest, but it's totally under her control. To actually confront a stranger and say "Excuse me, Mam, you're hogging the armrest" seems absurd. You are stymied. Then she turns to stow her briefcase. Quickly you assume possession of the armrest and feign passionate interest in the newspaper, rejoicing inwardly at your triumph. But then she turns to you and says, "I'm sorry, but I was here first."

That armrest scenerio is a classic symbol of a person's willingness to assume control. Until recently, women never would have challenged a strange male so boldly. Control, or at least overt control, would have been the man's.

Demanding control is a sign of the increased power struggle between couples. But there is a down side. Control is intensely seductive, tickling the mind with a sense of self-importance and power. As a result, many people end up fighting simply to achieve that captivating power, both when it's appropriate (how you'd like to spend your birthday) and when it's not (how she ought to want to spend hers).

Compromise, on the other hand is not nearly as gratifying as out-and-out victory, and that makes it easy to forget that your triumph represents someone else's defeat. The result: You might gain more control than you really want.

Many a man has transferred his control to the woman in his life. His attitude: You want the house to look a certain way? Fine! You decorate it. You want the pots and pans cleaned a specific way? Fine, go do them. I won't interfere. You have strong ideas on proper birthday celebrations, ideal Christmas festivities, a well-planner social life? "Great. Take care of it." he says

On and on the list goes. The controlling woman does get her way, even though she doesn't feel particularly good about it. What she does feel is exhausted and unappreciated. But when she complains to her partner that she always has to make the weekend plans and he suggests they take a drive in the country that Saturday, she adamantly resists that suggestion. "*It's not a good day for it, honey. We have Kaye and Palmer's dinner party at seven. We'd need to be home by five to change. That would put us in a rush.*" So she's in control-and miserable-once more.

If You Loved Me, You'd...

Many times it is believed that love means the other person should put us first and be devoted to making us happy. This seems perfectly logical, and so you dig in your heels when decisions come up, just to test her devotion. You mention going out for dinner, but she says she wants to stay home-and you feel your anger rise. Doesn't what you want count for anything? Is she taking this relationship for granted? Suddenly, you really, really want to go out. When you first brought it up, you were merely thinking about shrimp scampi-now she's got to give in to you, as proof that she cares.

Too many couples put themselves and their partners through this kind of love test, and don't even realize they're doing it. But it can easily backfire and damage, or destroy your relationship. One reason is that you become your least attractive self--anxious, needy, or bratty-when you force your partner to prove her love in this petty way, and it rarely brings out the best in her. What started out as an unconscious push to feel lived ends as a fight, and after enough fights, you might just find you've "tested" yourself right out of a relationship. In the end, insisting on your own way as an unconscious love test is much more likely to make you feel uncertain, insecure, or even rejected than truly loved.

WILL THE REAL MEN PLEASE STAND UP

Asserting Your Personal Power

It's true some of us fight for our way because we need to be the one in charge, and sometimes we insist because being indulged proves we're loved. But the battle for control is often a battle for equality.

For example, Ann's mother-in-law has been running a huge and complicated family for decades. When Ann married Bob, she took her place in line with the other daughters-in-law, who refuses to participate in any Christmas celebrations. Ann decided to rebel in her own small way. She knew she couldn't respect herself if she followed family orders all the time. Therefore, every so often, she gathers her courage and says a gentle, polite no. Over the years, her refusals have ranged from "No, I don't want to bake the ham" to "No, I don't think that's the best summer camp for the kids." The no's don't come often, but they are frequent enough to remind her mother-in-law and everyone else that Ann is a person operating under her own terms.

Getting your way for the sake of registering your presence is a reasonable interpersonal technique. The trick is not to overdue it. Don't create a family catastrophe be asserting your personal power in a careless, dramatic, and extreme way. Try to equalize your relationship instead of destroying it. Don't be too pushy nor a pushover, and it get the respect you know you deserve.

When Getting Your Way Gets In Your Way

The following strategies will help you keep your controlling impulses in check: Keep Score. When a couple gets stuck in an endless power struggle, both people often perceive themselves as the loser, so they fight even harder to win the next time.

One way to break the cycle is to keep score. I don't mean the kind of mental score keeping in which so couples secretly engage, tallying everything we give and waiting to see if we get it back. I mean doing it openly, making a written note of who won each time a decision is made, even if it's just which television program to watch. Many times, you'll be tempted to say "It was mutual., but force yourself to choose, and give the point to the person who made the suggestion.

This exercise has several positive outcomes: It puts your power struggle on the table, and that can drain a lot of emotional poison. It also helps you and your mate become more aware of the balance of power in the relationship and recognize which areas each of you control. You may always feel like the loser because she often gets her way about recreational plans and spending. But this can be balanced by her frequent victories in scheduling, parenting, and vacation planning. You may both want to renegotiate, once you have an objective measure of how you operate.

Delegate.

It's amazing how incompetent people can be, plus why do you always have to be the one to decide everything. It seems no one else can take any responsibility. Nevertheless...you need to learn how to delegate! And once you have (take a deep breath), live with the job the other person does. Don't critique it, amend it, correct it, improve upon it, upgrade it, or in any other way put your stamp on it. Just live with it!

This means if your partner has the job of washing the pots and she leaves a crust of dried egg yolk on each and every one, smile sweetly and say nothing. Don't redo them to your satisfaction. Don't let her know you disapprove. Don't insist the pots and pans be done the right way i.e., your way. All this will earn you is an opportunity to spend time in dirty water. Think about it.

If your partner has already made brunch reservations, don't mention the newer, better place you read about. If you prefer it pick up the check but if she offers, let her. Surprise yourself. Act out of character. I promise, you'll have some fun with it.

Giving In.

Giving in is the most difficult to do. Your assignment is to look for the opportunity to let someone else win. For a normally assertive, not to mention competitive, man like yourself, this will feel unnatural. But remember, all change is "unnatural: by definition.

Giving in means adding a little shock value to it. Giving in means letting your partner have her way with something you've been fighting about forever. If you two

WILL THE REAL MEN PLEASE STAND UP

always argue over her passion for morning television, turn it on for her. Look for opportunities to call cease-fire in some of your ongoing power struggles. Does Mom still insist she needs to know where you'll be staying every moment you're out of town? This time, call her with the phone numbers before she asks.

Giving in befuddles your opponents. They are primed for battle, but there you are, sweetly handing them victory. They will hardly know what to do with it. Quite often, what they do with it is try to thank you for it. You may worry that other people will grow with triumph if they get their way. Sometimes they do. (Sometimes, you have to admit, you do too.) When your friends, lovers, colleagues, get their way, sometimes they like you better for it. In fact, they may feel so grateful to you, they'll work miracles to make you happy. And that's the best way of all to get your way. So when you really think about it you're getting your way in the long run anyway.

Male Ego: Measure it three times, cut it once.

Step 4:

Improving Your Relationships

18

CREATING ENDURING RELATIONSHIPS

Teach others by setting a good example.

Do you ever wonder why you get into a big hurry the second you step foot in the airport? You rush to buy your tickets, only to wait in a line filled with people who are also in a hurry. You walk quickly to your gate, but you still have to sit there and wait until the flight attendant calls your section of seating to board. You jump up to get in a line so that you can get on the plane, only to encounter another line of people in the tunnel gate waiting to board the plane. Once you get on the plane you slow down a little until the plane lands and then you feel a need to hurry once again. You jump out of your seat and reach over people to get your too large luggage that you should have checked in, but you felt it would help you reduce some time. You squeeze your way down the isle only to wait until the plane's doors open so you can exit. Once in the terminal you make a mad dash to get your remaining luggage in the baggage claim area. Of course once you get to the baggage claim you have to wait another fifteen minutes until your luggage rolls around the bend. Then you wait to catch a shuttle to the nearest rental car area, only to wait in line again. All this rushing, pushing and running rarely speeds up a person's travel time but that still doesn't stop them from repeating the process every time they travel. And even though they know their going to go through the same lines, same delays and same hassles, they still think this time I'll beat the odds.

Similarly; the second some people step into a relationship, they feel the need to rush through the dating process as if they were running late to catch a plane. If you thought your plane was going to crash, you'd probably be a little more cautious. You probably wouldn't want to fly again, but just like rushing to a plane everyday people rush into unhealthy relationships and all the way to the alter, knowing that their relationship has a fifty-fifty chance of crashing and burning. Their reason, "I know what the divorce statistics say, but this time I'll beat the odds.

The risks of marital failure diminishes significantly with longer dating periods. "Couples who are friends for more than two years before marriage, scored consistently higher on marital satisfaction." Yet in face of all the evidence couples still think, "Our relationship is unlike any other, we're different so we'll beat the odds."

Friendships Create Healthier Relationships

Relationships!!! Does longer friendships really create enduring relationships? They don't come in a bottle and you won't find it at the end of the rainbow. Look no further than your closest friends because they may be the key to a longer and healthier relationship.

For many couples when juggling a job, a family and housework the friendships gets lost. There's no such thing as an eight hour work day for any couple who has children. Couples rarely get quality family time and inevitably they're friendships get put out with the trash. Here's news that will encourage you to put your friends back on your priority list. Ignoring your friendships not only diminish your quality of life but could also be a health hazard. Close relationships act as an ounce of prevention, bolstering the immune system and reducing the risk on illness like colds and flu and perhaps even heart disease in many people, and other serious disorders. That makes maintaining friendships a priority, right up there with exercising and eating right.

Bert Uchino, Ph.D., an assistant professor at the University of Utah in Salt Lake City, who did this research while at Ohio State University suspects that it is a real possibility. They discovered people with strong ties to family, friends, colleagues and community has a significantly longer than average life span than isolated individuals did. The lack of supportive relationships is a factor that is almost as dangerous as well-known risks such as smoking, high blood pressure and or obesity. Scientists still don't know why love and friendship give us a healthy glow. One theory is; they act as buffers against stress, which itself can take a toll on your body. People are less likely to take unhealthy risks if they are loved. People with good friends were less likely to smoke and that those who belonged to a church, professional group or parents association were less likely to smoke or drink heavily.

What kind of relationships are good medicine? They seem to be the ones offering true intimacy, which means your friends accept and love you for who you really are. And the quality of the friendship matters more than the quantity. "Simply having one person you can get deep support from may be enough" says Uchino. "In fact, being involved in a social network that's too large is a double-edge sword because it puts added demands on you.

Still cultivating different kinds of relationships in your life is probably a good idea. Try to make friendship a priority. If you don't have as many friends as you'd like, try to get involved in activities you enjoy. If you've moved away from your friends for some reason get involved in community activities, volunteer or church groups to bring a sense of belonging into your life. You'll probably still miss your friends, but you will began to feel like a part of your new community.

If an overbooked life is your problem, use your creativity to schedule dates with yourself. Resolve to make one lunch date per week, and dedicate one half hour each weekend to checking in with a different friend by phone. Carry stationary, post cards, and stamps with you so when you can jot down a brief note while waiting at the bank or while commuting. When you do something with your family, ask a friend to come along. Have a impromptu potluck meal once in a while with a group of your favorite buddies.

Ultimately you may need to shift your expectations. Free up your schedule a bit by arranging your priorities. Be more relaxed, even if people want to drop by unexpectedly. They can make themselves a cup of coffee or tea. The point is not to show off your house or your cooking, it's just to share time with your friends.

Always remember, even the best dates will sometimes show their character flaws.
Don't panic when your date turns out to be human.

19

MAKING HEALTHIER RELATIONSHIP CHOICES

Your happiness starts with you.

Do you ever feel like your quest to find The Right Mate is like that never ending search for the Holy Grail? In the movie, Indiana Jones and The Last Crusade, Indiana Jones and another character named Donavan are searching for the Holy Grail, which is also supposed to be the fountain of youth. As the movies comes to an end, Indiana and Donavan find the room where the Holy Grail is kept and being protected by a seven hundred year old Knight. They have to select the right grail from choices of about thirty. The Knight informs the both of them if they select the right grail they will be rewarded with eternal life. If they choose the wrong grail they will have eternal damnation.

Donavan allows his side kick to make his selection. She looks about for a moment or two, then quickly grabs the most beautiful chalices she can get her hands on, and hands it to Donavan. He holds the cup above his head and says "Surely this is the cup of the King of Kings." He dips the grail into a pool of water and quickly gulps it down. After a breathing a sigh of relief, positive that he has chosen the right cup, he notices the reflection of his face in the pool. Suddenly, he begins to age and wrinkle, his hair grows out, and his face rots away, he turns into a skeleton, and explodes across the screen. After Donavan disintegrates into a thousands pieces, the old Knight slowly turns to Indiana and the woman and says, "He chose ... poorly."

How many men and women across the globe have had their hearts and lives torn apart because they chose poorly in the dating process? Why do more than half of all marriages end in divorce? Why do so many couples divorce each year before they have a chance to celebrate their second wedding anniversary? It's partly because men and women are simply choosing poorly! They're selecting the wrong people to date and then marrying one of them.

You can make a lot of bad decisions in your life and recover. Believe me I've been there, done that, and have several T-shirts to prove it. You can select the wrong car and trade it in after a few months. You can choose the wrong college and transfer if you don't like it. You can pick the wrong major and revise it later. You can take the wrong job, but later land another that you like better. You can make foolish financial decisions and end up in debts, but you can recover by wising up and paying off those debts. You can relocate to the wrong city, and move to another one that suits you better. All of these decisions may carry some adverse consequences but pale in comparison to the consequences of bad decision making in an intimate relationship. If you date and then marry the wrong person, you will live with significant, negative and lasting consequences of that decision for the rest of your life. If you choose poorly in the dating arena, that choice can affect every area of your life.

Are You Making Healthy Choices?

Many times you make the wrong choice for several reasons: you were impulsive and desperate, you allowed the "beautiful woman" to influence your choice, and, finally you assumed that her choice was the best based on the external beauty of the chalice. Just as Donavan chose poorly in his quest for the Holy Grail, so do scores of people during their quest for a mate. We have identified four of the most common reasons people tend to make poor choices. Each of these reasons serves to keep people from discerning the true character of those they are dating (which is their reason for dating in the first place).

If you really want to have healthier relationships you must first begin to make healthier choices -- that is choices that make you feel good about yourself and your mate rather than choices that rob you or make you feel bad about yourself. It is wrong to think you can fashion a new, healthy relationship on the false, traditional beliefs. Most of the problems we encounter in relationships derive from the beliefs these relationships are based on. We make mistake; none of us is perfect. Unhealthy, traditionally structured relationships exacerbate those mistakes and allow little room for improvement or change. If anything these relationships actually thrive on healthy dynamics. In contrast, the new relationship nurtures and supports expression, equality, fairness and consideration.

To have the relationship between equals that is deserving, a new set of beliefs and teachings should reflect the issues we face today and encourage us to have the relationships we want now is needed. One piece of good news is that a new, healthier, more realistic way of viewing relationships is evolving. The other piece of good news is that our generation is at the forefront of this seismic change. Where's the bad news? I don't believe there is any, but I will tell you that to have the relationship you want and to keep your love alive, you must make a serious commitment and give great effort. It's all within your power if you are willing to work at it. Before we chart our new course, let's look at some good examples of great relationship builders:

1. Choose partners who make you feel good about yourself.
When you choose partners that don't treat you with respect and care, but instead are critical, demanding controlling, or even abusive you are likely to feel bad about yourself afterwards. And when you are with someone who criticizes your body or your sexual performance, who blames her sexual inadequacies on you, or is rejecting afterward, you will end up feeling bad about yourself sexually.

2. Choose to have equal relationships.
True intimacy is based on mutuality and equality. When there is a lack of equality in a relationship, one person has more power than the other. Equality means that neither partner has more power than the other.

3. Choose sexual activities that are fulfilling without feeling shame or guilt.
It makes sense that if you continue negative or esteem-robbing behavior it will only serve to make you feel worse about yourself. This is especially true when it comes to participating in sexual activities that cause you to feel shame or guilt.

When you become involved in behavior that causes you to feel bad about yourself you are creating and perpetuating shame and guilt. An activity is a healthy one if it makes you feel good about yourself, and it is an ego-robbing one if it makes you feel guilty, ashamed or disgusted with yourself.

There's no question about it, relationships today are different from those of the past. Our expectations are different also. Unlike previous generations women do not cast their self-worth simply in terms of how successfully they marry and how many children they have. Couples are more likely to desire a healthy relationship for what it can do for them than for the ways it can enhance their lives and facilitate the goals in their life.

Avoid The Common Relationship Mistakes

When a relationships starts to experience problems, couples have a tendency to replay every conversation, analyzing what happened and sorting out who's right and who's wrong. Maybe they swear they will never go out with someone like that person again. Maybe they just give up on people and vow to never fall in love again. However it ends, it is often because -- no matter how smart they are -- they have repeated some of the dumbest mistakes that people make in a relationship. To avoid making mistakes that will hurt your relationships you must:

1. Identify and admit your mistakes, and then vow to stop.

Most people are in such denial about their own behavior that they lack the awareness to make changes. When we assert that our problems are not all our fault, we are correct to a certain degree. We go strong when we begin thinking that not being completely at fault relieves us of the responsibility to do anything to correct the problem. Everything and everyone around may be wrong, but until you change nothing else will.

2. Separate your identity from your mate's.

It's hard to separate ourselves from our mate's life sometimes. When we do not complete the separation from our former mates, we continue needing their love, support and approval. This emotional dependency pushes us to seek mates and relationships that replicate the dependent-controller model rather than a healthy, balanced man-woman partnership of equals. Rather than develop a romantic relationship based on equality and mutual respect, in the dependent-controller relationship we trade in our identity and our share of control for our mates love.

3.   Admit your mistakes to your mate, and require her to do the same.
When you learn to admit your mistakes to your mate, you are making yourself vulnerable to her; you are letting her know that you care and that you want the relationship to work. Once you admit your mistakes, you are also letting your mate know that you are not forgetting the part you play in the relationship. To maintain balance, be sure you receive the same treatment.

4.   Know yourself.
When you know who you are and how you really feel, you'll be less likely to repeat your mistakes. Spend time alone staying in touch with your feelings, needs and wants. Look into your past relationships to figure out your patterns, the issues and behaviors that really upset you (push your buttons), and the reasons why you are the way you are. Then vow to be your true self around others instead of who you think they want to be.

5.   Express your feelings and wants.
Most of us were taught that it's selfish to tell people how are feel and what we want. As a result, we usually express ourselves indirectly and hope that our mate can figure out what we really mean. Developing an intimate relationship requires emotional honesty. Emotional honesty involves expression of your full range of emotions -- from tears to anger. Without this, your mate can't really know you.

6.   Establish and respect your own boundaries.
There are probably things your mate and others in your life are doing that hurt you. You may respond by nagging those people, avoiding them, or getting defensive in a variety of

ways. These behaviors never solve the real problem, and they often exacerbate your resentment and anger over the real issue. Instead you need to learn how to set boundaries and clearly communicate them to those around you. You should be able to determine which behaviors are unacceptable and which boundaries have been crossed.

7. **Resolve issues from the past.**

You cannot change the past, but you can change whether and how it affects your current relationships. Cleaning up baggage from the past gives you the strength and the confidence that put and keep you in charge of your own life. Resolve past issues. In an ongoing relationship, it often involves going over the resentments you and your mate have built up over time and work to find better resolutions.

8. **Be willing to take risks.**

Without risk taking, you cannot change your behavior or your life. But let's be honest: It's difficult to change when old habits feel so comfortable. In order to change old habits we must be willing to try new behaviors and new ways of looking at things, even if these innovations do not at first feel normal or right.

9. **Control yourself, not your mate.**

We always want to change our mate. We think that we could be happy only if our mate did this or that. By changing your own behavior, you will affect your mate's. Instead of expecting your mate to read your mind, tell your mate what you want. When your behavior is healthy others only have two options: respond in a healthy manner or stay away from you.

10. **Build intimacy.**

Set aside bonding time for your relationship; time to hug, talk, touch, share, talk, laugh, dream and even debate. The sharing of good and bad feelings builds intimacy. Sharing success as well as handling crisis together build a bond that no one else can destroy. Do not allow work, children, family, friend, or unresolved issues tear your relationship apart. Develop an attitude that says 'It's our world."

Obviously, we cannot change the past. But we can learn to identify the real cause of recurring relationship problems, the reason why we end up with the same type of mate again and make mistakes. We can learn to crack the code that masks the reason why we behave as we do, and we can learn how to break the cycle.

If you can't understand it, change your attitude toward it.

20
RELATIONSHIP BOOSTERS

Bring passion and lots of fun into your relationships.

Last month I bought a desk calendar with a page for every day of the year. You know the kind that you tear a page from it as the days pass. It's June now so it's still good for about six more months. Actually, the calendar may never be useable -- as a calendar that is -- even when January arrives. This is because I can't keep my hands off of it. I flipped through it frequently, laughing at the cartoons revealing wit and skewed perspectives on life. In fact, I have already torn out several pages containing favorite cartoons and faxed them to friends. By the time January rolls around I won't have much use for my calendar.

We love to laugh don't we? Humor eases tension. It diffuses embarrassment. It enlarges our perspective. Smiling frequently reduces the odds of us getting old before our time. Even the bible tells us that a cheerful heart is good medicine. Our relationships should make us smile too. When we are in love and full of romance and passion we can help but keep a smile on our faces.

There are no confines when it comes to romance; yet many couples are in a romantic slump. In any season, in any weather, romance can be found. All it takes is an imaginative mind and a persistent heart. For those who would like to enhance their relationship but are confused about where or how to begin, there are ways to make your relationship come alive. Why not bring some of the magic healing power into your life with these common sense relationship rules. They can help bring passion and a whole lots of fun into your relationship.

1. Go slowly.
After about the ninth grade, courtship should be a gradual process. Falling desperately in love with someone after two or three dates only says that you are desperate. Instant love

is not a real compliment to women. It is a turnoff to any mature woman. Take time to bond. Get to know a person before you fall in love too soon.

2. Don't pretend.
We're all grown-ups. If it's just sex you want, don't pretend it's something else. A mature woman will respect you more if you don't pretend you want something other than sex if that's truly all you want.

3. Show that you appreciate her.
You are not going to impress her with the things that make *you* special. She'll spot those in time; you'll impress her more with your appreciation of the things that make her special *to you*.

4. Become friends first.
When she says, "Let's just be friends," feel complimented and take her up on it. If you can't be friends with her, why should she bother with you in the first place?

5. She might not want a deep relationship.
If she shows no interest, it could be because you're repulsive, but more likely it's because she has better things to do right now than fall in love. Consider the fact that she may already be involved with someone.

6. Develop True Intimacy.
Don't fall into the trap of giving too much too soon and take a chance of sabotaging your relationship before it gets off the ground. Develop true intimacy with her before you allow a physical relationship to take over. "True intimacy provides a shelter in which we can be vulnerable and open, feel safe, and truly be ourselves. True intimacy develops over time and although the timing varies from couple to couple, true love never happens overnight.

WILL THE REAL MEN PLEASE STAND UP

7. Don't force intimacy.

Forced intimacy makes a woman feel unnatural and uncomfortable. Because of this unnatural, uncomfortable feeling, at some point, most likely she'll withdraw from you. When she does it will only send signals that you need to try harder to win her love. As long as you are chasing after her and trying to win her love, she'll always be in control.

Don't allow yourself to fall into the trap of giving her too much too soon. Stand your ground and take your time to develop a special closeness with her before you leap into intimacy without placing your relationship on a solid foundation.

8. Take your partner out to dinner.

Inform your partner that formal attire is required. On the way to the restaurant, forget your wallet and go home to retrieve it. To your partner's surprise the backyard or living room floor is set up in a romantic picnic scene. Candles, wine etc.

9. Encounter different places together.

Romance should not be limited to the bedroom...be open to other possibilities.

10. Have a happy relationship by boosting your partner's confidence.

The right compliments can give your partner the confidence needed to branch out into new areas. Here's how:

* *Be direct.* If your partner did something you really appreciated tell her. Don't assume your partner knows how grateful you are.

* *Be indirect.* Tell a close friend how much you love you partner. But of course, make sure your partner is within earshot.

11. Be realistic. Love is not always blind.

Being romantically involved with someone who has irritating ways does not mean you have to keep hoping your partner will change. It's more likely she will not. No one is ever going to be 100 percent perfect, not even you.

WILL THE REAL MEN PLEASE STAND UP

12. Choose and use nicknames.

Bestowed out of love, pet names are meant to reassure your partner that he or she is special. Nicknames that make your partner feel uncomfortable should be avoided. Also, never use nicknames in the heat of a dispute. Nicknames are intended to show endearment.

13. Give the keys to your heart.

Give your partner the assurance that you are theirs exclusively.

14. Leave secret notes.

Leave love notes in your lover's pockets, briefcase, lunch bag or box or in various places around the house. Little notes with words "I'm thinking of you or I love you or I miss you will give your partner reassurance that you really do care. It will give a sense of comfort in knowing no matter how difficult things get you'll still be there.

15. Take a soothing bath.

Surround your bathroom with scented candles and flourish your partners bath water with rose petals and wonderful scents. Create lots of bubbles too.

16. Use body massage.

Give your partner a sensual body massage from head to toe. During the journey intimate stops are definitely permitted.

17. Have heated phone conversations.

Call your partner on the phone and tell one another about your hottest fantasies. Make sure yours is the previous event the two of you recently shared.

18. Perform the mirror exercise.

To enhance your relationship sometimes it's good to know that your partner finds you attractive. Undress your partner and have them stand in front of the mirror while you verbally express their beauty. The nakedness is not to arouse your partner but to emphasize contentment with every aspects of their attributes.

19.   Flirt with your partner.
Find reasons to flirt with one another on a regular basis. If sitting at a distance from one another send silent signals of affection that only the two of you know what they mean.

20.   Serve breakfast in bed.
What a wonderful way to start the day off. A lavish breakfast of strawberries and crepe is not necessary, a breakfast of orange juice toast and cereal will also bring a smile to her face.

21.   Be dependable.
Men as well as women appreciate partners who do not take them for granted. Partners who can be relied upon for anything from returning phone calls to paying the bills on time are more likely to be trusted. Partners who respect each other by being dependable have successfully learned one of the ground rules of building a strong foundation of love.

22.   Take fun seriously.
Laughter can be a great antidote to your problems, particularly when coping with relationship woes. Focus on the laughter, the here-and-now attitude, to get a stress free relaxed mind and a good nights sleep.

23.   Show your affection in public.
Stroll though the streets holding hands, lightly kissing. Let the world know you're proud of your partner.

24.   Understand that communication is the key.
Express to your partner what he or she means to you.

WILL THE REAL MEN PLEASE STAND UP

25.   Encourage independence.
Enjoy time apart as well as together.

26.   Take an interest in her hobbies.
Express an interests in what excites your mate (football, sports, car racing, horseback riding) whether it appeals to you or not.

27.   Keep romance alive.
It's important to keep romance alive. Giving her money and roses is not enough. Spend the time to pick out unique flowers to express your love and devotion. Do lots of other things too.

28.   Laugh and lighten up.
There is plenty of reason to have laughter in your life. For starters, humor is wonderful resource when it comes to coping with some of life's more awkward moments. Laughter builds a bond. Something is created that belongs to you and your partner and no one else.

A cheerful heart is good medicine.
All it takes is an imaginative mind and a persistent heart.

21
WHAT DRIVES THE SEXES CRAZY?

Don't keep repeating the same mistake; learn and try a different approach.

Some men without even knowing it, are driving the women who love them right out of their lives. For the most part men are getting information about women straight from the source. They're asking other women, listening to relationship experts and comparing the statistics. Even though, most of these sources are helpful and provide information, nothing is as accurate as asking men how they feel. Just for fun I developed a list of things that drive us crazy about one another. This list of the things that drive women crazy about men, and what drives men crazy about women was compiled from interviews and research with real men. These are everyday people: college students, firemen, police officers, construction workers, computer specialist entrepreneurs, mechanics and attorney's.

What Drives Women Crazy About Men

When I got couples together I asked them what are things their mates do to drive them crazy. These same things were listed as the top things that drive them away. I asked them to be as blunt and as candid as possible. I asked them to tell me what are the things they want their mates to know most of all.

This was a light hearted look at men through a scrutinizing microscope instead of rose colored glasses. If you know anyone whose been kissed enough by toads you'll probably find this list very intriguing.

1. **Self-centeredness.**

Also known as genetic inability of the male to understand that he is not the center of the universe and it is actually farther away from him than he thinks.

WILL THE REAL MEN PLEASE STAND UP

2. Dysfunctional communication skills.

A man will talk to a woman for hours on end about the importance of a football game that happened five years ago or how the engine of a car is designed but if a woman asks him about his feeling he can't think of anything to say.

3. Poor eyesight.

This has been proven to be the case with many mature men because they still can't seem to determine a woman from a girl.

4. Competitiveness.

If you decide to play a friendly game of scrabble with him, he gets angry. And if someone try to help him he refuses to acknowledge or talk to you for the rest of the evening. If you make up a word he doesn't understand he starts to sulk or pout and swears he's not pouting he's just taking his time.

5. Self-obsession.

If a man is sick, he can barely get to the toilet without being helped by his wife or girlfriend. His wife now spends at least four days trying to nurse him back to health, but now she has a cold that turns into the flu. Her fever is high, her eyes are watery, her joints, muscles and bones ache. When she needs help he remembers he's feeling better and he's made plans to play golf with the fells and he's gone.

6. Priority distortion.

Man is ruled by not what lies in his head but what lies in his pants.

7. Domination complex.

You've cut the grass ten times over. She enters and before you know it she's telling you what you're doing wrong.

8. Lack of intuition.

Men lack real curiosity about other people and how they might be feeling.

9. Self-dramatization.

When a woman does the shopping, preparation, cooking, while still trying to entertain, her daily job and duties like taking care of the children, taking the dog back and forth to the vet and manages to keep everything in order and in place. John decides to cook breakfast it takes three hours and by the time everyone sits down he has used every clean bowl in the house, pancakes all over the walls, only one perfect pancake is seen and he insists on flipping it to show his talents and as soon as it hits the floor he continues to do it again just to prove he can do it.

10. Self-delusion.

Anytime a man swears he likes women you can bet he likes them undressed with something in their mouth other than words.

11. Insensitivity.

No matter how angry a woman gets at a man he will swear he can't understand why she's mad.

12. Absentmindedness.

He can never remember to replace the toilet tissue or put the seat down, but he'll never forget where the refrigerator or good sex can be found.

13. Selective Incompetence.

His inability to work the household items like the washing machine the ice maker, the dishwasher or the garbage disposal, tend to the children or make a bottle is quite surprising when he can drink a beer, talk on the phone, barbecue and make bets on the fights all at the same time.

14. Silence.

Value it .

What Drives Men Crazy About Women

Here a few ways men have said that women drive them crazy.

1. She makes lists.

Things to do, things to buy, people to call, If it's not on the list it doesn't get done. Once to be funny my wife put sex on the list.

2. Everything smells too much like a woman.

I'm convinced she sprays the closet and my sheets with her perfume. Everything I own smells like flowers.

WILL THE REAL MEN PLEASE STAND UP

3.   She steps in front of me too much.

If I'm doing the dishes she gets in between the sink and me and she does them too. If I'm cooking she gets in between me and the stove, stirs, taste adds pepper, The only place she doesn't step in front of me is at the toilet.

4.   She keeps old food too long.

If you open the refrigerator you take your life in your own hands. There's leftovers, turkey on top of pizza, on top of casserole on top of steak, on top of cheese. If you're looking for the mustard you've got to unload the entire shelf to find it. And then you've got to get it all back in.

5.   She makes me repeat things.

I hate it when she turns to me and says, "What was it you were going to say?"

6.   She forces me to go on her diets.

No matter I feel, I have got to go on her diets. There's nothing to eat but diet food.

7.   She argues in front of people.

She's always fussing with me no matter where we are or who were around.

8.   She straightens my clothes in public.

She's always picking stuff off my jacket or brushing my face. She'll lick her finger and smooth my eyebrows, right in public. It's embarrassing.

9.   She's too tidy.

She clears the table while I'm still eating, gathers up the newspapers while I'm reading it and has my clothes in the washer before they hit the floor.

10.   She bothers me while I try to sleep.

She rearranges me while I'm sleeping. Turns my head, covers me, uncovers me. Pushes me onto my side.

11.   She tries to beat me when I'm in a tight.

She races ahead of me trying to get to the toilet first. Tells me she's quicker and I take too long.

12.   She brings the wrong things to bed.

She insists that the dogs sleep with us. When we make love, they sit and watch, panting and waiting for us to finish so they can jump in bed.

13. She's a pack-rat.

Her purse weighs more than she does. Whatever you need, its in there: Band-Aids, aspirin, chewing gum, a tooth brush, matches, anything you need.

14. She's a little too eclectic for me.

She dyes her hair all these wild colors. I have no idea what color her hair is.

15. She's into blood and guts.

She loves slasher movies, it makes me nervous.

16. She waits too long before she buys groceries.

She won't go to the supermarket until the refrigerator is completely empty.

17. She makes me feel like I have bad breath.

She can't stand for anyone to breathe on her face. Sometimes she puts a pillow between our faces when we make love.

18. She doesn't open up enough.

She never tells me she wants to make love, she just looks at my crouch and smiles.

19. She makes me feel unsanitary.

She leaves notes on the toilet seat to remind me to use Lysol after I'm done.

20. She doesn't keep up with our money.

She balances the checkbook to the nearest one hundred dollars.

21. She cries for everything.

Happy things, sad things, weddings, funerals, movies, furniture things, jewelry things,, things that just happened, things that might, television commercials, new baby's good grades whatever.

22. She loves to go bare feet in public.

No matter where she goes she takes her shoes off. In the theater, restaurants, in her office, at the movies.

23. She's too perfect.

To let her tell it nothings wrong with her, she has no faults, and she actually agrees with me about that.

24. She speaks of people as if they were food.

Her dad is a clam, her daughter is a peach, her brother is a prune, her sister is a dead meat depending on her mood.

25. She uses the term we all the time.

We like such and such. We think so and so. As if were on brain in one body and one person.

When you've kissed enough frogs you'll find your princess.

22

IS SHE REALLY THE WOMAN FOR YOU?

Don't quit after the first sign of problems. Or the second.

A couple of weeks ago my husband I snuggled onto the den couch with a bowl of popcorn to watch one of our favorite movies. Before the movie began, we watched the commercials that advertised all sorts of products. One of them referred to the difference in male-female perspectives. When my son didn't understand some of the nuances of the commercials he turned to me and said, "They're fighting because men and women think differently about life." "Not really," I said absently, watching the television. My son looked and me and said, "tell me how they think different." "You'll understand it better when you get older," I said. I was trying to quiet him, the movie was about to begin. By now my son was growing impatient. "I don't want to wait. Just tell me real quick. In ten words or less. What's the main difference?"

People have been writing about the sexes and it still doesn't make us any more perfect than the next person who appears to know nothing about the sexes. Take for instance, the way a man can emerge from a bathroom ready for love making and a women emerges ready-to-get-ready for lovemaking. (Brushing and flossing doesn't count as foreplay.) Yet sometimes couples find it difficult to understand, accept and cherish one another's differences. Of course this may seem easier said than done, but let's consider some insights and suggestions that just might help us reduce the battle between the sexes to a few drills now and then rather than a civil war.

Most people put more time and energy into planning a dinner party or shopping for a car than they do seeking a mate who is right for them. Unfortunately, there are serious consequences when romance is left entirely to chance. Oh, I know it sounds businesslike to talk "strategy" when it comes to dating. "You should just let it happen," we often hear. But that's a cop out. If you're hoping to date smart you have to think smart.

Have you considered the kinds of things you want in a dating relationship? What qualities are you looking for in another person? What traits, skills, abilities would fit the bill for you? Whether you've made your "shopping list" or not, I've got to tell you that it may be deceiving. Unless you are practicing smart love, what you think you're looking for may be off the mark.

When asked to indicate the most important quality in a dating partner, men don't hesitate. Many times "Looks" is the first word they utter. Whether we admit it or not, physical attraction tops the list of desirable dating qualities. Sex appeal is part of God's design, but here's the clincher: there's far more to a dating relationship than looks. The truth is physical attractiveness is a good spring, but a poor regulator. It gets love going but it doesn't keep love going.

Smart love understands this and looks beneath the surface. Smart love looks beyond beauty to find sustaining principles for lasting love, a love that may uphold lifelong marriage. After all, the divorce rate is so high because they are drawn together by reasons that matter less as the time goes on. In other words the force that brings a couple together -- physical attractiveness -- has little to do with what keeps them together.

There are always going to be compromises, you won't ever find a perfect relationship, even though many times it will feel perfect to you. First, you'll have to figure out what really matters to you, and there are some issues that you'll need to resolve ahead of time. Let's examine a few of them:

1. Background.

No two people have identical backgrounds just as no two families are alike. Still according to many men getting involved with someone who was raised in an entirely different culture can present problems in the long run. Here are few bad reasons to love a woman who grew up different from you.

a. *Pride in your heritage.*

Many times we date people of different cultures, but after marrying them we find that they don't have lots of things in common with us. Though they love them dearly they admit that part of the initial attraction was the color of their partner's skin. It's not okay to run from your own culture without first working out your feelings.

b. *Rebellion*

Some son's will do anything they can to upset their parents. It's their way of saying I am my own person and I'll do what I want to. Many times in order to gain independence a man will find a woman who he knows his family will disagree with. Driving your parents crazy may be a great satisfaction now, but in the long run you may be the one to get hurt. You'll have to live with her after their anger dies down.

c. *Religious Background.*

Gaining a relationship with women who are outside the confiding force or what the church feels is right is one way to get away from all the things you were taught to believe in. Many of us have at least some type of tie to our faith -- whether we're believers or not. The more willing you are to integrate each others worlds the easier your lives will be.

One small note, even when a couples isn't marrying outside of their faith they can still be confronted with differences. It soon becomes clear, however that neither was going to give in. Many times rituals have more meaning to one partner than it does the other. So if you get caught in a relationship with a person whose stuck in their ways maybe marriage is out of the question. The less extreme the easier it is to bridge.

2.   How to work out your differences.

Okay, there are some simple ways that we can work out our differences. When you come from different cultures it's best to equally socialize. By this I mean in order to create a more balanced relationship make the effort to meet people from both of the cultures or backgrounds. This keeps your relationship from becoming socially unbalanced. Moving into neighborhood where there are both cultures is a good way to assure your children will get the proper exposure also.

An interracial marriage stands a much better chance of surviving if a couple can incorporate each other's backgrounds into their lives. Another way to help a mutual effort to explore as much about the others world as possible. Once you really get to know each other and the differences between you can forge a unity that's based on commonalties you've created.

3. How much does money matter.

Women have a tendency to write off good men because their more interested in the size of another mans wallet instead of his qualities. Never mind that you are surprisingly bright and goal driven, or that you are still young and had plenty of time to be successful. Or that you came from a wealthy family with great connections. Some women never bother to sleuth out these possibilities in a man, all that matters to them is a man's present net worth.

Keep in mind that there are many good, eligible, worthy women out there. Before you chose her ask yourself this: Could she be using your earnings as an excuse to get close to me. You don't have to marry her but you should at least check her out. Who knows she could be a life long friend instead of a wife. Before ruling out a struggling woman don't forget she might just be Ms. Right.

Men and women are both looking for a mate who is fun to be around.
Get rid of the gloom and doom attitude.

23

SIGNS THAT POINT TO MS. WRONG

Visualize successful outcomes.

My mother once told me a story about the man who took the wounded snake home with him only after it promised not to bite him. To the gentlemen's dismay, immediately after he had patched the snake up and given it nourishment and everything else it needed to survive, the slick creature bit him hard.

"But you promised not to bite me!" the gentlemen screamed.

"Ha, ha, ha!" the evil snake cackled. "You knew I was a snake when you brought me here."

Though I'm sure my memory has failed me, as I don't remember the tale word for word, the moral is one that for some, should be applied to their everyday lives. Everyday that I'm out in the city interviewing men they go on and on about the latest woman whose brought mystery to their lives. More often than not I hear these men say, "but she seemed so nice at first."

It happens all the time, in small towns and big cities across the country. A man meets a woman that he thinks is "Ms. Right", he's looking for the ideal woman, and he feels it's love at first sight. As days dissolve into weeks and weeks into months he discovers his dream girl is more a snake than a perfect woman. She's not all she appeared or pretended to be. Among males and females there are hundreds of so-called good catches who upon closer inspection, turn out to be Ms. Wrong. Men sometimes overlook the small flaws in their lovers that reveal the big picture.

Overlooking these habits prevent them from assessing women and situations accurately, and it keeps them from moving on to healthy partnerships. When spending time with a less than valuable partner you should be able to recognize these warning signs.

1. She won't give you her home telephone number.
There is difference between elusiveness and convenience. If a woman that you've met won't give you her phone number, then you have reason to believe that she's probably already involved and doesn't want to be bothered or is running a game on men. In addition some women like the ideal of keeping track of men that they date, but prefer that he's not able to pin down her whereabouts.

2. Incompatibility in simple values.
It's expected that two individuals will have different opinions and will not share fully all the same values, but if most of their values are different, the relationship is in serious jeopardy.

3. Hectic schedules leave limited time for you.
Men often complain when their woman don't have enough time for them. The mistake that many men make is thinking that marriage will change their bad habits. If you find that your love interest has a greater interest in her job or her social life, than she does for you. She might not be the right person for you.

4. Past relationships can leave emotional baggage.
The girl that you just met seems intriguing but constantly brings up nasty tidbits about her ex-husband. Or the attractive woman who at first was like a breath of fresh air can't have a conversation without mentioning a past lover. When there are violations of trust in prior relationships, emotional trauma is transposed into the new relationship this carrier poses problems to the compatibility of the new relationship.

5. Violent behavior and jealousy.
Men should be cautious about partners who are possessive, jealous and violent. If your

date has a bad temper or angry outbursts, you should be very careful. Excessive jealousy in a partner could mean insecurity and she could possibly become physically abusive. Look for traits such as paranoia, the need to control, quick anger and constant criticisms. Women with this profile fit the abuser profile.

It should be noted that women are and can also be violent. Men interviewed told me that it took all of their inner strength to walk away from a woman after being hit in front of their friends or relatives by her. Men should also make it clear that they will not take this type of behavior. Disagreements are to be expected and are sometimes healthy for the relationship and discussions about them are normal. If every disagreement escalates to an argument in a very short time there may be serious underlying problems.

6.   **The drug addict or alcoholic.**

The drug abuser or alcoholic is the wrong choice of a mate. Many substance abusers are adept at masking the severity of their problem. She may drink with you socially, but also keep a bottle hidden at her bedside. She might slip into the bathroom to snort her cocaine or smoke her crack out of your presence. Be aware of your partners actions, reactions and mood swings. There might be a problem if responses are slowed, words slurred, or eyes are glassy.

7.   **Too many nights out with her girlfriends or her mother.**

Strong messages are sent by women who spend several nights a week out with the girls or who spend excessive time with their family while you spend time alone. Obviously they fear the idea of forming a solid relationship. Men are turned off by women who consult with their mother or friends on every aspect of the relationship, or who always tend to be on the telephone with the girls when he calls or wants to be alone with her.

8.   **Ms. Tease or Ms. Flirt.**

If she constantly flirts with your brother and male friends, you are headed for trouble. If you date the type of woman who is always up in some other man's face trying to make you jealous you need to reconsider having this relationship. With her it might be cute at first, but eventually it will drive you crazy. If she flirts with your brother she will probably flirt with your son.

9. Communication problems.

Communications are a must for any good relationship. Talking and sharing your feelings, needs, desires, and fears are keys to bonding with a potential mate. While it might not seem like much of a problem at first, in the long run the lack of communication can pose a serious problem with intimacy. If you have problems talking or your conversations tend to get shorter and shorter there are probably incompatibilities. If you find that you just don't have anything of common interest to talk about and your interests are different from one another or there are few sparks to keep the relationship alive you are probably with Ms. Wrong.

10. The control freak.

If your partner must always be in control of you, and the relationship, you constantly feel criticized, judged or scrutinized, or she has an intent on correcting your behavior, even in front of others you'd better start running. Stay away from partners who are determined to change you or those who feel you must change. Besides, if drastic changes are needed she might not be the right person for you.

11. She has trouble keeping a job or the likelihood is unable to be seen.

If you are involved with a partner who can never seem to keep a job and they are always depending on you to keep the boat afloat, to foot the bills or make a loan to tide her over, then you have a Ms. wrong. There are the women who float from job to job yet they frequent the hangout of hardworking men in hopes of getting themselves a meal ticket. If you find a woman that can keep a job and carry her weight you are less likely to end up with a woman that's looking for a meal ticket.

12. The gold digger.

There are some women who expect to contribute virtually nothing into a relationship, and they may also have unfair expectations of what they should receive. These types of people are usually called gold diggers. They expect their romantic partners to give them more than they are willing to give others. They are typically free loaders.

Breaking Up With Ms. Wrong.

The good thing about breaking up is that you might shed ten pounds in a short time. The bad thing is, it's usually painful. Thomas thinks while curled in a fetal position on his side of the bed. Tea, maybe. He makes his way to the kitchen. On the counter are two cups. One red, one blue. *"Sex 'R' Us"* is stenciled on both. A gift from her on Valentine's Day. He breaks them in the sink. The anger starts again.

He goes back to the bed and says aloud, "I'm going to be all right. I am going to be all right." Once in a while he whimpers, like a small, lost puppy.

When she told him, Saturday night-how long ago was that? Two days, two weeks? ... he remembers a weird sensation in his temples-as if something had broken. The electric pain got all his attention. When it passed, he was not certain she'd spoken, then unsure he'd understood. Did she say, "I just don't love you anymore"? "Could she have said that?" He'd taken her to a restaurant that last evening they would ever spend together, chosen to take her there because he wanted to propose to her.

He has a vague memory of her leaving. He ought to have been the one to leave, but he sat still like a stunned rabbit, lost in the bright white light of rejection. He thinks she called him names. The vilest she could summon. "Scumbag," maybe. But the only thing he is heart-shatteringly clear on is those six little words: "I just don't love you anymore." She did say them. As he left, with his tail between his legs, he could see her behavior had confirmed for him that he was right. He saw her shake her head sadly. He kept his eyes lowered as she left the room. She had really left him.

"I'm all right," he says into the pillow he now holds. "I am. I am." It is four o'clock in the morning. He's been in the bed in his green FUBU shirt for two days. He often wore it to bed with her because it symbolized to him what they were like. Perfectly designed, beautiful. They wore well, they'd get better as they grew old together. Now he has chewed the buttons off the right sleeve. Suddenly, rage cramps in his stomach, then overwhelms him. He gets out of bed, tears the sheets off of it, and shreds them. It is not easy to do, but anger has given him strength. He imagines the sheets are her arms, her legs, her heart.

I've called him hundreds of times and got no answer. Because I have left messages and he has not called, I've go to see what's the matter. He's my friend, and I sometime stay in his apartment when I'm in St. Louis. It is odd to hear his voice say, in its deepened, normal way, "Please leave only good news at the sound of the beep ."

Finally, he answers the intercom. I tell him it's me and convince him to open the door. When he does, I don't talk. I just sit with him on the sheetless bed, holding him while he cries. From time to time he pushes me away and says, "You're all bitches."

He's is twenty-six years old; this is his first major disaster. He tells me what I've told you. I tell him not to hang on. I looks at him and say, "But, you know hanging on is part of letting go," although he didn't see it then. "I know you're right about that, often, people need to hang on for a while, to be sure there is no way to fix the relationship.," he says .

I don't mean they should do so indefinitely, but after a breakup, I think you should try to communicate with each other as completely as you can about what the value of the union was. It helps to know it wasn't meaningless."

God knows, he's tried to find out what went wrong. He did get her to talk to him. He wanted to know if there was something left, if they could be friends. After several painful, forced conversations, he was able to see that whatever caused her to leave him had more to do with her than him. He has now, after a year, accepted that they will never get together again. Well almost.

When a relationship ends, you come out of the cataclysm in stages that are well-defined. Millions of people go through this trauma every year (by the way, it's more often the man who gets dumped, according to a New York Times survey). And no matter what their gender, people get through breakups in very much the same way.

Here's the nine-step path most psychologists agree leads to healing after a break-up:

WILL THE REAL MEN PLEASE STAND UP

1. **Bargaining.** Usually with fate or God. You offer something (to change, be a better person, let your hair grow, diet) if only she will be brought back to you.
2. **Grieving.** Tightness of the chest, difficulty breathing, emotional numbness, feeling desperate and abandoned.
3. **Pain.** Anguish over your loss, a sense of unendurable deprivation.
4. **Fear.** Night terrors and sweats; certainty you cannot extricate yourself, that you be alone forever.
5. **Sadness.** Deep sorrow that your life has lead you to this point and a bleak impression that your love affair almost worked, could have worked, if only. . .
6. **Anger.** Rage that you were undervalued by your lover or at the "other man" or the circumstances that brought about your breakup.
7. **Depression.** Moping, feeling you can't make the effort anymore, can't make small talk with women. Terrible lethargy and weakness.
8. **Acceptance.** The beginnings of wellness. You start to think that you can and will survive. You appreciate what you had in the relationship and understand that it is over and that your intimate experience with your lover has truly ended.
9. **Hope and rebuilding.** You begin to take better care of yourself, start to have a good time when you're on a date, are eager to meet new people.

If she looks like a snake, acts like a snake and talks like a snake, she probably is a snake.

24

OLDER WOMEN - YOUNGER MEN

Age really doesn't matter.

Marie and Allen held hands as they ran up the steps to the large wooden doors of the church. This was the most important Saturday morning of Marie's life. She wanted her entire family to meet the man she had fallen deeply in love with. They tried to catch their breath as they took a moment to straighten themselves out. They were greeted by her mother who was also an usher at the church for the past thirty year. Her mother looked Allen up and down. As she looked her eyes widened. Then she looked at Marie, turned to look at Allen again, and then perched her mouth as she looked at Marie with a puzzled look on her face.

Marie felt an uneasiness about the way her mother was looking at Allen. She knew that within the next ten minutes everyone in the church would know that Allen was younger than she was. This young man that Marie had been bragging about for months didn't look a day over twenty-five. Only seven years older than her youngest son. And worst of all, he was about the same age as her daughter Tee, whom her mother had been trying to marry off for the past two years.

Why was this such a show stopper to Marie's mother? It doesn't raise as nearly many eyebrows when the man is much older than the woman. The taboo associated with older women, younger men carry's negative gossip. In fact a man gets constant praise for having a younger woman, whereas a woman gets ridiculed for having a younger man. It's a stamina medal to let the world know you have a younger woman or a girl twenty years younger. But the woman has to deal with the world, family and friends telling her she's too old to sleep with a younger man. They constantly say she's not acting her age. Jokes are made about her robbing the cradle. People even imply that she's possessed by an uncontrollable lust.

WILL THE REAL MEN PLEASE STAND UP

Women aren't paying attention to the rumors or the taboos. They are reaching back finding partners that are five, ten, fifteen, and twenty years younger. Women are no longer taking the jokes lying down. They are changing the rules of what it takes to be happy. And if it takes a younger man, then so be it. These ageless wonders are not a fad. Taking a younger man is a new way of life for many women.

From the time they become teenagers, men are fascinated by older women. Everybody has found an older woman to have a crush on at some point ion his life -- a teacher, a baby-sitter, a friend's mother, or a next door neighbor. To a nine year old boy a teenage girl is considered an older woman to have a crush on. For ages men have been told that an older woman has a secret that can transform boys into men and believe me the younger men are trying their best to find out if there's any truth to it. It's not the Oedipus complex either. For younger boys and men it has more to do with hormones than anything else.

I remember several times when my college students had crushes on me. They seem to stare at me with a boyish kind of charm that made me nervous. As they tried to get their schedules changed to be apart of my class I found myself trying to steer their hormones, minds and bodies towards other teachers classes. Everything they did seemed to suggest hormones out of control. They found reasons to stick around my class or stay after class to ask questions. I must admit I found myself looking at their fathers instead of them, but they didn't care. I just couldn't see where we would be able to communicate with one another. To me their talk of fraternity parties and nightclubs was a turn off. They didn't have the level of wholeness I needed as dating single woman. But they still tried to convince me that they were the one for me. They felt that I had it so together. At least that's what young men have told me. They feel that an older woman has more to offer to them. Intelligence, experience, and most of all understanding. They feel that older women are already whole. To help you understand this better, let's look at some of the dynamics involved with younger men and older women.

Younger men are usually ambitious, sexy, focused and goal oriented to mention a few. He's either trying to establish his career or attempting to complete advanced education classes. With his dreams come the harsh realities of the world. He sees that there will be years of sacrifice in order for him to reach his goals. These are the men who want to get married and raise a family. They just don't want to do it right now. He wants a non-streessful relationship with a woman of low-maintenance. A woman who already has it together, so to speak.

Usually he's dating someone very close to his age, but women in his age bracket are usually ready to get married or pressuring him to make a commitment. It's not to force him, she's just trying to live the American dream. A husband, home, family and live happily ever after. He feels the pressures from her and all this does is add pressure to his already full life. He says "lets wait." She says, "for how long." He says, "Until I'm more established." She says, "I'm ready now, we can get established together."

On the surface all of this getting together sounds good, but most men like to plan their future a little better. They map it out year by year. They want certain things by twenty five. He wants to have seen the world by thirty and a wife will only slow him down and add pressures to his life. They are afraid their dreams are sacrificed. This fear makes men look noncommittal in their relationships. A woman sees him as unwilling to make the sacrifices necessary for commitment.

On the other hand the older woman has already evolved. She has her own life. She already has a home. Her children are usually grown and on their own. She has more experience in making relationships work. She doesn't stress out when you can't see her. She knows love and doesn't take it for granted. She will often times have a tight body and high energy levels to compete with younger women. She doesn't appear to fit the term of "older woman" because she doesn't carry herself like an old or outdated woman. She lives her life to the fullest and she lives in the present. She doesn't allow the people she associates with to live in the past because she knows that life is full, fun and free. She knows how to enjoy her life and the people in it because her years of living have taught her well. In fact she has aged gracefully and she's not in a hurry to grow older. All of these qualities are appealing to the younger man.

It's not the age that matters. It's a woman overall wholeness that attract a man and it *is* attractive to him. Those fine qualities such as her outlook on life, her patience, and her self-confidence often come with the wisdom of years. But not exclusively. She's like all other women who are growing in life, not just in age, she is an evolving women.

An evolved woman doesn't have to have a younger man, but he sure wants her. He naturally feels more comfortable with her. Some women do seek younger men for their youthful vim, vigor and vitality which closely matches their own lifestyles. These same women might be looking down the road to youthful companionship in her later years, or she may have already tried conventional marriage and decided that she was experiencing the same pressures men have with women. Many times she wants a low-pressure relationship too.

Many younger men have a fantasy of being seduced by an older woman with a terrific body and great legs. In some ways the differences in sexual aging is more beneficial to the man than is to the woman. Relationships between younger men and older women would seem to be a near fit, sexually speaking because of the notion that men tend to reach their sexual peak in their late teens, while women peak later in their early thirties. It turns out that that notion isn't really true.

All in all sexual differences are relatively minor and nothing that can't be handled. The most important thing to remember about these intergenerational relationships is not the sex at all. If your relationship is based on sex in the first palace then it's already doomed to fail. What really matters is what else you have in common when the sex is not there. The older woman can also teach a younger man about what women enjoy most in sexual intercourse. Being more experienced is an advantage within itself.

Since I'm in no position to argue with moral issues of young-old relationships, I think the best thing for me to do is investigate it a little more. One thing I can say sexually speaking is there are legitimate benefits to this type of relationship.

Many times the opinions of people who feel a older man should not be with a younger is because of deep rooted. There are known beneficial sexual and psychological reasons for age differences. For one: the problem of human sexuality is that men tend to become aroused and reach orgasm much more quickly than women do. As men age their sexual responses tend to slow down. It takes a man longer to reach an erection and he requires more manual stimulation, more foreplay, to become aroused. They began to have a sexual harmony and it begins to emerge at mid-life, for no other reason than the passage of time.

A younger woman's youthful body excites him over and over again. Her vagina tends to be tighter than a older women which also adds to his excitement. An on his part the older man contributes calmness, confidence and skill to their lovemaking, something younger men have not yet learned or earned. That's why some younger women prefer a smoother and more steady gray beard to a feisty too-fast younger man. Both of these men have their experience in both the joys and sorrow of loving and have thus learned through the years the true meaning of tenderness.

Let's assume she has a few years on you. There are several valid reasons that age difference doesn't have to mean much.

Why Age Shouldn't Matter

a. **You've already grown up.**

Many men are looking for older women. This need for an older woman to many men is their salvation from having to do everything for themselves. Many young men graduating from college actually look for a woman that resembles his mother in care taking. One who would tie up all the lose ends and make his problems go away so to speak. And many times when he finds this type of woman he also finds that he doesn't have to worry about taking responsibility for the relationship. If he decides to take a vacation or leave town for a while she usually waits patiently for him, with no strings attached.

The promise of this type of security is very inticing and seductive to a young man who is just starting out. The problem with grabbing hold of a replacement mother is that many of these men never grow up. Since all of their emotional and financial needs are being taken care of they gain their independence slowly. These men also grow restless because as the relationship grows they began to realize what they've been missing in life. They even result to having affairs early in their marriages because of unfulfilled feelings. There's nothing inherently wrong with marrying an older woman as long as you see yourself as equal. Don't allow her to control your every move, your every thought or your every decision. Be sure to keep in mind, however, that the wider the age gap, the harder it is to keep the balance of power at an even state.

b.   Friends won't take you seriously.

The trouble with dating an older woman is that their friends might not take you seriously or treat you with respect. Going to parties, functions, and get together can create feelings of insecurity if her friends are ignoring you or worst than that they talk you down. Her friends may see you as a jock especially all of the friends who knew the first husband. They will also wonder if you are the signs of the times and feel insecure that their marriage is soon to be threatened.

Overcoming The Social Stigma

What may be more difficult to overcome than physical differences is the social stigma attached to this type of relationship. Society seems to be lot more skeptical of a younger man who develops a thing for an older woman than the other way around. An older guy who marries a much younger woman is said to add vim, vigor and vitality to his sex life and himself. But a younger guy who falls in love with an older woman leaves people wondering what's going on and they just can't seem to figure it out.

Since most societies are male dominate they favor older men with younger women. However an older women and younger man isn't favored. By societal standards a older woman doesn't have much to offer a younger man. She might already have kids and can't offer him children of his own. If you add the huge premium society places on beauty, youth and fertility it's difficult for the world to understand how a younger man would want to settle for her. As a woman gets older it becomes more difficult for her to find a mate because men her age group start dying off for one reason or another.

If you are trying to be romantic don't give a practical gift.

Step 5:

Learning

To Romance

25

THE MAGIC OF ROMANCE

Have an understanding of what romance really should be.

"This is it. It's over, It's for real this time." Are you listening to me?," she asked.

"Yes, I hear you. You're breaking up with Buster for the 100th time in four years."

"This time I mean you, "she screamed, her voice raised in disgust and anger. He's been seeing his ex-girlfriend again. Somehow she has my unlisted number and she's calling here harassing me. "She said she was going to take Buster away from me." "Now she says they have a child together that I don't even know about." None of this would have happened if Buster had kept his pants up. It's hard enough to deal with his parents, now I have to deal with his baby's mother." "She's been trying to get him back, and I think they're seeing each other again." "I won't be disrespected like this by another man." "I've been good to him. I help him with his bills, I cook a for him, I clean his laundry and I helped him get his phone turned on in my damn name. I'm not taking this bull anymore."

"I warned you not to date him." But every time I talk to you it's the same old story. You'll just leave him and then go back to him as soon as he sweet talks you. You'll forget he did you wrong. Your life is a romance novel. Why don't you get a man whose less dramatic and confused?"

Her phone rang before she could answer my question. When she came back to the phone her tone of voice was different. She sounded happy now.

"Donald I've got to go now, Buster is on the phone and he wants to explain what happened."

WILL THE REAL MEN PLEASE STAND UP

I've known Marie for ten years and she's been running after Buster for more than five of those years. She acts as if he's the only man on earth. He treats her bad, forgets important dates, and doesn't return her calls. She rationalizes his actions by making excuses for the way he treats her. She spends lots of time at home waiting by the telephone, but he seldom calls her. She forgives him for all this and then she's the one to try and salvage the relationship.

Romance starts in the early moments of the relationship. Women are guilty of falling for the *idea* of romance. No matter who the woman is or what positions she holds she'll always long for romance and passion. It has an alluring effect on women all over the world.

Couples spend billions of dollars each year trying to find new ways to enhance the romance. To fulfill a woman's need to have romance a man must first have understanding of what romance is. Walking hand in hand, playing footsie, exchanging gifts, cut flowers, and sharing moon lit nights all spell out romance.

Men are more than happy to create romantic atmosphere's they just don't understand why it's so important or why he has to keep doing it. It has become a learned skill that men have to think about in order to keep it going.

Becoming More Romantic

Asking her if she wants romance is not the key. Hints and subtle gestures that push her romantic button will help her fall in love with you. Pay attention to the hints she will almost always give, then you can take credit for doing those things. Not only will she see you as a romantic man, she will feel that you care more for her. You will feel closer to her as well. When you see the happiness on her face from your romantic gestures it will make you remember to do it again.

Small Details Count

When you take care of the small details a woman feels romanced. She likes it when you handle the tickets, drives the car, opens her doors, and protect her. When you take the responsibility to take care of things she feels she can relax and enjoy being taken care of. It allows her to enjoy her feminine side and it gives her a mini-vacation from being in charge all the time. Romantic moments are particularly helpful for women who don't feel comfortable sharing their feelings. On a romantic date, without having to talk about her feelings a woman can feel understood, and supported. She enjoys the benefits of talking without having to say a word.

Responding To Your Partner

Of course you want to please your partner. And you'll be happy to know that you benefit from the romantic responses as well. Women are more inclined to please their men when he gives her the romantic attention she wants and needs. When you fulfill your mates desires she'll take care of your needs as well.

Many men have a hard time expressing what they want because they don't know how to express their feelings. Women have been taught to express their feelings whereas men are taught to suppress them. With men, their feelings might come out an hour, a day or a week later. What women feel on the inside is often expressed on the outside.

Men want what they want in terms of outcome. They want to feel good. They want to feel wanted. They just don't think in terms of process, how to make it happen. So how can a man discover his woman's needs. One of the best ways to discover what your partner wants is through play. Playing games allows both partners to let down their defenses and become more vulnerable to one another, which is the key to an open relationship. Once a man begins to discover his partners needs and desires he can incorporate different methods for satisfying her.

Whether you've just met a terrific woman or whether you've been married for a long time. Get to know and understand your partner better. Each day should be a day of awakening for you both. After all, you do want to continue fueling your flames don't you? Let's work to find your inner romantic. There's a lot of romance and passion within you that's trying it's best to get out, all you have to do is help it come out.

WILL THE REAL MEN PLEASE STAND UP

Getting To Know You

While you're working to satisfy your partners desires be sure to include your own and don't lose sight of your integrity and self-respect. You don't want to resent something you did only for the sake of pleasing your partner. The best way to ruin a romantic relationship is to be filled with guilt.

Since we all have different tastes, likes and needs we are unique. Everyone is! What your mate wants may be completely different from what you want. We are all pleased in ways that may differ from one another.

If you feel embarrassed, offended or otherwise compromised by something your partner wants you to do, don't do it. As you will see in this book you can do many things that aren't offensive to stimulate your partner and to satisfy your romantic needs. If you say yes to something you really don't agree with or want to do you'll regret it later. Keep in mind that your partner wants you to be happy and if you're unhappy she feels that it's her fault. If you can please your partner and she can please you there's a lot more romance awaiting the both of you.

Keep the Momentum

Keeping a steady rhythm it not as difficult as you might think. By doing at least one little romantic thing a day for your partner you will bring intimacy into your relationship. Remain consistent and persistent. If your partner doesn't notice the new romantic you right away don't give up. Believe me she'll notice. And when she does she'll return the romantic favor with some romantic moves of her own. Whenever she makes the smallest gesture to romance you, respond in positive ways. Each time she tries she's moving your relationship toward a happier and more intimate union. Tell her how much you appreciate what she's trying to do. That way she will want tolerant more about what pleases you.

Be sure to give yourself credit for this wonderful progress, no matter how small. Congratulate yourself. Keep up the good work, expand on it and celebrate the new found happiness you've brought to your relationship.

What Is Romance?

Romance isn't something that happens only once in a while, when everything is working right. Romance is an attitude that can be created anywhere at anytime. If you start it, your partner is sure to follow. One small romantic act can serve as a catalyst, and soon your relationship will resonate with an electrifying glow. The trick is to make it a habit. Giving your partner a little TLC every day strengthens your relationship, expanding its romantic power.

Lasting romance and passion exists in a small, loving actions carried out on a regular basis. Opportunities to romance your partner are all around you. Something as small as adding her name to the conversation can add intimacy to your relationship. Giving her a special greeting without complaining about your problems can trigger romantic feelings. One of the most important things you can do for your partner is move toward her in romance and then move away from her so that she can respond to you in return. In this way you create an easy-flowing reciprocal interplay that will develop the intimacy of your relationship. If, on a daily basis you make her feel better with you than she feels when she is with anyone else, she'll want to spend most of her time with you.

Let Her Be Your Heroin

From time to time your partner might have something to say to you or maybe even a fantastic story to tell about a special award or achievement. Maybe she finished her report by deadline, or discovered something wonderful. During these times try your best not to interrupt her. Let her tell her story and listen to everything she says. Give a smile or appropriate facial expression from time to time and then give her a big hug for reaching her goal.

WILL THE REAL MEN PLEASE STAND UP

A Weekend of Romance

Has your love life become routine, hurried or boring? It happens to the most passionate of lovers. One great choice: a weekend of sheer romantic joy. Shared meals, massages, open and loving intimacy. Lavish attention on one another for two days and two nights.

Give yourself a weekend of sexless pleasures and the thrill of being in love. This can be the greatest adventure lovers can share with one another. You can concentrate on each other for two and a half of the most wonderful days of your lives. And the good thing is you can do it as often as your heart or your libido desires.

One of the romantic myths to be set aside is that making love should always be spontaneous. On the contrary, you will prepare well for this special weekend of joy, love and intimacy. Here's what you should do to make it pleasurable, exciting and sensuous.

Plan to go away together or to stay home for the entire weekend. If you have children make the proper arrangements to have them taken care of for the weekend. The first commitment of a weekend of romance is to concentrate only on each other for two days and two nights. In advance, arrange to have the following supplies and any other personal favorites you may think of:

*candles (scented, different colors, and sizes)   *colored light bulbs
*freshly scented clean sheets   *beautiful arrangement of flowers
*jojoba oils and lubricants   *your favorite poetry
*a weekend supply of food for two.   *your favorite beverages
*fruit/ sweets   *minimal preparation foods
*skimpy underwear

Plan a small, inexpensive, loving surprise of some sort for your partner. Also plan what type of weekend get-a-way it will be so you will know exactly what you need to bring. Comfortable, partly transparent, revealing clothing is usually the best and most sensuous. Prior to the weekend tell your friends or relatives you will be unavailable from Friday until Sunday evening. Tonight and through the weekend, unplug the telephone or leave the answering machine turned off. Agree to leave the television off the entire weekend.

WILL THE REAL MEN PLEASE STAND UP

Remember this is a weekend of romance and all the busy gadgets that remind you of work and other parts of your life should be obsolete. Now let's begin.

Thursday

Double check your list of things to do so that you won't forget anything important. Check off the things you have done as you go. Assure your children that you will be near if they need you or that you are only a phone call away. Let them know that you are going to spend some private time so they won't feel neglected or left out. Preparing them openly and honestly will assure you a successful weekend of joy.

Friday

Wake up early today. When the weekend finally arrives complete your preparations. Order in fresh flowers or go pick them up. Air out your home by cracking windows as you freshen up all those necessarily places you'll spend most of your time. Deodorize your home, light scented candles and freshen any areas that you feel should have special attention placed upon it. Clean and beautify your bedroom, using fresh clean sheets on your bed. Add beautiful linens, dust your furniture, the fixtures and place fresh fruit in your bedroom in romantic places for your guest to have at her leisure.

Clean, deodorize and sanitize your bathroom: the tub, shower and toilet area. Make it as sensuous and pleasant as you can. A good way to do this is imagine being in the finest hotel and set your bathroom up in the same way. Comfort and cleanliness is the key.

Set up a supply drawer near your bed with lubricants, massage oils, and objects that are pleasing to the touch. Prepare some light delicious snacks and have them ready for sharing romantically later.

Officially begin your weekend with a sensuous bath or shower taken separately. Consciously relax for the rest of the day. Take your time. End your day with a cool dip in cold water to revitalize and increase your energy level. Put on clean, loose clothing such as a robe or night clothes. Use your favorite body oils and or fragrances to help entice romance.

When you both are ready, come together with calming music. Light several candles, sit down together and gaze quietly into each others eyes silently. The flickering of the flame from the candle will help set the mood and the music you choose will help set the tone. Make silent and physical contact spending a few moments doing nothing but touching one another. These gestures of friendship, love and care are what so many couples forget about once they get into a relationship that has been going on for a few years.

Bring out the food you have prepared and offer gratitude for having it and one another to share it with. Throughout the entire weekend feed each other. Eat and drink lightly, take your time and lavish your time with one another. Eating heavy will make you drowsy and sluggish. Light foods that are also eaten lightly will help you to enjoy each other for longer periods of time this weekend.

When you both feel at ease and comfortable enough offer one another a loving massage and caresses. Take turns giving each other back rubs, foot rubs or other touches that's meant to nurture and release body tension. Do not touch each other's erogenous zones yet. Focus more on nurturing each other rather than on trying to arouse. If you feel like touching each other in an intimate way slowly move away from each other, sit facing each other and touch in this way. Use pillows to make yourself more comfortable. Change positions at any time you choose to. Play and stroke and make love gestures but don't have intercourse at this time.

After this time of sharing with one another begin to move toward sleep. Don't discuss any of your problems at this time. Remember this is a get-a-way, which for all purposes means to be with one another, yet away from all the problems that cause problems or frustrations in your life. Pray or meditate together for a while and then cuddle as you settle in. Talk softly to one another allowing sleep to come at will.

Saturday

Wake up refreshed, comfortable and deliciously aware of a weekend day alone together. Whoever wakes first should make a simple breakfast in bed for the two of you. Don't cheat, if you wake up first pamper the other one. Begin acknowledging your gratitude for your food and each other. See how many mutual acknowledgments you can offer into one breakfast. Recite things like "you're great to be with, a great cuddlier, waking up to see you brightens my day." Try to recite those things that you really feel in your heart. After breakfast connect with one another. Hold each other silently in the spoon position or other positions for a few moments. Begin to make it a habit to reflect on the deeper purpose of your relationship when in this position.

Move into intimacy and lovemaking when you both feel inclined to do so, but try not to have intercourse yet. Continue to make intimacy the most important part of lovemaking. Position yourself to lavish love and affection on one another. Experiment with touches and positions that are unfamiliar or new to you and your partner. Make it priority to stop short of orgasm, but if an orgasm should happen spontaneously see it as a good sign instead of premature. Just enjoy the outcome, this will let you know how much you have turned your partner on, or she has turned you on. Enjoy it and don't stop, continue on.

Whether or not you have become accustomed to making eye contact while making love, include this now, for at least a little while. Allow yourself to see and contact the inner being of your partner. After a while of petting and making non-sexual love relax and spend some quiet time together. By mutual agreement, take a break from lovemaking. Exercise separately or together, indoors or out. Run, dance, swim, walk, or bike; especially if you have a beautiful outdoor area to enjoy. Afterwards come back to your indoor space and prepare to enjoy your next planned events. Here are a few ideas:

1. **Dance For One Another.**

It can be seductively or casually. Take a few minutes to change into your chosen costume. If you have no costume, undergarments or nude or maybe even a scarf will do. Whoever is moved to begin first can put on the music of his or her choice. Be as outrageous, silly, erotic or as serious as you want to be. Dance from your heart, forgetting about criticisms and evaluations. As soon as one finishes the other one begins. Dance to together at the end if you wish.

Put on soft music and sit down facing one another. Make silent eye contact for a few minutes allowing soulful contact. Begin to touch when you feel inclined to do so. This should be your time for experimental touching.

Choose some of these favorites: Give hand or foot massages. Tell each other what feels best. Kiss romantically and experimentally for a long time. Choose who will give and receive first and experiment with oral stimulation. It can be as simple as sucking fingers and bottom lips to something more daring. Invent your own; and then try them out on one another.

2.   Have a Ceremonial Meal.
When you both are hungry choose a ceremonial time and way to eat that you'll always remember. Prepare a simple meal together or one of you can do it for the both of you. Light a candle and decorate the table with flowers or your favorite centerpiece.

Include tasting of fresh fruit with this meal. Feed each other pieces of your favorite fresh fruit. Savor these moments and these edible delights as well. Do the same with other foods. Try closing your eyes as you taste and feed one another. Have fun with it. Swallow slowly. It gives you the gift of savoring sensational mouth watering eats.

3.   Resume Intimacy.
When your meal is finished, go back to the bed or couch. Use the various means of connecting with one another to help you also bond with one another. When you are ready began to make love again, this time going for higher states of arousal. You can use this moments to experiment with different types of intercourse, but don't have an orgasm yet. Try positions that may seem silly or impossible, or positions you have avoided because they don't lead to orgasm. Stop and rest when you get close to orgasm and only resume after your arousal has subsided a bit. Take your time and enjoy the company of one another for as long as you can before orgasm.

Sunday

Waking up together, savor the prospect of another day to explore and enjoy each other. Have a light breakfast prepared by the one who was served on Saturday. After grace or giving thanks, feed each other, savoring your food.

Then have a period of stretching your bodies. Take an extended bath or shower together. Give each other some massage, communicating your wishes clearly to each other. When you feel ready it is time for you to honor your man. She should now receive your attention for half an hour or more this means not responding or giving back right now. Touch, feel and give to her concentrating on those things she loves the most. Suck her toes, massage her scalp, stimulate her orally. Do everything you are willing to do to her but don't bring her to orgasm this time.

When you both feel ready change roles. You can now receive from your lover until you feel moved to initiate a time of unrestrained lovemaking. Do anything and everything now, no holds barred. Approach everything with gratitude and openness to new experiences with one another. Enjoy making love without a goal or a script. Let orgasm occur or not as they will. Ask each other for anything your heart desires. Give and receive freely, noticing how in lovemaking, as in life everything you give comes back in multiple.

A get-a-way, means to be with one another,
to go away together or to stay home for the entire weekend-together.

26

KEEPING THE MYSTERY ALIVE

Sexuality is not a leisure or part-time activity. It is a way of being.

A major mistake made in relationships is revealing too much too soon, whether it's tight clothing that leaves little to the imagination in order to attract a mate, or stripping down to the bare souls. Often, men see revealing life stories, daily schedules, and their every desire as establishing intimacy with a woman. Women like a challenge, something to fight for, a mystery to solve. Reveal too much, give too much, be too easy, become too available and it will cause her to move right past you after she's gotten what she wanted. She'll soon be calling it that much needed space.

That fact that men desire women who provide a challenge may seem archaic, not to mention a sexist concept; but let's face it, they've been socialized that way. Here are steps to keep your relationship alive and full of mystery:

1. Don't be easy to get.
Women and men both love the thrill of the chase. The more efforts taken to get what we want the more we try to get it. We're at our best when our wit is called upon. Don't play standoffish or too hard to get. Never be too anxious, available or accessible either. Show your interests and enthusiasm, but don't show it all at once. Give it to her piece by piece.

2. Don't be desperate.
Maintain some mystique, but not aloofness. Avoid anything that looks like either desperation or lack of interest. If you are perceived as being too eager to date others, the romantic value become less, and will come across as a desperate grab for an exceptionally good deal.

When you desire to be with a woman make sure it's because you *want* to be with her. A confident man, one who loves his life and is not desperate to have a woman in his life to fill some void, is far more attractive. The men who are happiest are the ones who can also be happy without a woman. Recognize that your relationship with her enriches and embellishes your life. It doesn't give you life.

3.   Be yourself.

Being mysterious doesn't mean hiding who you are or what you want in life. How will a women know who she's sitting with if you are editing yourself and trying to look like someone you're not. And how are you going to know she's fallen in love with the real you? If she doesn't like who you are and how you think she's probably wrong for you.

A loving relationship with a woman should never mean that you give up your unique personality. Loving her doesn't mean losing yourself either.

4.   Don't reveal too much.

Too much personal disclosure too soon is threatening, especially if you've just been introduced to someone. Discussing very personal information very early in the relationship seems to reduce a couples attractiveness to others. Prematurely discussing your personal business may later reveal things about you that will reduce true intimacy and cause her to no longer trust your judgement to handle such information.

5.   Don't be predictable.

Always keep her guessing. Give her daisies or tulips instead of roses for a change. Reveal a new side of yourself, you know the side you kept secret by not revealing too much. Learn about her hobbies or interests. Keep her guessing what you might do next.

6.   Do not give too much.

Giving expensive gifts, catering to a woman too much, sticking like a piece of toilet paper on her shoe, can take away the mystery and the adventure in a relationship. Getting too much is like not getting enough; it can damage the relationship. Although partners who receive too much may be delighted with the things they get, they also are likely to experience feelings of guilt, being obligated or entrapped. Don't overdo it.

7. Get a life.

Don't abandon your own life and friends for her. Don't break off dates with friends just to be with her or forgo functions just because she can't attend. Women are attracted to vibrant, happy, confident men who have lives of their own. They must know that you don't need to be with them, that you want to be with them and that you will not cease to exist without them.

8. Make her work.

Men do not have to be the caretakers of relationships. Make her put some time and effort into the relationship. Show her that if she doesn't want to make the effort to do things with you, you can do it without her and then do it.

9. Discover yourself.

One of the fundamental attractions between men and women is the fact that they can never fully sum each other up. Getting bored with each other is much less likely to happen when a little mystery remains between couples. When you are continuing to grow as a person, you are more interesting. Try to spend time away from her so that you can discover who you are and what you can bring to the relationship. Become a mystery to yourself, constantly learning new things about yourself. If you enjoy solving the mystery within you, slowly take your time to unlock the new you.

Women like a challenge, something to fight for, a mystery to solve.

27
SEARCHING FOR REAL LOVE

When you think about it, everything is a miracle.

Lee and Louise were infatuated. They couldn't get enough of each other. They had found their respective soul mates, the fulfillment of their wildest fantasies. At any given moment, they could be found joined at the hip and locked at the lips. They were in love. But everyone else knew better. Everyone insisted these two did not belong together. Lee and Louise had nothing in common, they had only known each other for two months, and at this point, it was too early for commitment to each other.

Sound familiar? Have you ever found yourself saying, "why does he stay with her?" Or how about, "I always thought you were smarter than that!" We have all experienced the frustration of watching someone we care about get involved in a relationship that just doesn't make sense. Worse yet, maybe you've even found yourself in the middle of a relationship driven by nothing but raw emotion, only to find later that the relationship was doomed from the start. How do you account for this bizarre activity? What is responsible for such behavior? The culprit is *romantic love*.

Romantic Love versus Real Love

Ah, the ecstasy of romantic love. Nothing beats the feeling you feel when you lock your eyes on the person of your dreams across a crowded room, falling head over heels in love, and spending the rest of your life in marital bliss. If you're not familiar by now how this thing works read a few romantic novels or watch a few romantic movies and see how everyone in a romance movie ends in a happily ever after scenario. It all sounds great doesn't it?

WILL THE REAL MEN PLEASE STAND UP

There's only one small problem -- romantic love is an illusion meant to give you the feelings of sheer happiness and contentment. For most of us it doesn't happen in our lives. Most of us know that romantic love has nothing to do in real life or with what real love is.

What is real love? What makes you feel loved and cared for? What is the right way for you to be loved? If someone were to ask you these questions would you be able to answer without feeling that you lack the real answers or solutions?

Let's face it our society is confused about love. We all think that love is just a feeling. As people put it, "It's feeling that feeling we feel that we have never felt with anyone else." Although deep down inside we all want to believe the fairy tale version of love, sooner or later we must face the truth. Love is not simply a feeling, it's much more.

When we think of all the positive elements of love in any relationships we have to think twice to see if we have these same qualities within our own relationships. Are we affectionate with each other, or considerate? Do we communicate our true feelings without hurting each others feelings? Are we respectful of each other's time and space? Do we have a sense of commitment, fidelity, loyalty, and trust? Do we have tolerance for each other's frailties, admitting, acknowledging, and appreciating each other's strengths? These are the necessary ingredients for a happy healthy relationship. But there's a new concept that encompasses all of the elements listed above. They balance our relationships to provide security, contentment, sovereignty and autonomy.

In the search for love we might often overlook the importance of real-love, perhaps the greatest love of all. With real love almost all experts agree we learn to lavish attention and seek fulfillment from within before we seek to bring another into our space. Before we can expect to give love to others we must learn to love ourselves. Love is complex and there are clear distinctions between *(Eros)* romantic love and *(agape)* real or mature love.

Eros is passionate forms of love which include all the elements of that initial attraction and romantic phase of a relationship: obsession, mystery, allure, excitement, passion. On the other hand *agape* is love that's demonstrated by two people who deeply care about each other and whose mostly concerned about the welfare of the other. Agape concerns a mature and stable kind of love -- solid, enduring, and providing a sense of security.

Real love is a decision to seek the good of another, whatever it cost. Agape includes nurture, support, encouragement, acceptance and companionship. When it comes to crafting a lasting relationship, real love far outweighs the fleeting passions of romance.

There is value in romance and plenty of it. Romance is a normal and natural part of healthy relationships. In fact I will be the first to admit I made a fool of myself while falling in love with my mate. I know what it feels like to be in puppy love. I know the ecstasy of having my world evolve around another person. I've felt the physical and emotional drive that made me want to spend every waking moment with my mate. I enjoyed every romantic phase, gesture and feeling that I experienced in the first 10 - 12 months of my relationship. But that's just the point: *the romantic love was a phase, and we did not allow it to dominate our relationship. Eventually we moved on to deeper kind of love -- a mature form of love, a real love.*

Real love can only began to grow and flourish when the infatuation diminishes. And it is only this kind of love that can sustain a relationship in the long run. Does this mean that romance is no longer apart of our marriage? No way! It just means that the romance and passion is just an aspect that enhances what we have rather than functions as the foundation for our relationship. We all love to get caught up in romantic love, however, it's time to stop giving romantic love so much of the credit.

Eros cannot measure capatibility. Romantic love tells you nothing about a person's character, and it's an extremely unreliable method of determining the viability or health of a relationship.

Whatever real love means to you, learning about yourself, accepting who you are, and learning to love yourself is critical to achieving a state of harmony with self and others. Perhaps you have found yourself in a relationship which you want more, but you realize it is not working for you. Finding real love means first taking a look at your own relationship and analyzing the union to find out what the roots of the problems are and how things may be fixed.

WILL THE REAL MEN PLEASE STAND UP

Sometimes couples who have been together for numerous years allow things to fall apart because neither of them can see past their own personal gripes or pin down why they aren't communicating any longer. Many times these same couples began to consider divorce as their only alternative. Even though they don't really want a relationship to end they often find themselves being worn out with the arguments and the growing distance between them. If it's going to work, both parties will have to work together at finding a solution. Some small but meaningful things couples can do to help their relationship move in a positive direction are:

1. Attend a retreat.
Accept the counseling services offered in the program. The fact that each of you are willing to seek counseling is a sign that you want to work on your relationship. These sessions may not be an overnight success for your relationship, but it will help each of you to communicate with one another again. The talks will help you to find better ways to get to know each other again and it will help you understand what each of you want in the relationship.

2. Become more aware of who you are.
Self-knowledge among couples is the first step toward building emotional well-being and healthy relationships. Each person should take an honest look at themselves. It is only after we get to know ourselves that we are able to truly love someone else.

Get in touch with yourself and all the things that dwell deeply within you. Find out why you're not happy or why you're angry, why you're secretive and why you don't trust your mate. The answer is within self first.

3. Get rid of effects of the past.
The examination of one's past is not easy. It's difficult for families to acknowledge painful events of the past. To move forward a person has to remember the things that actually happened to her or him as a child. A person may also need to go to their parents or someone in the family who is older and ask some questions about things that happened

in their childhood. Only when we dig into our past can we figure out what baggage we carry into our relationships that are unhealthy and unresolved.

4.   Contribute emotional security and commitment.
All of us need to feel secure in the knowledge that we will be able to afford the basic necessities such as food, clothing, and shelter. Both partners must be prepared to contribute to the emotional, physical, financial, social and spiritual security and contentment of the relationship. While no one can completely make his or her partner feel secure, each partner should make a sincere effort to alleviate his or her partner's anxiety.

5.   Be attentive.
Do not be an overbearing flirt especially when you're with your partner. You should be mature and considerate enough to create an environment that makes it safe for your partner to reveal his or her needs. They must know that the things they feel serious about not be laughed at, scorned, or humiliated in any way. Make every effort to cater to your partners needs and maintain emotional contentment.

6.   Try to minimize conflicts and disappointments.
Each partner should have a calendar with little boxes big enough to enter both partners activities. This helps to remind you both of important dates. It hurts when important dates are forgotten.

7.   Speak well of your partner in their absence and presence.
Don't bad mouth your partner to your relatives and friends when you have a disagreement. Negative speaking poisons the listeners mind and these opinions of your partner may backfire on you. Some of your listeners may agree with your partners perspective. And if you decide to stay with the person despite all the negative things you have shared you leave yourself open to ridicule and your judgement will be questioned.

8. Willingly demonstrate your affection.

Holding hands and exchanging an affectionate peck in public reassures your partner that you love him or her and you don't care who knows it. Doing all of these things contribute to your partner feeling emotionally secure and confident.

9. Sovereignty and autonomy.

Where men-women relationships are concerned, we would all do well to remember that a relationship is not a prison; nor is it only a mother-son; father-daughter relationship. Just as we prefer autonomy for ourselves, we should be willing to grant sovereignty that is freedom for our partner that he or she agrees are within reason. There should be no long lists of do's and don'ts; no interrogation series; no intimidation tactics. The negative behavior smothers your partner and kills the positive spirit of the relationship. Both partners must allow each other the room to grow and blossom as a person.

Love is not simply a feeling, it's much more.

28

HOW MEN ARE ATTRACTED TO WOMEN

Don't rush, all things come in time.

Is it love or something else? You can become attracted to a woman in several ways, but how will you know which ones are real signs of love, and which are signs of lust?

What is this attraction-love-lust thing anyway? Is it when you wake up in the morning with her name beating inside your head? Is it when she buys you expensive jewelry and you wonder if she can really afford it. Is it when you feel safe and warm and giddy when she's around, and cold, dry and nervous when she's not?

Love is not necessarily that funny feeling you get in your stomach. There are other more important signs of what is and what isn't love. There are fifteen reasons that contribute to attraction, love and lust. You'll probably recognize more than one of them. They are:

Love-Lust Attractions

Love-lust (horniness) can manifest itself in several ways. Four key signs to look for.

a. When introduced to a woman do you find yourself wondering what it would be like to make love to her?
b. You often consider setting a small fire in the fireplace, changing into something sexy and then calling her up.
d. Even the ugliest woman you know begins to look good to you.
e. Instead of having a healthy snack you decide to masturbate.

Your physical yearning receives temporary relief when you have sexual encounters. Just because a woman gets turned on does not mean she's in love with you and just because she desires to go to bed with you does not mean she loves you either.

WILL THE REAL MEN PLEASE STAND UP

1.   A Crush.

Crushes are risk free and they're great when you have lots of work to do and no time to recline in someone's arms. Often the person who you have the crush on has no earthly idea of your intentions. In a crush there are elements of fear, but it's still okay to ask her out to a movie or a dinner.

2.   Infatuation.

Infatuation is tricky. Your heart begins to palpitate, you look deep into her eyes, you suddenly want to rip hers clothes off at every opportunity. Every moment you spend together is fabulous. Is it love? Probably not. The problem: 75% of this relationship is based upon infatuation. Infatuation and fantasy are very closely connected: You want everything to be true about her, so you convince yourself that they are true, even though you have no evidence they are.

3.   A lot-of-like.

You like her, she likes you. You're not in love and neither is she, but she sure does brighten your day. She makes you feel good about her, about yourself and the two of you together. You enjoy going on fun dates with her, and you want to be with her all the time. But still you know she's not the Ms. Right you've been looking for.

Maybes she's so close to being Ms. Right that she'll do just fine until the right person comes along. So why not relax and enjoy your moments. Stop talking yourself out of great relationships.

4.   Obsession.

Staring at the phone, waiting on it to ring won't bring you love and happiness. It will only stare back at you. So you turn nonchalant and uncaring. When you finally fall asleep you wake up feelings even worst because you didn't get a wake up call throughout the night. You look at the phone again and you began to play tricks on your own mind. You convince yourself that something must have happened to her since she didn't call you. Obsession is a mighty master and it takes no prisoners.

5. **Love madness.**

She treats you badly, but you keep her around. You even feel like you'll throw up if you have to look at her breastless chest again. So why can't you get rid of her? You convince yourself that she's better than nothing and you decide to keep her around until something better comes along. Wake up and smell the misery you are putting yourself through.

She treats you in a way that you hate but you still stay. Seek professional help and realize that you deserve more than she has to offer you. Understand also that she's not better than nothing.

6. **Waiting all your life.**

Sometimes dramatic, you have no earthly idea you're in love until you realize you're at home watching reruns on television and you say "I've got to talk to her. She's the only one that will understand how I'm feeling or what I'm saying." Then suddenly you realize you've been in love with her since the moment you met her. Nobody else will do for you. Falling in love is something that will happen to you in your lifetime. And when it does you'll know it.

Physical Attractions

A woman's soul alone won't spark your attraction. She should have a divine sense of humor and show inordinate caring. Here are the ways physical attraction can make love happen (and a few words on when a guy's being too picky.)

7. **She looks good.**

Packaging does figure into the chemistry equation. You have the right to demand that your mate looks presentable. Still, some women feel guilty about keeping up standards. If the idea of walking down the street with her makes you cringe it would be out of the question for you to get intimate with her. You learn to fall in love with the whole person, not her body parts or her looks.

8. Her voice is attractive.

Physical attraction isn't solely on a woman's appearance. In fact what turns you on -- or off --may seem trivial. For instance, a woman's voice can be a major lure. Just hearing her voice can be enough to spark your attention and attraction. Nothing is wrong with this criterion, still don't be too quick to judge the blind date who leaves a slightly nasal sounding message on your machine.

9. She smells good.

Smell has a potent effect. If she doesn't smell good you might not be able to get close enough to hug her. It might be petty, but if you can't stand the way she smells you won't be able to endure her for long. Some cultures don't believe in wearing deodorant because their custom denotes that natural body odor is more alluring.

Most people are born with a distinct smell that can be eradicated but which you shouldn't feel forced to love. Other considerations are bad skin, hands that are too sweaty, or rough. If you find yourself turned off, don't feel guilty just be sure you're not using them as excuses for *not* getting close to an otherwise delightful woman

10. The power of good sex.

If you're unhappy with what's happening between the sheets don't throw in the towel right away. Try to understand that the problems may have nothing to do with the lack of chemistry. If she's lousy in bed she'll probably be more than willing to learn. Just because sex is barely satisfactory at the start, a relationship is not necessarily doomed. It's normal for a relationship to be a little awkward at first in the area of lovemaking. You have to get to know what each other likes before you give up on her lovemaking and vice versa.

Whose Problem Is It Anyway

11. Her problems could be holding you back.

Okay suppose she makes an effort, but after a while she forgets, it's sort of like that for the rest of your sex life too. She's awkward continuously, gawky and no matter what you say to her she shows no signs of improvement. Her refusal to hear you or understand your misery can leave you frustrated and left without answers to your problems.

Sometimes a woman's discomfort with sex makes itself far more obvious than a boorish bedside manner. Plenty of women suffer one dysfunction or another. There's no shame in having these problems -- only in refusing to resolve them. You deserve someone who's willing to try her best to make sure you're satisfied so don't settle for less.

12. When you have the problem.

You could just as well be the cause of the problem. If you are madly in love with her yet you never feel a desire to make love to her chances are it might not be the amount of chemistry you have between one another. Fear of intimacy is a biggie and fear of being revealed is another. If you sense such problems could be plaguing your relationship as well as your love life, get help. The problems won't just disappear.

For couples starting out in a relationship, there's fear of the unknown. If you've never had any real intimacy it can be terrifying. We all behave in familiar and predictable ways. New territory always bring fear.

13. Have a heart.

Frequently the demise of an old relationship can keep you from seeing a potential match. Pay attention to the little things that you've come to overlook in others because of your former commitment to someone else. You'll have to tune in to those things that your senses have ignored for a while. Remember: The woman who's making herself available now may or may not wait for you to recover from a breakup. Don't allow your unhappiness after breaking up to drag you so low that you keep from attracting the love you deserve.

14. She doesn't meet your expectations.

Frequently inappropriate notions of what's proper "wife material" can also keep you from recognizing a potentially great love. The new idea of who would be right for you might need to be changed or at least revised.

The best time to examine a woman is when you are in a non-sexual relationship. How does she acts when she's tired or sick? Is she thoughtful? How concerned is she about you? Slowly, you may find yourself totally is in sync with someone you initially thought you could never love.

15. Chemistry.

Okay, so what about chemistry with the wrong woman? Chemistry can grow between you and someone you didn't first think was right for you. That's why a relationship can blossom and work out wonderful when two people expect less than more from one another. The spark that's ignited with inappropriate mate material has nothing to do with healthy attraction. There are those who mistake love for something other than what it is.

It's not the situation, it's how you react to the situation that counts

29

CREATING YOUR OWN PARADISE

Happiness is a do-it-yourself project.

Recently my daughter and I made an interesting observation. We were sitting in a rocking chair on our front porch, her hand on my belly, talking about advice she'd like to give the new brother or sister who was still several months away from birth. One of the things she plans to say to our new baby is that, of the first eight years of life (which is the particular segment of time that T'Juanna can discuss firsthand), the best age happens to be three.

When I asked T'Juanna why being three was better than being eight, she rolled her eyes and breathed an exasperated sigh as if I should know.

"When you're eight you have too many responsibilities," she said.

Too many responsibilities. Where does she get this stuff? No, wait, I know. Just yesterday my husband was complaining about having no free time. I was sitting in the room, absorbing every word. When he was through, she looked at him and nodded sympathetically. "I know what you mean," I don't have any free time either." When my husband looked at her, T'Juanna explained, "I'm doing something EVERY minute, Dad! There's school, homework, gymnastics, piano, roller skating, playing with my toys, watching cartoons, feeding our dog, playing house, playing computer games, coloring, reading books..."

Oh, the leisurely life of a child. You and I can smile, because we know what responsibility really is. It's mortgages and car pools and overdue bills and signing up for one too many committees. It's working long hours on the job and longer hours once you finally get home at night. It's falling into bed too tired to change your clothes. It's never having enough time to wash your hair and shave during the same shower.

Finding Time For Paradise

When my friend Don and Debra describes their hectic schedule they expresses sorrow for the lack of time available for some of life's most basic requests. They laugh together stating, "Sometimes I need to go to the bathroom so bad, but there's no time to spare. I'm running car pools, getting snacks, supervising homework, making dinner, keeping house, putting to bed, reading bedtime stories. When I finally get a minute and head down the hall, little voices follow me even then. I find myself shouting through the locked door, "I have to go to the potty! Can I have a single moment to myself just to go to the potty?" With all the hectic schedules, work, the children, balancing finances and other responsibilities how can we manage to find quality time to spend with one another. There is paradise in spending time with each other. Here are a few simple, inexpensive ways of creating your own paradise.

1.   Communicate quietly.

Take a stroll in a nearby park, museum, art gallery, beach, on a city bus, take a train ride together, or just sit on a park bench. Walk hand in hand and share your goals, thoughts, dreams, and feelings. You and your partner can let each other into your lives and begin building an inseparable bond as you hold each other and talk quietly together. You receive a small taste of paradise just by indulging in it.

2.   Have romantic candlelight dinners.

Prepare a romantic, candlelight dinner on your roof, terrace or in your backyard. Complete the scene with easy listening music and a blanket. Have small portions of your favorite dish handy. Feed each other. Gaze into each others eyes; smile occasionally as you gently touch each other's hands. Sip your wine. Lie side by side gazing up at the stars. The sky is your ceiling; the world's at your feet.

3. **Dance romantically.**

Dancing together can be part of your romantic candlelight dinner outdoors, or you can save it for another occasion, indoors. Again silence is golden. Keep the music slow and turned down low. Dance together with a gentle sway; while holding each other. Feel your partners warmth against your face. Imagine no noise, no time, no space -- just the two of you, beneath the stars, the moon, floating on a summer night's breeze, existing as one.

4. **Have an early morning picnic.**

Wake up early on a Saturday or Sunday Morning, pack your favorite blanket, a light brunch and go fly a kite at a nearby park. As you fly your kite, marvel at the heavens, the trees, the grass, the rising sun. When you tire, get relaxed on your blanket with your special someone by your side. As the sun warms your heart, you'll find paradise.

5. **Chase your lover.**

Play *'catch if you can'* in the privacy of your home. Play catch me in the park during a romantic early morning picnic, or frolicking in freshly fallen snow. Laugh hysterically like children; run and play; sneak up on each other; play and enjoy child like innocence of the lover's chase. The light hearted fun will bring joy and laughter into your lives.

6. **Take a lover's shower or soothing bath.**

You and your partner can relax together in a heavenly embrace while standing face to face in the shower or nesting in the tub. As you slowly lather up, caress and massage each other. Allow the warmth of the water and your partners embrace to soothe you. Close your eyes and imagine that the two of you are beneath a beautiful waterfall or nestled in a natural whirlpool. Smell the fragrance of exotic flowers, hear the love song of the beautiful birds; feel the gentle breeze; feel the warmth of your partner's embrace and know that you've found paradise.

30

FINDING HEALTHY INTIMACY

Develop relationships with people who are helping you develop.

Darryl was a shy man. Gloria was reserved and a loner. When Darryl was in high school he went through a phase where he was afraid to get close to women. Ironically, the more emotional distance he put between himself and women the more intimacy he longed for. When he did meet a woman (Gloria) he rushed her into intimacy. Both of them usually spent all their free time with one another. They didn't go out with friends and they didn't make time for their family members. They had sex very early on and they worshipped each other so much that they really began to believe that they had found "the one." Of course neither of them were in love. They liked the *idea* of being in love. They barely knew each other of course, but thought they were in love because of the intensity of the relationship. To say the least they loved it. When their relationship burned itself out they couldn't figure out why because they couldn't see the mistakes they were making.

Their relationship never had time to build. It was a fantasy of what a relationship should be. They chased that wild exciting infatuation stage of intimacy that they thought was love.

Intimacy, we all want it, but what does healthy intimacy look like, feel like, and act like? Somewhere between constant clinging and no - strings, free agency lies in the center of what we all seek, where both partners feel wanted and connected, yet not stifled or stuck.

Finding that middle ground -- together -- is like trying to stand still in the middle of a see-saw. One minute your life is full of balance and the next minute you're struggling with the force of nature -- hers and yours. Yours can create closeness without cling, autonomy without distance, but finding that place where intimacy intersects takes practice and patience.

Healthy emotional intimacy is the heart of a good, healthy, long term-relationship; it is the one element without which real love cannot survive. It develops over time and although the timing varies from couple to couple true love never really happens over night.

When we say "intimacy" most of us automatically think "sex." But there is more to it than that. True intimacy - healthy intimacy involves the expression of both positive and negative feelings, the revelation and consideration of our own partner's strengths and weaknesses. Healthy intimacy provides a shelter in which we can be vulnerable and open, feel safe, and truly be ourselves.

Within the confines of healthy intimacy an intimate relationship, (the real lifeline of love) honest, open communication flows. Here are five great intimacy builders that can help keep your love alive.

1. Talk about your relationship.

Check in regularly to see how your mate is feeling toward you. Is she harboring any resentment, hurt, disappointments. Hear her out, and share your own feelings. Let her know that doing this makes you feel closer.

2. Reminense about the good times you've shared.

Continually remind each other of the incidents that have made the two of you become closer. Discuss those things that made the two of you fall in love with one another?

3. Share events of your life, past and present with your mate.

Talk about those memories that affected you the most. Discuss the good times and the bad time with your mate. It opens the door for understanding. Ask your mate to do the same for you.

4. Check in with each during the day when possible.
Ask how your mates day is going and give information about yours.

5. Be spontaneous and get away from your daily routine when you can.
Stay up late, go for a midnight stroll, meet your mate for a dinner after work, or prepare a surprise meal.

One of the healthiest delights is revealing passionate attachment we feel for each other. But insecurity or immaturity, can lead us to define that intimacy too narrowly, as in true love means never having to spend an evening apart" (never mind disagreeing or saying you're sorry.) When partners demand closeness at the expense of their separate selves, dependence not intimacy is created.

Finding your way through intimacy is liking taking a shower together and looking for perfect water temperature. One person's ideal blend of hot and cold, connection and freedom doesn't always suit the other. But a little fine tuning will allow both of you to bask in the warmth of each other in healthy ways.

Making Intimacy Sweeter

Autonomy can seem odd when the urge to merge hits you. It's easy to forget that a healthy independence is intimacy best friend. What creates a truly rich togetherness is the experience and knowledge you bring -- separately to the equation. You know you've found nourishing independence when...

* You grant each other key escape clauses: any non-essential birthdays, non-boss impressing functions, occasions one of you deems meaningful.
* You can fall asleep after a fight even if it wasn't resolved, even if it was over the bathroom, the telephone, the last piece of toast etc.
* You share expenses but not all of your money.
* One of those couples who likes to touch yet you don't feel at all competitive.

WILL THE REAL MEN PLEASE STAND UP

* You've adjusted to the idea of her falling asleep before you do.
* You know that you don't have to share your deepest secrets or give up your travel-the-world fantasies to make the relationship better.
* You can't stand golf and she can't stand to talk on the telephone for extended periods of time, but that's okay because you don't need each other to change or explain why.

Independence That's Really Intimate Distance

We all need our space, that's just the way we are. We need our space to live, to think, to be who we are, but some couples disguise their lack of closeness by calling it autonomy. When the need for separateness takes precedence over human needs of either partner, the results is a relationship becomes lacking in it's basic nutrients. You know there are too many spaces in your togetherness when your relationship is based on the following equation:

* She doesn't put demands on you therefore you can't put demands on her.
* You've got a mental list of things you hide from her because you feel they are too petty, personal or embarrassing -- and the lists never gets any shorter.
* You stopped asking if her to go to parties because her answer is usually no.
* You find yourself lecturing your friends about the importance of freedom in their relationship.
* You mention her to a co-worker you've worked with for years and he said he assumed you were single.
* You've been dating her for six months and she still introduces you as her friend.

Intimate Love Signals That Tell You She's For Real

As a man there will come times when you'll surely want to know how to tell when a woman really cares for you or better yet, you'll want to know when she really and truly loves you. This is a questions that's easy to answer yet difficult to define. Trying to come up with good reasons can usually be followed by sober and useless discussions to

WILL THE REAL MEN PLEASE STAND UP

emotional risks and rewards. It is important to listen to your heart when it comes to questions about heart, life, love and the meaning of either.

Even if you think she loves you how can you be 100 percent sure? The answer of course is you can't ever really be 100 percent sure. When it comes to relationships and love there is are no guarantees, relationship + affection X care does not = love.

As I began to ponder and research this question from real men who have been in love and gave love because they thought they were in love they all gave me tattle tale clues or love signs that you can clue in on to help you decide is he's in it for the thrill or for the love. Here are ways she'll show you she's for real, She...

1. Tells you she wants to date you exclusively and no one else.
2. Stops dating other people and she plans all of his extra time with you.
3. Calls you every night.
4. Calls you at least three times a day just to say she was thinking of you.
5. Gets allergy shots instead of letting you get rid of your favorite pet.
6. Calls your mother to wish her a happy day for no reason at all.
7. Treats your mother just like she treats her own.
8. Makes you the beneficiary of all her belongings if something God forbid should ever happen to her.
9. Runs you a warm bubble bath the morning after sex.
10. Invites you to a romantic dinner she prepared with her own hands.
11. Watches your favorite football team instead of watching her favorite show.
12. Goes to the store to get your favorite foods without argument or hesitation.
13. Takes off work to nurse you back to health when you are sick.
14. Uses the words we, us, our, and love whenever she talks about the future.
15. Is genuinely glad to see you excel and succeed in your career.
16. Gives you your space when you really need it.
17. Give you your way when you really want it.
18. Keeps several photos of you on her desk.
19. Gets up right away to check when you say you hear funny noises.
20. Keeps her promises.

WILL THE REAL MEN PLEASE STAND UP

21. Doesn't tell you things and then gets caught telling a lie about it.
22. Gives you priority over her friends, work and relatives.
23. Stocks her refrigerator with your favorite foods and drinks.
24. Cuts your grass without you asking her to.
25. Hugs, kisses and snuggles you for all the right reasons.
26. Changes your oil and gasses your car without you asking.
27. Stares at you for long periods of time.
28. Looks at you as you walk away and she watches you walk away before she takes her eyes off of you.
29. Doesn't allow other beautiful women to grab her attention away from you.
30. Acts if no one else is in a crowded room when you are with her.
31. When you back into another car she still lets you drive her car.
32. When you look like you're sad she's overly attentive and protective of your feelings.
33. Recites your name with love, affection and poetry.
34. Ask you more than once a day if you doing okay.
35. Brags about you to her friends over and over again.
36. Helps you with your coats and pulls every time there's an opportunity to do so.
37. Never takes you for granted.
38. Gives you the keys to her place.
39. Gives you a set of keys to her heart.
40. When she says no to you it means no limitations.

Know the importance of living your moments.

Step 6:

Practicing

Hygiene & Ethics

31
HYGIENE AND PERSONAL ETHICS

Hygiene: It's your attraction device.

Every person's body smells slightly different, just like finger prints we all have a special odor print. It's just as distinctive as our voice, our hands and our intellect. As infants we recognize our mothers by their smell and as we grow up we are able to detect thousands of different odors. Men are susceptible to odor lures. Take the vagina for example...it has a sensuous lure that brings a man to heightened sexuality when he smells it. It's sort of like a homing device.

All this means is, that special someone can lead us by the nose with their body odor. When you meet someone who you're especially attracted to, you will find that you probably likes her body odor too, which helps predispose you in romance. Sweet smells are a continuously feed for your aphrodisiac. It's the best stimulant to a great love affair.

When a pleasing aroma comes your way it gets wilted up by thousands of odor receptors that are lumped together in a small patch of tissue in your nasal cavity, right behind the bridge of your nose. Another place is your limbic system, a primitive region developed early in our evolutionary past that controls emotions and sex drive. Among the five senses, smell is unique because it has a nonstop flight to your brain. Your limbic system is also the seat of long term memory, which is why you can remember odors years later, while sights and sounds disappear after a few weeks.

Smells and emotions overlap the brain so if you smell something you like it *can* make you feel better. Smells have been found to improve a person's moods too. In pursuit of this interest food odors can boost the immune systems. Nice smells actually can make you feel better. If colognes can make you feel better, calmer, and more confident and therefore sexier, it proves to be money well spent. If one person doesn't like the other person's smell they've got trouble. Adding smells to your natural body odor makes initial encounters more neutral. They don't mask the odor they simply meld with it.

Odors may also be useful in treating impotence. Smells like cinnamon have been proven to increase blood flow to the mans penis. Lavender and pumpkin pie has been found to increase their penile flow by 40%. Donuts and black licorice (32 %) and pumpkin pie (20%) Why these particular smells are so potent is anyone's guess.

Odors can help you lose weight. In one study overweight people were instructed to sniff inhaler containing banana, mint and green apple scents whenever they get hungry. Those who felt bad about being overweight, but did not feel bad about themselves overall were able to lose nearly five pounds a month.

Odors can make you spend money faster. One of the latest trends in retailing is the subliminal odor strategy - pumping just enough scent into air so that we don't notice it, but our moods improve and we open our wallets.

Loss of smell can be linked to other maladies. People who suffer from migraine also suffer disproportionately from an impaired sense of smell. And 35% of people who have smell problems are clinically depressed. Odors can affect people with anxiety disorders, the smell of green apple and cucumber eases pain of claustrophobia.

Odors That Turn Women Off

What turns women off? I'm glad you asked that question. There are several odor issues I feel that I should mention that women have stated are the primary turn-off's. There are personal habits and attitudes that are causing many good hearted men to miss out on being with the woman they desire. These same habits irritate women and keep her at arm's length or far beyond your arms. If your hygiene habits are keeping her at a distance, you'll have to change a few things.

WILL THE REAL MEN PLEASE STAND UP

If you are an intelligent man (and I hope you are), you will realize that all women are more than two breasts and a vagina. You'll understand that she's loaded with many sensitivities much like yours. You can minimize being refused by her if you eliminate those terrible things that are turning her off. Here are the most wide spread odor irritations that women of all nationalities have expressed to be the worst in a man.

1.   Bad body odor.

If you are one of those people who never use anything to freshen yourself you might want to reconsider it. Bad body odor is the most grotesque form of offensiveness. If you fail to use deodorant or you wear a pair of socks until they are stiffened by the odor you will never attract or land a lover. If you've been fooling yourself and think that your animal smell will turn a woman on you're wrong. Let's face the facts, sweaty, musty, offensive odors ruin relationships.

No woman in her right mind will allow a man to touch or kiss her if he stinks. Unless there's a particular medical problem, eliminating bad body odor is pretty simple.

2.   Use a little water.

All you have to do is use water on your body. When added with a good soap it will remove dirt, grime, oils, grit and odor. No need to cover your natural body odor with load of fragrances, working to smell fresh is all that's needed.

Upon getting out of your bath or shower, dry yourself and then wait for about five minutes. Apply deodorant generously under your arms for best results. Sweat glands are heavily concentrated in the underarm area, therefore you need to spread deodorant over the entire surface of the armpits. You should feel very safe and secure now.

3.   Change your clothing.

Don't wear the same clothes over and over without washing them. Bad body odors on clothes you have already worn linger on and on. When you have bathed again the odors on your clothing from previous wear will still linger. Odors cling to underwear, shirts, suits, coats and the only remedy for pulling those old odors out are regular cleaning and

WILL THE REAL MEN PLEASE STAND UP

laundering.

4. Bad breath.

If she kisses you once you feel she'll kiss you again. Not true. If you have offensive breath, chances are she probably won't want to see you again, let alone kiss you again. When a man has bad breath and kisses a woman with his bad breath he transfers that smell to her lips, gums, tongue and even face. Wherever you kiss her with bad breath rest assured your bad breath will linger onto her breath.

Certain foods and seasonings can knock a pig on his ass, so if you have seduction or intimacy in mind you'd better check your breath. Lay off the foods with garlic, onions and lots of seasonings unless she's eating them to. Bad breath can be attributed to...:

- * medications you are taking
- *vitamins
- *bad dental hygiene
- *morning breath
- *cigarettes, pipes or cigars
- *infected sinuses
- *foods you've eaten
- *hair products
- *rotten teeth
- *false teeth
- *alcohol or liquors

Leave nothing to chance when you are trying to get close to her. If she doesn't smoke or eat the foods you eat her olfactory senses will be much keener than yours. When you smoke or eat spicy foods you build up a resistance to smells and anyone who hasn't indulged in these scents will be able to pick them up quickly. Regular trips to your dentist or doctor can help prevent bad breath and also help keep it under control.

5. Hair stubble.

Most women have soft, tender skin that can't withstand hair stubble without screaming in pain. When you decide to affectionately rub your stubby beard across her soft skin she might scream ouch. It really does hurt her and it can leave red abrasions or her skin feeling inflamed.

WILL THE REAL MEN PLEASE STAND UP

Stubble against a woman's skin feels like coarse sandpaper running against the skin of your penis. The best way to avoid ruining a great moment is to remove all stubble before getting intimate with her.

6. Dirty hair.

It is also offensive to have dirty hair. Bad grooming consists of hair filled with dandruff, too oily, to thick laden with sprits or other hair products. Women like to sniff and run their fingers through hair. Extra ear hair that hold ear wax is very distasteful. Some of the same hair products used on your scalp can also be used on other body hair.

7. Rough spots.

Rough spots on your hands such as golf calluses or the like, can be an unwelcome invitation to her. Jagged and split nails can make her run in the other direction. The worst thing a man can do is fail to manicure his nails and try to caress her love button and end up cutting her. You'll never be able to make love to her again, and if she does take a chance she'll be so frigid with fear you won't be able to satisfy her.

Leave watches, rings, bracelets, sharp edged metals and eyeglass rims off during any intimate contact. And whatever you do don't take her to bed with these items on.

8. Foot odors.

Many a man has suffered from athlete feet fungus or some sort of sweaty feet problems, especially if he's a jock. This can be combated with over the counter foot medications, clean socks on a daily basis and proper care of shoes. Many times when athletes feet fungus breaks out it's due to wearing colored socks in sneakers. Try your best to wear white socks in sneakers. (Sweat + colored socks + sneakers = athletes feet).

Make a woman want to be with you by looking good and smelling fresh all the time

32
YOUR SEXUAL ETHICS

Develop a great code of ethics, then use them.

Sexual ethics are a very personal thing, yet a woman considers them the most important part of a man's character. Your ethics will set the tone for the entire life of the relationship, and you will be judged on that basis by both men and women.

Every man, consciously or not, has a code of sexual ethics. And no two men have the same codes. Many ethical matters relate to your whole approach as a lover. Here are a few sexual ethics worth discussing. They are not the "law" by any means - you have to answer to your own conscience - but they can serve as a model for your code of sexual ethics.

1.   Don't gossip or name drop.

Nothing is more worthless than a man who lets the gang know his conquests. This is the first sign of an immature man. Sexual intimacy with a woman is beautiful. She is giving you her most precious commodity - herself. But your knowledge of her intimate sexual habits should be strictly privileged information. You have no right to jeopardize her reputation by immature bragging in the company of others. Keep your mouth shut. A loudmouth is usually a liar on most accounts. A man who respects a woman and her privacy is more likely to succeed with her. Put more simply, "the doers don't talk, and the talkers usually don't do."

2.   Protect her and she'll love you for it.

Sex is equal between a man and a woman, and while she loves it as much as you do, there is one outstanding difference - a woman can become pregnant, men cannot, This is probably why men take the possible consequences of sexual affairs more lightly than most women. This type of attitude is short-sighted. You should be prepared to assume your fair share of support too.

3.   Leave married women alone.
She may be one of the best sexual partners you've ever been with, but when it all boils down it's not worth the trouble. There are plenty of loving young women who are available and desirable. They can do many things that a married woman cannot do. They can sleep over on weekends, they can go away with you for days at a time, you don't have to slip into hotel secretly and you don't have to play hide from the husband at far away restaurants.

A man should work very hard to never interject himself into a married woman's life, because he has little or no control over his own presence in her life, and there is no future in it. Men who break up marriages intentionally or unintentionally by seducing a married woman is doomed to a failed relationship. If you are determined to be with a married woman then all I can say is be prepared to take the good along with the bad.

4.   Don't flirt with other women or try to come on to her girlfriends.
This damages the respect level you might hold with your partner and it makes you look like an uncaring fool. It casts you as fickle, an ass hole, insensitive and brain dead. If the woman you're coming onto has any sense at all she'll ignore you and move on to more caring men.

Don't try to have a romantic relationship with your wife's or your girlfriends friends. It's a true violation of her space and friendship and it makes you look unfaithful. Your personal devotion to your partner ought to be enough to discourage you from pursuing a woman who is devoted to someone else.

5.   Don't say "I love you unless you mean it.
These days you don't have to lie to a woman in order to get her in bed. Most of the time she wants it just as much as you do. If she appears to be hesitant you need to resist the lies in order to convince her that it's the best thing for her to do. Everyone wants to be

loved and women especially like the sound of being told "I love you." It's not fair of you to lie about loving her. Don't load her down with false promises just to get her into bed. If you have to result to these tactics you still have a lot to learn about being a real man.

6.   Don't make her feel guilty.
Nothing is worst than trying to make a woman feel guilty about not having sex with you. It goes something like this ... "What do you mean you won't have sex with me." After all the things I've done for you!" I bought you drinks, took you to dinner, paid for the play and then drove you home. I gave you a great time and you can't do the same for me? When I spend my time and money on a woman I expect to be appreciated."

With lines like these you are sure to loose. Dating is a social convention in all respects. If you play by the rules you'll get more praise and rewards than not. All a woman owes any man for a good time is a polite "thank you."

7.   Don't be a grabber.
Some men feel that it's important to advertise that they have intimate relations with a woman. They claw and paw the woman in public. They grab her breast, her butt, her crotch and try to prove they have a possession. They are only proving they are crude, insecure, immature, and stupid. This display of possessiveness makes them look worst than what they probably feel. No woman likes to be grabbed sexual ways in public.

You can touch her all you want while making love, but it's not necessary to display or demonstrate it in public.

8.   The Crusher.
Not only does this person crush her clothing he crushes her in doing so. This type of man is inconsiderate and not conscious of the fact that she went through a lot of trouble just to look good for you. The crusher is the type of guy that gives bear hugs that mess up her hair, ruins her make-up, turns her neat look into a crumpled and untidy look. She wants to be admired by you, not mauled!

9. The Double Standard Guy.

This guy lives by all the double standards he can find. He pressures a girl into bed just to satisfy himself, and then he calls her a tramp for being there. He won't respect her if she gives in and respects her less because she doesn't. He wants to prove he has a super dick and he goes around trying to label every women he meets as a whore. Even though he's trying to lay every woman he can find he also thinks sex is dirty. He feels any woman who has sex with him is a dirty slut. He wants a virgin for a wife, but all he ends up getting is a frigid woman. A guy with double standards will sleep around on his wife, but tell why she shouldn't sleep around on him. He talks out of both sides of his mouth, but mostly out of his a--. He's a hypocrite.

10. The Tantrum Thrower.

He punishes women when he can't have his way. He pulls temper tantrums, sulks, and insults the female. Believe it or not there are women out there who falls for this rat. Even though the woman he gets might submit to his unpleasant ways, she regrets the fact that she ever did and in the end she finds a way to get even with him.

The tantrum thrower never has anything good to say about women and he makes sure the whole world knows she's no good. He wants to tear her down before anyone else gets a chance to build her up. He makes other men think she hates men and in the long run it's really him who hates women as well as himself.

11. The Bad Timer.

Many men get turned down because of their timing. They don't put enough thought in when or where they just go for it. If he would only tune into what she's doing before he leaps on her. Be more considerate of her and her duties as a mother, a wife and a woman. Remember if you want things to go more your way timing is of the essence.

12. Sloppy Table Manners.

This is the guy who sits in public and wolfs down his food like a wild animal. He washes his hands from his dinner glass cleans his knife with his napkin, slurps his soup, and spears a dinner roll with a fork. Please learn table manners before you take a woman out to dinner.

13. Men who spit when they talk.
If you are one of these who does that you are pitiful. Enough said.

14. Men who allow spit to form in the corners of their mouth.
This is called the "mad dog" syndrome. There are men who talk continuously and with it comes foam in the corners of their mouth. To make things worst they act as if they can't feel it. It's disgusting and to say the least a turn-off.

15. Careless Smokers.
Men who have a habit of smoking, dropping their ashes, burning holes in a women's clothing, grinding the butts out on table tops and he's so inconsiderate he gives her a kiss with a mouth full of smoke. He even kisses her with an embrace while the cigarette is next to her skin. Many a woman has been burned because of a man who smoke and was inconsiderate of her as he did so.

16. Men who don't identify who they are.
When you answer the phone instead of him asking for you he says "Guess Who." This is childish and elementary. Don't play on the phone. It's not attractive.

A woman considers ethics the most important part of a man's character.

33

TAKING CARE OF YOURSELF

Work to improve yourself so that you will be attractive to others.

The most important way to change your life is by changing the way you think and react. For total wellness, there is another half of the health equation: changing the way you take care for your body. Remember, your mind and body are inextricably linked. This chapter will show you how to meet and conquer those daily demands that would otherwise sap your energy and stamina, so you can have some time left for yourself!

Body Images

There's a character in War and Peace who never realizes how beautiful she is. Her most dazzling attribute is her glance, her wonderful spiritual eyes, but when she studies herself in the mirror her eyes go dead. People don't discuss beauty in men as fluently as they do women. To say he becomes rigid and disapproving-and he remains ignorant of what everyone else knows, that he is the man with the beautiful eyes is just not politically correct.

Many men fail to perceive their looks clearly. Men carry around in their heads a sketch, if not a finished painting, of how they appear, and too often the sketch is unflattering. Sometimes the sketch may be redrawn along more attractive lines, but the next time we're ignored or rejected, the sketch turns into a caricature.

Not every man goes through these agonizing fluctuations in ego about his body, but there's bound to be some correlation between the way men react to your body and the way women regard it. It's not bad to be affected by what others say, but it's terrible to be ruled by it. It's worth remembering that what you consider your worst feature may strike others as your best.

Men with poor body images convey a sense of insecurity to the people they meet.

A few men use their poor body image almost deliberately to keep other women at a distance. The scenario goes like this: "I'm ugly; she couldn't possibly like me; no one could like me; therefore I needn't risk getting close to anyone. I'm not going to deal with the rejection. This is an awful way to live.

Poor Body Image Can Be Improved

One way to see the light is, simply ask a friend or friendly acquaintance what she likes about your body. Have your friend sit in a chair and look at you while you stand and study yourself in the mirror. Tell her all the things you like about yourself-your smile, your big eyes, your powerful neck, your skin color, even the chipped tooth that you secretly pride yourself on. This will embarrass you at first, but it is curative. You can look at yourself in the nude or clothed. If you don't want to do all this in front of someone else, find your longest mirror and do it alone, but make sure that you say the complimentary things about yourself out loud. This works best when you approach it with an attitude to learn.

If you wish to do something to improve your body, do it. Swim, take up a new sport, cut back on sugars and fat intake, join a gym or whatever it takes for you to do. When you begin to show your physical gains, show them off with more revealing clothing or by going to a pool or beach; give people a chance to tell you about yourself. Set your own standards for your looks rather than submitting to the standards (either real or imagined) of others. You must begin by yourself. After that, the good feelings you radiate will be magnetic to women.

Healthy Eating

Whether you're working long hours, raising a family, or training for an athletic competition, if you're going to be a healthy person you have to eat like one. Poor nutrition practices have been related to every major health problems. Good nutritional practices can play a vital role in enhancing your health happiness and quality of life. To help you reap the benefits of a healthy diet you must first learn and understand the importance of good eating.

We are constantly reminded on a daily basis our government's nutritional guidelines: eat a variety of foods, watch our fat intake, get regular physical activity and maintain a healthy weight. They tell us to choose a diet low in fat, with plenty of vegetables and fruit, and to consume sugar, salt and alcoholic beverages in moderation. Sounds easy, but when you're rushing off to work, eating whatever won't crumble or drip in the car, or visiting the vending machines, it gets a lot more complicated. Once you've learned the ground rules they will become second nature and eating healthy can become an integral and painless part of your lifestyle.

Water: The Secret Ingredient To Living Healthier

While you may not consider water a nutrient, it's actually the most critical one in your diet. Drinking water is one of the easiest things to do, and it serves a greater purpose than just quenching our thirst. Your blood is 85% water and water makes up 75% of your brain and 70% of your muscles. Water is the essential element that helps your body function properly. It helps cool, it helps digest food, it lubricates your joints, it cushions your insides and it washes out waste from your body.

No matter what your activity, even if you're a couch potato you're still loosing enough water to fill approximately eight glasses of water a day. Water sneaks from your system without you noticing it too. You lose water just by breathing all the time. That's why the eight glasses of water rule hold so much weight in our lives. By drinking eight ounce glasses of water you help your body stay in tip top condition. Most people drink less than half that per day.

Many people walk around in a state of chronic dehydration, never realizing it, and when they began to feel fatigued from that lack, they blame it on low blood, exhaustion or being run down. Many times it's due to their lack of drinking enough water. They often drink coffee to boost their energy not realizing that coffee really further dehydrates them.

You may need more than eight glasses of water daily depending on how much you weigh, what you're doing and what environment you are in. If you live in a warm or dry climate you probably will need more than eight glasses of water a day. If you live in a high altitude or you breathe dry air from a heater, dehumidifier, or an air conditioner your fluid loss increases drastically. Plane travel also induces a large amount of water loss. Sunburn can also increase your water loss.

A good way to check if you're loosing too much water is to do a quick check when you visit the rest room. Lots of pale yellow urine is good; small amounts of dark urine means the digestion of more water is necessary. If you're drinking large amounts of alcohol it's important to carry a bottle of water with you.

Water and Exercise

When you exercise you loose a lot of water from your body which must be replaced. An hour of working out can cause you to lose at least one to two quarts of water per day depending on your body style. Don't wait until you're thirsty to drink water, hydrate yourself for no reason at all. Drink when you're not thirsty. When working out keep water available and you won't tire so fast. Here are a few tips to keep your body hydrated while working out.

1. Drink at least two glasses of water before you work out to set your water level in place. It prepares you for the sweat you'll lose.
2. Drink water after exercise. Drink three glasses of water after you've quenched your thirst.
3. Drink cool fluids. This keeps you cool. Despite the myths, cool fluids will not cause cramping.

Cutting Down On Fats

One of the best ways to decrease the fat in your diet is to use the shrink-and surround strategy; take a smaller portion of your favorite high-fat food -- say steak -- and surround it with bigger portions of low-fat foods such as steamed vegetables.

Try using less of the fatty food you really love and substitute the low fat foods for others. Use less margarine and butter on your foods and less mayonnaise in your tuna and salads, or put mustard on your sandwich instead. Have a sorbet or nonfat frozen yogurt instead of ice-cream.

Another trick that many people use is to eat more fiber filled foods. Fiber not only leaves less room for fatty-foods but helps push fat through your system faster, so you naturally absorb less of it. Bran muffins, for example, are a source of high fiber, but they are not always low in calories. As a source of fiber you might prefer extra fresh fruits and vegetables, which are naturally low in calories and fat, or you could try a low-fat bran cereal. The simplest ways to cut back on fats is to eat more fruits and vegetables.

Carbohydrates versus Proteins

Because people are feeling so let down by the fat-free approach to weight maintenance and loss, we're seeing a new interest in protein-heavy diets. Many experts advise caution. One of the things that's particularly unhealthy about them is that they're very low in carbohydrates. That's not healthy for your body or your brain. Another problem is that high protein diet leads to diet and binge cycles, since any diet that excludes basic food groups isn't healthy in the long run.

There's not much bad to say about carbohydrates," says Dr. James Rippe especially the complex carbohydrates we get from fruit and vegetables, beans, and whole grain pasta, breads, cereals, and rice.

Dairy gets sort of a bad reputation, but it's actually a great source of protein. Nonfat milk and yogurt are great. And a piece of cheese from time to time is not going to kill you. And dairy products are great for supplying our bodies with large doses of calcium.

Salt and Sugar: Those Terrible 'S' Words

The message is two-fold. We all carry some type of salty food with us to snack on from time to time, and then we work our butts off to cut down on our salt intake. Experts say the average person who has a normal blood pressure does not need to worry very much about salt in their diets. There's a debate about whether people who have high blood pressure need to worry about salt.

New research has confirmed that the more salt you eat the more calcium you lose from your body and the more likely you are to break bones when you're older. If you eat less sodium (table salt is 40% sodium) you'll keep more bone density, but you should make sure to include lots of calcium rich foods in your diet and even take calcium supplements if your doctor recommends them. If your body is sensitive to sodium you are probably retaining fluids, making you look and feel bloated.

Okay what about the other "S" word sugar? By itself sugar is worst. But sugar contributes in a major way to tooth decay, which is also something that we tend not to think about. Sugar nutritionally equals zero. It fills you up and out, and is loaded with lots of calories. The best way to help yourself is to recognize whether its the sensation or the taste you're craving. Do you really want something sweet, salty or crunchy? Then look for a calorie-reasonable alternative to fulfill that taste you're seeking. If you're in the mood for something crunchy, for example, there are plenty of healthy and nutritious cereals that you can snack on, or try pretzels which are usually fat free. You can help yourself more if you make it a habit to become a label reader.

Recognizing the actual effects that a certain foods have on your body will help to better understand , avoid, and combat their consequences. Paying attention to the negative effects foods have on you, you might be surprised at how even the slightest adjustments to your diet can make a frantic difference in how you feel.

Exercise Benefits

Exercise isn't about suffering; exercise is about finding something you enjoy doing that also happens to protect your health, lift your spirits and gives your energy level a boost. if you're in your twenties and finishing school, starting a career and perhaps looking for a mate, exercise is something you do for cosmetic reasons, to look your best. By the time you're thirty years old you began to realize that exercise has emotional as well as physical benefits. The best benefits come from women who reassess why they're exercising.

When you enter those fabulous forties all those diseases that men in their forties get become more real to you because some of your forty year old friends have suffered through one of these diseases or they've died from it. It hits home real fast when someone you know suffers from osteoporosis or heart disease. Life begins to get a little more serious for you. Heart disease is six times more likely to kill a man after 40. After heart disease all the other deadly diseases are only a step away from occurring in your life. However the good news is exercising helps prevent heart disease.

Exercise Creates Good Mental Attitude

While improving your health is the primary reason for exercise, it also helps you feel better about yourself. And I don't just mean feeling good about the way you look. Getting off your emotional treadmill and onto your physical one you can stop being critical of yourself. Exercise reduces stress, increases energy, and gives you feelings of accomplishment.

Accomplishing your physical goals have always been known to help your self-image. That's the best form of motivation. Ultimately you have to feel good about yourself based on who you are inside, not because of your weight.

Walking Your Way To Fitness

Walking is no longer the craze of seniors, sightseers, or walk specialist. It has become an activity for anyone who wants to get in shape. Whatever walking pace you choose, here are some simple steps to take to get you started.

1. Keep your back straight, head up, stomach in and chin parallel to the ground. Look straight ahead, not at the ground when walking.
2. Don't over walk, take natural and comfortable steps.

3. Swing your arms freely from the shoulders and slightly across your body. Move each arm with the opposite leg. A full arm swing will use upper-body muscles, increase the heart rate and help you walk faster.
4. To pick up the pace even more bend your arms at a 90 degree angle.
5. Wear a shoe that has good arch and heel support, moderate cushioning and plenty of flexibility in the forefoot.
6. Lunch hour mall walking.
7. Early morning treadmill walking or jogging.
8. Push ups in your office at various times throughout the day.
9. Sit-ups in your office at various times throughout the day.
10. Sit down or lie down on the floor while watching television and do your favorite exercises.

Exercising doesn't require a gym, but it does require clothing that is comfortable.

Exercise Goals

Before you decide what your goals are you must first make sure they are realistic. And before you can meet them you must have some sort of goal-map. If you know that you haven't been working out on a regular basis, start with simple goals that you'll achieve, so that you won't get frustrated and give up. If you've been working out, but need a goal, find a reason to train by seeking your interests. Have a purpose and then stick with it. The results will follow.

Be sure to see your doctor before you begin a workout program to make sure you are healthy enough for what you want to do. If you haven't been physically active for a while it's best to find out what and how much you can do.

An important part of setting your goals are realizing a realistic exercise program is not a fad program that you go off and on in a few weeks. Your work outs are now your lifestyle, it's a new way of life. You are deciding to take care of yourself because you need to and you deserve to.

WILL THE REAL MEN PLEASE STAND UP

Once you decide what you want to include in your program you have to also add variety to it so you won't get bored. Try something different to add to your workout or exercise plan. Some of the best places to enjoy the results of your workout is in all facets of your life.

Get Some Sleep

Are we a nation of drowsy people? Research shows that Americans get less sleep and frequently exhausted. Can a sleep deprived man be efficient? We spend one third of our lives sleeping, but we know little about why we sleep. We do know it's important in repairing worn-out tissues, renewing brain structures, and relapsing growth hormones. It's true: your kids really do grow overnight!

When you don't get some sleep one of the things that start to happen is your ability to process information begins to stop. Your brain acts as if its losing IQ points. In fact when you lose an hour of sleep it's equivalent to losing one IQ point. If you lose an hour below seven hours you lose two points. Add these points up. So if you are loosing two hours of sleep five days in a row you've lost ten hours worth of sleep and fifteen points of IQ.

The amount of sleep you need or get is going to change with age. Have you ever wondered how your children can sleep for lengthy periods of time? At mid-life you'll recognize that most people sleep approximately seven and one half hours per night. As you get older it's normal to sleep less than seven hours, take more naps and wake up more often throughout the night.

Some people feel great with only four and one half hours of sleep and others need at least eight hours to feel satisfied. The problem is many people don't know what amount of sleep they need to feel refreshed, alert and efficient. If you don't have the slightest idea of what your sleep time should be here are a few sleep suggestions:
1. Try not to exercise right before bed.
2. Give your muscles a rest from the middle of the day to later that night.
3. Try to exercise early in the morning.

WILL THE REAL MEN PLEASE STAND UP

4. Omit caffeine from dinner. If you have caffeine too late; like chocolate, tea, coffee or cola's you'll toss and turn most of the night or you might not fall asleep at all.
5. Try not to eat heavy meals late at night. A spicy or gas producing meal contributes to restless nights. Alcohol also causes you to have interrupted sleep.
6. Foods containing an amino acid called tryptophan (found in protein) can aid in sleeping. A glass of milk and a couple of aspirin has been know to help you sleep.
7. Actually trytophan helps to induce sleep and calming effects on your body. Small amounts of starchy carbohydrates, low in protein and fat consumed an hour or two before bedtime is great for inducing sleep. Here are a few favorites:

Pretzels	Baked corn tortilla chips	Breadsticks	Plain biscuit
Animal crackers	Toast	Baked bagel crisps	
Popcorn	A cup of hot oatmeal	Lowfat waffle	
An English muffin			

8. Give yourself at least an hour to relax before you sleep. Whatever your favorite relaxation techniques is use it one hour before it's time for you to go to bed. It works.
9. Create an environment that's easy to fall asleep in. Keeping your bedroom a little cooler than the rest of the home is best for falling asleep. Make sure it's dark and quiet. Too much light or noise can affect your quality of sleep even if they don't wake you up or keep you from falling asleep. A sleeping mask and ear plug will help you if you can't find dark and quiet.
10. Consider buying a better mattress. If your mattress is too taunt saggy, thin, or old it may be the cause of your sleepless nights. When shopping for a new mattress lie down for at least five minutes to test it before you buy it. You deserve a decent nights sleep and finding a mattress that you can cuddle up into is the key to a good nights sleep.
11. Forget sleeping in. You'll feel much better if you go to bed early than try to sleep a little later in the day. By sleeping an hour later you actually reset your body clock and end up dragging on the day you need to be up on time. Early afternoon naps help you catch up if you don't sleep more than an hour.
12. If you travel and suffer from jet lag, talk to your doctor about ways to prevent it.

13. If you can't sleep after twenty minutes, get up. Read a dull book, or do relaxation exercises. Try going back to bed when you're sleepy. if you're not sleepy at all don't get into bed because you'll only toss and turn.

If you really want to appreciate your body treat it well and it will serve you well for years to come. Getting started with a healthy routine of diet, sleep and exercise can sometime be intimidating, but it's your body, your health and your life. One day you'll thank yourself for taking good care of your body.

Set Your Priorities

There will never be enough time for everything you need to do or want to do in your life. And some things -- that extra dinner date, that party, serving on that new committee, -- will have to go. Concentrate on your priorities for the optimum health, minimum stress and maximum efficiency. Your priorities are:

1.   Health.

Keep up with health news and see your doctor regularly. See that your family eats and lives right. Your health must come first because it determines everything else in your life.

2.   Sleep.

Lack of sleep on a prolonged basis can weaken your immune system, and even prevent your body from warding off colds and flu. If you can't get enough sleep at one time learn to take short naps, catching 15 - 20 minutes here and there or at least an hour from time to time. You can sneak in naps while waiting n your plane or any other time you have the freedom to squeeze it in.

3.   Exercise.

For every half hour you exercise, you'll gain about two extra hours of energy. It organizes the mind, orders the thought processes and makes you stronger. Exercise keeps your weight in tact, your skin glowing and it keeps you looking good.

4. **Work.**

Every successful person I know does what is needed of them to keep work on schedule; otherwise tension sets in. If you love your work be grateful for it. If not do it diligently while looking for something better. be sure to recognize that work isn't everything.

5. **Fun.**

A giggle with a friend dissolves worries like nothing else. If fun is what's missing in your life, then life is what you're missing. Try your best to laugh at least eight times a day. It's good for the heart and the soul.

Exercise has a positive influence on all other parts of your life.

Step 7:

Discovering The Arts

34

THE ART of TOUCHING

To have power you must be clear on what you want.

Men like to be held, kissed or touched, just as much as women do. It can be out of compassion, sensuality, or to console. In laymen's terms touch means to cause or allow a bodily part, especially the hand or fingers, to come into contact with, to feel or bring something into contact to eat or drink, to reach, to have an effect on. Touching in a person in an intimate way can excite or relax the body. Many people feel touch also relieves stress to both the body and the soul. Then, there are also other's who crave to be touched for emotional comfort.

Your partner may be deprived of being touched and think she wants to have sex; when what they really wants is to be touched. The pleasurable experience comes when touching not only expresses caring but also sparks genuine sexual desire. So before going all the way, stop touch, and caress your partners body.

Touching actually has health benefits. Getting a massage slows down the heart rate and relieves muscle tension. That's why so many people go to spas to rid their bodies of stress. Touch is also sensual. It has become synonymous with eroticism and the quality of pleasure that people experience. Couples can become proficient in stimulating each other's bodies with their hands, and fingers, in ways specifically geared to increase their partners passion.

Touch is a major force in communication. It's a reassuring hand on the shoulder or a hug when you feel a need to express your feelings. Different types of physical touching while making love can similarly produce differing emotional and physical reactions. The types of touch -- rough, gentle, tickling, scratching, teasing -- and the areas that respond positively to being touched in particular ways reflects each individual. Don't make a big thing of it; don't even call it a massage if the idea seems too corny. Try slow, deep relaxing, you-feel-terrific touching. Some couples recommend scented oil or baby powder to amplify the sensations.

The Power of Touch

A man reaching out to touch or hold hands is a turn-on for women. While they generally hold hands in the courting stage, they stop after a while. This is a big loss. A woman loves to feel that a man wants to connect with her in his way. She doesn't feel loved if the only time he wants to touch her is when he wants sex.

If a man wants his partner to feel receptive to sex, he needs to touch her in an affectionate way many times each day when he is not wanting sex. He can hold hands put his arm around her, stroke her shoulders and arms, all without implying that he is wanting sex. If the only time he touches her is when he wants sex, she begins to feel used or taken for granted.

When he is holding her hand, he should remember to be attentive. Many times a man will forget he is holding her hand and she is left holding a limp, lifeless hand. When he needs to shift his attention, he should just release her hand. She doesn't want to hold hands all the time. It is just a way to connect for a few minutes.

By being more affectionate and touching most of the time, it will make a tremendous difference. One simple shift can make a big difference. Women need to be touched at least twenty times a day in non-sexual ways. Start out with at least ten times a day just to see how it works. Learn to be much more affectionate when you are around her. Not only is touching her a fantastic way to connect and feel close at any time, but it also softens the rough edges at times and brings us back to feeling love for each other.

Touching Through Massage

Massages increase the blood circulation to the soft tissues helping them to heal with oxygen and nutrients. Massage has been shown to boost immune functions by increasing the number of natural killer cells to the body. Massage should be as important to you as exercise and a good diet. Here are some basic massage methods that will help you and your partner discover the art of touching:

1. **Swedish Massage** - is the most common practiced method in the US today. It uses long strokes, kneading and friction techniques on the superficial layers of the muscles over the entire body. It also happens to be the best for increasing overall relaxation, ridding the body of toxins and improving the circulation.

With your partner, start at the shoulder, then work over the neck to the center of the back, then back to the shoulders and down the arms and hands. From the back go to the buttocks, down to the legs and feet. To do massages it's better to use oils and lotions with water base or in different flavors. Always remember that both partners have to be in tune with each other during the massage process, regardless of whether it's serious or playful.

2. **Deep Tissue Massage** - uses slow strokes and deep pressure to work on tight areas to release specific muscle tension and restore flexibility. Trigger-point therapy or neuromuscular therapy helps ease chronic pain. A therapist applies concentrated finger pressure to trigger points to specific areas of intense muscle tension and breaks the cycle of pain caused by spasms.

3. **Sports Massage** - focuses on specific muscle groups to eliminate factors that interfere with performance, such as muscle spasms, tendinitis and muscle fatigue. Sports massage can be used before or after participating in an event, or as an adjunct to training or to help recovery from soft-tissue injury.

4. **Shiatsu (Japanese) Massage** - works under the same principle as acupuncture. This system teaches that energy (qi) flows through the body along set pathways. When pathways become blocked, pain or illness result. Practitioners apply firm finger pressure points to blockage to restore a balance in the energy flow. Don't forget when doing a massage what makes it more pleasurable are oils lotions, and aromatherapy.

Touching is just a way to connect for a few minutes.

35
THE ART of KISSING

Become 100 % committed to the kiss.

The old song that was created to make us believe a kiss is just a kiss can be quite understated. Manners and morals may change and this world can turn upside down, but the romance of two people kissing remains a constant.

Kissing is a fine art. But because we do it so often and for such divergent reasons, sometimes we forget just how erotic a deeply felt kiss can be. If you approach each kiss with a sense of wonder (you are actually putting your incredibly soft, sensitive lips on her soft, pliant and very personal mouth, and you may even touch tongues), you'll be well on your way to creating a very sensual experience. Concentrate on the sensation of lip against lip, tongue on tongue, wet against dry, and you'll startle her into a passionate kiss. She too will remember the excitement and electric discovery of a first kiss, the voluptuous magnetism of a pair of ripe, pouty lips. Be inventive. Use your lips, your tongue, your teeth. Press hard. Brush softly. Suck, lick, and bite. Linger lovingly, press passionately. And respond sensitively to her lip maneuvers. This is not a solo tune but a lovely, harmonious duet.

People really do like to kiss and will seize the intimate moment of a good kiss for as long as their breath will allow. Kisses can be used to greet as well as to say good-bye. We accept innocent kisses of affection, but crave those of intense lust. Kisses can be dry, wet, fulfilling needed, desired, good, bad, sensuous, erotic and sincere social gestures as well as deeply felt expressions of love and passion.

Kissing is more than a means of conveying emotion - it is a crucial part of the transition to adult sexuality. Maybe that's why people often remember their first kiss. It's cliché that women remember their first, while men can't remember their last. The heat of the summer sun, the cold of a winter morning, and the moisture on our lips creates such excitement that we can't help but want to kiss. It's a real connection between the two of you. Kissing comes way before passion, intimacy and sex in a relationship. It's the meter by which couples judge passion. A good kiss will literally take a persons breath away. Some men claim to remember the smell of the room when they first kissed." The erotic potential of kissing is often underrated by those in a hurry to get to the main event. Some women feel this is a mistake. If the kiss is right, and the attraction is there it arouses couples to pleasures of great heights. The eroticism comes not only from the intoxicating sensation of bringing soft lips and tongues together, but also from the anticipation of further pleasures that run through your mind at the moment your lips meet.

German biographer Emil Ludwig wrote: The decision to kiss for the first time is the most crucial in any love story. It changes the relationship of two people much more strongly than even the final surrender, because a kiss already has within it the surrender.

Kissing is, in many ways, the ultimate act of intimacy, bringing lips, bodies and minds together. Unfortunately, some people kiss less often as they settle into their relationship. "That's the shame, I think, because kissing can be as sensuous and as sexy as making love. Women usually get lost in their kisses. They report loosing track of everything else. Women like the warm, moist intimate feeling a good kiss leaves them with. They like everything about a kiss before they sleep with a man. Sex to most women does not feel comfortable or complete without a tantalizing kiss.

Enthusiasm of the kiss to a good key. You can have your kissing technique down, but if you aren't happy, eager and willing to kiss or be kissed what's the point? Many times a person can love to kiss, but not love to kiss the person who wants to kiss them. If you aren't attracted the person you're kissing it can leave you feeling uneasy and cheated.

There are different types of kissing though. The kiss after a date with someone you love dearly. The little peck of a kiss to someone you like, but have no romantic interest in. The long lingering romantic kiss that sets your soul on fire. There are so many kinds of kisses you've probably tried and tested, but if you don't like the person no matter what your technique is the kiss won't help it.

Others place great importance on style. Some men have suggested an approach that is gentle at first, flowing naturally into the more harder and intense kiss with slight wetness. Kisses that are too wet and sloppy are a turn off for many women. No one likes getting sticky and wet from slobber. Most kissers prefer the sensual, lingering exploration of every inch of your mouth as long as it's not too juicy.

Should you make sounds while you kiss? Slurpy, smacking noises are definitely a turn off, but the occasional sigh, light moan, or murmuring of your lover's name can be very sensuous and appealing to the human ear. Silence while kissing is often interpreted as lack of enthusiasm. Expressing your pleasures openly is great for both partners. At times kissing and open eyes are expressive and erotic and words might create a sense of interruption.

Experienced kissers often have favorite things they do while kissing. Sitting close to your lover, or sitting on his lap is especially favored by women. While standing a kiss can be very sexy, especially if you allow your body to gyrate and move sensuously against her pelvis. Men like the feeling of their body being pressed against a woman's body. As the kissing gets more and more intense men have said that their knees get weak. Reclining while kissing makes for long pleasurable kissing when the circumstances are all right.

Touch is a major component in kissing, extending the experience from the mouth to the entire body. Men and women alike enjoy having their face held while being kissed. The feeling received by the hands on the cheeks or running through the scalp is very soothing and pleasurable. Another turn on while being kissed is having the fingers sucked into your lovers mouth. Its also pleasurable to be caressed firmly and kissed in that spot where the neck and the shoulders meet.

Couples who have been in their relationship for quite some time have a tendency to forget the delicious twang of a good kiss. It can be the beginning of new life into a lifeless relationship. Women states that men use kissing as the only means of touching them before they have sex. It becomes more of a demand than an expression of love. A simple kiss soon becomes "I want sex now." Thus the downhill slide begins. Both partners then began limiting the casual kiss or any other physical affection for fear that it's an interpretation as an invitation to sex. When your relationship begins to loose it's sensuous battle it also begins to loose it's appeal, zeal and wet your whistle effects. It's like a meal with no meat or vegetables or Kool-aid without sugar and that's not good.

Here's a simple exercise you can try to help you experience the true joy of kissing along with other sensuous undemanding touches. To pull this one off you have to forego intercourse. Instead restrict yourself to kissing, hugging, petting and cuddling. You can even have manual or oral stimulation, but remember no sex is allowed. If you can do it, this exercise will feel sort of like a time machine. It will make you discover and rediscover great ways to turn each other on without sexual intercourse. You will find yourself being fulfilled in other pleasurable ways. Believe it or not you'll discover new ways to use your mouth as a sensuous tool that will create lasting impressions of care.

If you are really serious about becoming one of the greatest kissers of all time you have to first understand how the tongue and the lips are characterized in all forms of gratification. They are so closely connected and compared to the vulva and the phallus that they can be used to bring about terrific orgasms. A really erotic French kiss to the clitoris can be about as close to intercourse as you can get without actually doing it.

The range of possibilities with your tongue are amazing - the gentle lip-brush, the probing kiss, the more like a question than a touch kiss, the deep, wet, yearning kiss, the deeply soulful kiss; and the rough almost overbearing kiss that doesn't leave a bruise can still be enjoyed by your partner. The *Kama Sutra* manual is great for learning new ways to embellish a kiss. It describes everything from the "kiss that kindles love" (when a woman kisses a man while he's sleeping) to the "kiss that turns away" (when she kisses him when he's upset or when he's working). You can always make up your own style of kissing - just remember to be creative, imaginative and sensual.

If you have broken skin, cuts or any form of blisters on your mouth, inside or out, avoid kissing because it can cause her saliva to enter your bloodstream and there have been cases where the HIV virus got in the blood stream. If you don't know her HIV status take the proper precautions and be very careful. Here are few practical suggestions for becoming a better kisser.

WILL THE REAL MEN PLEASE STAND UP

1. **Make it gentle.**

Relaxed lips and facial muscles are more soft and sensuous than hard and determined lips. Kissing tight, taunt and non-relaxed lips are like kissing a piece of corn on the cob.

2. **Practice movement of the lips.**

Use your mouth as if it were a gift to be enjoyed by any woman that comes in contact with it. Don't be too forceful or so determined to kiss that you forget the most important ingredient of a good kiss. "Flexibility."

3. **Brush your teeth.**

When it's your own breath you won't be as in tune with how it smells. The person on the receiving end of the kiss is usually the one who get the worst of it all. People who smoke or eat spicy foods have a higher tolerance level for smells than a person who doesn't. This makes a great difference in when, how and if you can smell your own breath.

4. **Freshen your breath.**

Many times you can brush your teeth, but miss your breath. There are many great breath mints and mouth washes on the market that will help cure your breath ills. The best thing to do is brush your teeth and your breath. The best way to brush your breath is to simply brush your tongue and the roof of your mouth. Brush your gums as well. Brushing your tongue is a favorite among people with dentures, partials and any other mouth work.

5. **Be kissed sometimes.**

There is a difference in being kissed than always being the kisser. You don't have to always be the aggressor in kissing. Try being kissed sometimes. If you allow yourself to be kissed during the act of kissing you'll learn a few things about how the person on the giving ends likes to be kissed. Women thinks it's sexy to be able to give the kiss sometimes, even if you were the one to initiate it. The best way to do this is kiss her first then follow as the kiss lengthens.

WILL THE REAL MEN PLEASE STAND UP

6. **Listen to her kiss.**

Fabulous kissers like fabulous lovers are sensitive to how their partner is feeling and how responsive their communication is with their mouths. Take a deep breath, relax, and try to imagine what she's thinking and feeling as she kisses you. Don't wonder off thinking about the daily chores or work while kissing her. Stay committed to the kiss.

7. **Add variety to your kissing.**

It a great way to try new ways of kisses when you imitate a celebrity or your favorite idol while kissing her. It doesn't mean you're trying to become that person. See it as a way to add variety to your kisses. The more ways you have of kissing her the better.

Don't.

There are certain things that a man can do while kissing his partner that will turn her off. Here are the top ten don'ts.

1. Don't crush her lips against her teeth to show your passion. Blisters have been caused by overly aggressive kisses. This kind of aggression only makes her hate to kiss you and if she does kiss you she'll only regret it afterwards.
2. Don't squeeze her so tight and hard that she can't breath or either body bruises result from it.
3. Don't try to ram your tongue down her throat in order to stimulate her. She can't breath in many cases and it hurts her.
4. Don't bite her lips too hard. Many a woman has had skin broken because her partner became so engulfed with her kiss that he bit down too hard.
5. Don't suck her lips too hard. Sucking too hard can creates painful red sections inside her lips if not done correctly. Short gentle sucks work best. Suck gently and let go, suck gently and let go. Do not pull her lips too hard.
6. Don't use birdlike pecking kisses that have no pressure. It's not affectionate nor erotic. Women complain of this type of kiss.

WILL THE REAL MEN PLEASE STAND UP

7. Don't kiss with your mouth wide open. It can cause you to slobber on her uncontrollably. This is most grotesque thing a guy can do to a woman while kissing her.
8. Don't turn your kissing into marathons. Don't kiss her so long that she has to push you away or gasp for her breath.
9. Don't drool as you kiss her. Get rid of it and make yourself aware of the type of kisser you are.
10. Don't began kissing her unless your breath is fresh, clean and appealing.

Do's

Now you've discovered some of the mistakes of kissing here's the best ways to kiss her.

1. Do use your kisses as a way to cushion her lips instead of pressing against them. This helps keep your front teeth covered so you won't hit against her mouth hard.
2. Do allow your tongue to touch the areas just inside her lips. Brush across this area several times, but don't go pass her teeth yet.
3. Do work your hardest to give her kisses that will raise her sexual desire more than your own. Remember you are working to please her at this point.
4. Give probing, sensitive kisses that will promote her to want more...more ...more.
5. Do feel free enough to proceed if she appears to be enjoying your kisses. Caress her face, the side of her neck, the back of her head, or hold her head and face between your hands as you assault her mouth with kisses.
6. Do let your tongue slip between her teeth and move to her tongue. Withdraw and see if she follows you as if to give and get more. Repeat this withdrawal method until she is physically begging for more.
7. Do cover the entire surface of her mouth while sucking, licking and biting her lower lip.
8. Vary your area of overage while kissing. Move from her lips to her ears, to her eyes and back to her lips again. One of the best areas on a man is where his ear, neck and jawline come into play.

9. Do stay alert enough to notice what areas she wanted you to kiss the most. Pay attention to her body language and watch her guide you to her sensitive spots. Understand where it is she wants your tongue to visit again.
10. Do continue to kiss her over and over again.
11. Lick only the corners of her mouth sometimes, two highly erogenous spots. Offer her the inside of your lips while kissing deeply; it's much softer and more sensitive and it's a deeply intimate gesture.
13. Run your tongue over her gums. Around his tongue, across his lips; then follow it up with a nibble or localized kiss. While enjoying some lovely open-mouthed kisses, pause for a while, mouths still open on each other, and simply breathe each other's breath. This is very hot.
16. Instead of one extended kiss give her many short, sucking kisses, one right after another. Kiss as if you want to reach inside of her.

Kama Sutra Kisses

1. Nominal Kiss - When your lips touch your lover, but do nothing else
2. Throbbing Kiss - When your lower lip moves your lover's lower lip but not the upper.
3. Touching kiss - When your tongue touches your lover's lip and closing your eyes your hands touch your lover's.
4. Straight Kiss - When you bring your lips in direct contact with your lover's lips.
5. Bent Kiss - When lovers bend their heads toward each other and kiss.
6. Turned Kiss - When you hold your lovers hand and chin and turn their face to kiss.
7. Pressed Kiss - When you press your lover's lower lips with much force.
8. Greatly Pressed Kiss - When you take hold of your lover's lips with two fingers and then after touching it with your tongue you press her lips with great force using your lips to do so.
9. Kiss of the Upper Lip - When you kiss your partner upper lip while in return she kisses your lower lip.
10. Clasping Kiss - When you take both of your lover's lips between your own lips.

11. Fighting of the Tongue - When during the clasping kiss your lovers tongue touches your teeth, tongue and palate.
12. Kiss That Kindles Love - When you look at your lover while she's asleep and kiss her face to show intention or desire.
13. Kiss that Turns Away - When you kiss in order to turn your lover's attention away from business, arguing, or looking at something or someone else.
14. Kiss That Awakens - When arriving home and your lover is asleep you kiss her to show your love and desire.
15. Kiss Showing The Intention - When you kiss the reflection of your lover in the mirror, in water or on the wall.
16. Demonstrative Kiss - When your lover is standing and you kiss her fingers, or if she is sitting you kiss her thigh or lower extremities.

Kama Sutra Biting (great when mixed with kisses)

1. Hidden Bite - When biting is shown by the excessive redness of the skin that is bitten.
2. Swollen Bite - When the skin is pressed down on both sides.
3. The Point - When a small portion of the skin is bitten with only two teeth.
4. The Line of Points - When small portions of the skin are bitten with all the teeth.
5. Coral and the Jewel - When biting is done by bringing together the teeth and the lips.
6. The Line of Jewels - When biting is done with all the teeth.
7. The Broken Cloud - When biting results in unequal rising in a circle and comes from the space between the teeth.
8. The Biting of a Boar - When biting consists of many broad rows of marks near to one another resulting in red internals.

Anastophobia - the fear of kissing.
Osculation - the act of kissing.
Philematology - the study of kissing.

36

THE ART of RELAXING BATHS

Bathing is essential to your soul.

I'd like to take you back through history to help you get a sense of passion, self-love and romance through bathing. Men of past civilizations have indulged in baths to relax and distress their minds, bodies and spirits. Many of us have all the necessary tools needed to create a spa in our home and don't even realize it. Most people are accustomed to taking showers instead of baths, because they are quicker. In the time it takes for your bath water to fill the tub, you could have already taken a shower, dried off and gotten ready for your next activity. Bathing served a dual purpose -- cleaning and relaxing.

To have renewed outlook on bathing, think of your bath as your moments to renew and rejuvenate your spirit. It can be a cleaning process, a relaxation process, a meditation process, a fun and games process or whatever purpose best serves you at the time of the bath. Be more creative with your baths and you will gain a sense of spiritual healing through them. Baths can also be used as a form of therapy, an avenue of beauty and a relaxation. They are used as a form of total relaxation at the end of a long day.

Baths have unfortunately become a sign of sinful retreats as well as great indulgent. Bathing is a lost art, a lost ritual that deserves to be rejuvenated. Bathing has been regarded as highly spiritual because it was believed to have divine powers therefore it was repeated highly by those who indulged.

Bath Pleasures for Men

Some bathhouses still do exist, and are, oddly enough, more prevalent in smaller cities than in larger ones, and mostly in the American South, Midwest and in Europe. Although recently the few remaining in large cities have expanded as a result of increased popularity. Lately they've been replaced by sex clubs. Should you happen to find yourself near a bathhouse, you may want to go in and at least look around. Lockers and rooms are usually available in a gym like changing-room area. The rooms are usually small plasterboard cubicles containing a bed, a lamp, a tiny shelf, and nothing else. Bathhouse amenities generally include a pool or Jacuzzi that can hold anywhere from four to twelve people. Also likely are showers, saunas, and steam rooms; sometimes there's a dormitory area or a small gym or workout room. Sometimes there's a lounge with a TV or video screen for porno flicks or even old movies.

There may be rare occasion's where you can mange to find one hour for a bath not to mention five minutes. The good news is a twenty minute bath not only pampers the outer you, but the inner you as well. Here are some helpful tips on how to take a relaxing bath.

1. Choose times to bathe when you can relax completely. Make sure there are no interruptions or appointments to disturb you.
2. Select all your favorite items, such as scented candles, matchbooks, lotions, oils bath pillows bubbles. etc.
3. Shower first to open your pores. Loofah in the shower with a long handed brush to scrub your back.
4. To add variety to your baths, try bubble bath one week and a milk bath the next. Milk products are great for protein rich baths.
5. Soak for at least twenty minutes or more each bath. This helps to relieve tired aching muscles, soothes joints, and wash away minor aches and pains.
6. Add your favorite extras to your bath to personalize it even more.
7. Listen to your favorite music, read or just close your eyes and relax.
8. Let the steam from your bath help open your pores.
9. Dry yourself by rubbing briskly with a terry cloth towel. Rubbing induces and promotes your circulation.
10. After you've soaked for a few minutes, scrub away any dead skin with a brush or loofah. Your bath is also the best time to manicure your toes because your cuticles are softer and easier to remove in warm water.
11. Hot water baths are great for relaxing (temperature no more than 85 degrees.) Warm water baths are best for soothing. Cold water baths invigorating and...

Cool water baths are stimulating.

12. Enjoy a candlelight bath. Candles softens the lines in your body through it's soft lightning. Others choose scented candles, the sense of scent is one of the five senses that we often take for granted, but frankly, it is a scent that can make your mouth water, eyes run your skin get bumps and even heighten your sexual arousal. Use scented candles as often as you can.

13. Enhance your senses with soothing baths. Smell your cleansed skin. She'll love to touch your clean smelling body. Sounds of water running, dripping and trickling from the faucet or your body soothes and calms you. The sounds of splashing water is tranquil also. Sights play an active role when rolling water slides off the body, and it also feels very good.

14. After she's showered, dry her off with your tongue.

15. After a hard days work, invite her into a hot bubble bath. Use several scented candles instead of harsh bathroom lights, put on some dreamy music and sip a heady wine or champagne. Lather each other up - and down.

16. For this one, you are the bather and she is the bathe. Get her wet but turn the water off while you soap her all over with sandalwood - pine or mint scented soap. Shower her off. Immediately run a very hot bath and let her soak in some feminine flavored oil. Bring on the candles and the mood music and read erotic stories to her, or do a striptease for her while you murmur sexy promises about what's in store after her bath.

17. Invite her to join you for a hot and sweaty workout. Follow it with an invigorating shower; lather her all over and give her a vigorous head massage when you wash her hair. Wrap her a Turkish towel and lead her to the bed for a relaxing baby oil massage.

For totally relaxing and soaking baths you should have a stretch out tub; a non-slip mat or posted nonslip strips, a large comfortable rubber pillows to rest your head; and large fluffy towels. According to the *Complete Herbal Guide To Natural Health & Beauty Book By Diann Dancing Buchman* some people prefer to wrap themselves into a rough cloth mantel or absorbent clothing and walk around or exercise until the body has returned to its normal temperature.

The important news about baths is they serve biological importance. The skin has four basis functions which are: sensory, excretory, heat regulating and respiratory. The latter two functions are most effected by bathing. In addition, bathing is also important to peripheral circulation in those tiny veins and capillaries close to the surface of the skin.

Skin is made up of several layers. The top layer being the layer which contains our pigment cells. The entire skin surface is shed every 28 days to be replaced by and healthy tissues. Dead skin must be removed frequently by washing to avoid clogging and sebaceous and sweat glands. Water cleanses, detoxifies and deodorizes the skin. The skin must have water to remain healthy, elastic and supple. To help enhance your baths here are a few resources:

1. **Bubble baths.** Available in powder, tablet and bead form. Bubbles act as insulation to keep the water warm and helps to prevent bathtub ring in many cases.
2. **Crystals and Salts.** They add fragrance to the bath and act as water softeners.
3. **Gels.** Gels are lightly scented, non soap liquid cleaners. Gels produce abundant lather in hard and soft water.
4. **Milk Baths.** Dry or liquid milk products give you a tub full of creamy fluff. This fluff is great for conditioning skin.
5. **Bath Oils.** Scented oils are available in several forms: foaming, fragrant and moisturizing. Fragrant bath oils are usually non forming products. Moisturizing oils replace the natural oils washed away during bathing. You can purchase oils at any bath and health food store. Dispersing oil is one that completely dissolves in water. There are very few of these, but the oil of the castor plant, when treated, can be an ideal bath oil, as it dissolves completely and does not leave a ring.
6. **Botanical Baths.** Dry or liquid vegetable, fruit, or herbal products, are available in a variety of flavors and scents.
7. **Aromatic Herb's.** In the seventeenth century perfumed baths became popular. Such fragrances as roses, lemon flavors, jasmine, bay, lavender, penny royal and

citron peel were used alone or together. They were sometimes mixed with a few drops of oil of spice and some fixative such as musk or ambergris. It's quite simple to obtain these oils and essences today, and you can certainly combine them for your aromatic baths.

If you prefer to use Herb's in your bath, be sure to use them in extract form or a bath pouch. You can make a herbal bath pouch by enclosing your favorite Herb's into a bag made of porous cloth, i.e., cheesecloth, colorful muslin or silk drawstring bags. These can be hung under the hot water tap and used for several baths.

Bathing is definitely a sanctuary. It's important to prepare your baths with the type of atmosphere that will enhance your bath even more. The ambiance as well as the foods, drinks, music, are all important in setting the mood you want to acquire in your bathing experience. Solitude baths are wonderful. They allow you the opportunity to listen to the inner you. You can choose an array of styles to help you enjoy your bath. It's up to you.

Bathing is a lost art, a lost ritual that deserves to be rejuvenated.

Step 8:

Practicing

Spirituality

37
HEALING RELATIONSHIPS THROUGH PRAYER

Get strength and wisdom from your spiritual beliefs.

In preparing this chapter, I took a break from my research and writing and called my pastor in Dallas, Texas. He was my friend as well as my pastor, and talking with him always provides a refreshing change of pace. Recently my conversation with him provided something even more -- inspiration for this particular chapter.

I now understood why my own marriage has lasted more than two decades. Not a small accomplishment in an age where sneakers last longer than the average marriage.

In light of me and my husbands milestone, I still asked my pastor for some advice. I asked him how a man and a woman might go about using their imagination in other ways to enhance their relationship.

In answering my question, he based his words on nearly three decades of counseling couples and receiving hard-won wisdom from them. He put it to me in days of the week, although he did tell me there's no need to attempt to put all of these days in a single week. In fact, I believe that any one of the principles mentioned will make a difference in your relationship and your life if applied with passion.

Monday: Stick to fact, not fiction.

Even though we already know denial isn't a pretty thing and telling ourselves we are in a relationship with the best person on earth when we know that it's not true will *not* transform our relationship. Rather than dwell on facts that you can't change, repeat over and over at least five thoughts that are positive and a truthful representation of your life and make a conscious effort to meditate on these thoughts throughout the day.

Tuesday: Take in consideration the positive qualities of your mate.

It's hard to be intimate with someone when your thoughts are consumed with negatives or faults. Keep in mind the principle of Monday and find time to recognize the positive qualities your mate possess. Ask yourself why you fell in love in the first place and pull from these thoughts the things you find the most attractive.

Wednesday: Make improvements in increments.

For two days now, you've generated positive thoughts that accurately represent your relationships, your mate, yourself, as they currently exist. This is not to say however that there isn't a time and a place to think about the future and the way we would like things to be in our relationships with our partners. Think about all the things you want to say and do that will encourage your mate to give you the kind of response you want. Use your imagination and in time look for the opportunity to treat your partner the way you have been getting treated in your thoughts.

Thursday: Imitate your role models.

My pastor told me that many couples tell him they meditate and fantasize about what they want their relationships to be like. This image not only foster many couples relationship it works as a model to imitate godly messages on a daily basis.

Not everyone is so privileged because many people don't ever use or see role modeling as a way to find success in their relationships.

Friday: Visualize positive difference in your relationship.

Spend quality time engaging yourself in thoughts, words, actions, and attitudes that you know would make a positive difference on your relationship. Visualize yourself making small changes in your communication so that you are more honest about your feelings airing and dispelling small hurts and wounds before they have a chance to create an icy barrier between you and your partner.

WILL THE REAL MEN PLEASE STAND UP

Saturday: Reminisce about the past.

I recall a time in my marriage when outside pressures were putting a strain on my husband. During this time, while cleaning out one of his drawers I uncovered receipts for diamond earrings that I had received from him, but lost on one of our many vacations. There was hosts of pictures and other momento's he had kept over the years. One of pictures in particular tugged at my heartstrings and filled me with remembered joy. This picture may not seem like much, but it was small black and white we took . It was in poor shape, poorly composed, faintly out of focus and faded with age. It's a picture of my husband, sitting on the couch at his brothers home. His sleeves on his shirt are rolled up, his belt is crooked, and his hair is filled with lint as the camera caught him by surprise. With one of his arms relaxed around my shoulder we are both holding my chubby new born son, Martin. Standing as close as they could were my daughter's Juanna and T'Juanna with the biggest smiles on their faces. Our happy times showed on our faces.

What's special about this photo is the period of time it represents. A time when babies were little bundles of joy and time were filled with love and sheer happiness. Life was also filled with promise. Several decades later finding the photo in the faded box reminded me of how much love my husband and I had for one another. Since those days I find my husband and I have thought of many wonderful ways to rekindle our love.

Find photos around your home that will rekindle happier times and memories for you. Perhaps the photo will be of you or your wife or the both of you. In any case put them where you see them often, and let yesterdays memories cast a golden glow on your attitude today.

Sunday: Say a prayer for your partner.

Last, but not the least, pray for your partner. Many times during prayer God will drop images into our minds that will guide us into praying for the things that he desires for us. In this way our prayers have the power to reflect back to us things that are being completed in the spiritual realm even though they have yet to be evidenced in the physical realm. After all our prayers are fueled by faith, which is nothing less than the substances of things hoped for and the evidence of things not seen (Hebrews 11:1)

Select verses that characterize godly traits you would like to see the Holy Spirit continue to cultivate in your mate. Incorporate these verses into your quiet times with the Lord, "praying" these scriptures over your mates as they go about their daily schedule. You may even want to insert your mates name into the verse as you pray.

All in all submit your imagination to the lord. Ask God to guide you in using the power of your thoughts to continuously build your life and your relationships.

Spirit Driven Dating

There is nothing quite as dangerous as deeply "religious" men or women who spiritualize their dating. I call this *"spirit driven dating."* Countless people are listening to "voices on high" instead of listening to common sense. Actually this is not being spiritual at all because spirituality is quite healthy. Spirit driven dating is really hyper-spiritual or pseudo-spiritual. The following story will help you understand.

When Joe and Leslie started dating, everyone wondered how this guy could have landed this incredibly righteous woman. We soon learned that Joe had used the "God told me to marry you" line to get her. Joe, a radically religious man, spotted Leslie at a singles Bible study. In a "spirit inspired" moment, Justin approached Leslie, and told her that God had revealed to him that they were to get married. Leslie responded with shock and excitement. She took Joe up on his offer to pray and fast for the next week.

Six months later, against the wishes of family and friends, she married Joe. From day one they were at each other's throats, fighting and bickering about everything. They had their relationship with God in common, but were incompatible in just about every other area. Finally, after years of marriage counseling, Joe had an affair, and their "spirit-driven" romance ended in a bitter divorce.

If you depend solely on your spiritual leading, and fail to use your brain, you may easily end up in a similar situation. There are so many wedding invitation "Led by the Spirit of God, John and Dora invite you to attend ... "Without question, this is one of the most common misuses of spirituality. If God is leading one of you, then He will be leading both of you. Don't let someone else interpret God's leading for you.

Does that mean I am opposed to spirituality in dating and making important decisions? No way! In fact, I vigorously affirm couples seeking God for guidance about getting married. The difference lies in true, healthy spiritual life versus pseudospiritual manipulation. God gave us our minds for a reason, and using common sense is indispensable when making godly decisions.

Do you see what happens to men and women when they allow themselves to be guided by emotions, sexual passion or heavenly voices? Hearts broken, dreams dashed, children stuck in the middle. This does not have to be your life story. You can make a commitment now to use your brain through the dating process.

There's are times in every single man's life that he needs a boost of confidence. There are times when he needs to hear that everything's going to be okay. That all is going to be just fine. Even the most confident, well-adjusted, happy man faces an occasional self-doubt on drop in his ego. Praying in the time of need, frustration, or grief is nothing new to men. What is new is the emphasis on using prayer to address health problems. Recent research has turned up a few surprising discoveries, but none manage to answer just how, and why prayer helps people feel better, fight off illness, and heal more quickly. As your mother probably told payer helps those who help themselves.

Prayer is said to be one of the best ways to get close to God. There's no right or wrong way to pray, but there are ways to pray more effectively. Here are six steps to for using prayer to the best of your ability. By using prayer effectively you can lighten your load, raise your spirit, cleanse your mind and set your soul on fire.

Step 1:   Relax and Cleanse Your Mind.
By taking the time to relax your mind, you learn to forgive yourself for past mistakes. You learn to forgive yourself for being upset because you couldn't face a particular situation or problem. If you want to handle your problem you have to start with facing it, and once you face it you can began to heal. Worrying about it is just another way of saying "I can't deal with this."

When you forgive yourself for not having the answers or being stuck in the same place with your problems you are able to move forward.

Withdraw to a quiet place, let go of your anger and irritability, breathe deeply and then relax your body. Use power words as you speak to your body. Know that these words do have the power to heal you. After you've relaxed, close your eyes for a moment and say this affirmation: "I am full of divine strength and that strength shall give me personal and spiritual power.

Step 2:   See Yourself In A Different Way.
Seeing yourself in a different way is sometimes difficult. You need to pray in order to expand and uplift your thoughts as you talk to God simply and naturally, as you would talk to a friend. Many times we lack patience with ourselves because we have so many things we need to do throughout the day. Once we get pass our physical pain our emotional pains takes place. Since many of us haven't learned to recognize our inner strength which helps us to find the answers that we seek.

You might also find that you are more tolerant of other people's opinions and differences than you once were. You never know how you might learn from the simple act of listening with an open mind -- knowing all the while that you can make up your own mind.

Step 3:   Unite With God.
So often when we are praying, we don't fully recognize that we can become one with God. The minute we still ourselves, our anxieties move out of the way. It is at this moment that we begin to feel no separation; then we know that or spirit is right where it should be.

Step 4:   Know What You Want.
Ask for what you want. Ask for your desires. Your desire is fulfilled through you. Once you make clear your desires, you might, as many people do, doubt whether you're

praying for the right thing -- even if you are seeking relief from a problem. Here, then, is help to clear up this doubt:

Pray for good with all concerned. Be willing to give up something that you have in order to make ready for your new good. Whenever something good comes in, something else moves out. Be ready for this to happen. Be willing to accept the responsibility for what is happening to you. With your desire comes the responsibility of making commitments and following through on them.

Step 5:   Be Grateful.

Give thanks for all that you have received. Take a box of your choice, maybe the size of a shoe box or an 8 by 11 inch. Call this your give thanks box. Write a line or two of your favorite scripture or scriptural message on one side of the box. Seal your box and cut a small hole in the top and then put it in a special place. Find something every day of the week that you can be thankful for, write it down and deposit it in the box. At the end of a week or month, take a look at all the good that's in your life. This box is simply a symbol that God is ever present in your life.

Step 6:   Believe In The Power of Your Prayers.

Take these five steps suggested here and you'll find that those worries -- whatever they are -- can be turned around and transformed. Use the power of your imagination that God and prayer is the answer to every situation, your refuge and your strength and are very present in your times of need. There is no need to worry when there is constant prayer in your life.

Men who place their lives in God's hands are empowered. Their relationships with God gives them strength, hope, faith, perseverance, joy, peace, and grace. Thus, they can handle any situation due to the power of God in them. With God in your life nothing is impossible.

Pray for God's leading and direction.

Step 9:

Celebrating Sexuality

38
COUPLES AND SEXUAL RESPONSIBILITY

Each partner should share in the quality of pleasure in the relationship.

A couple of weeks ago Martin and I found ourselves sitting in our favorite seafood restaurant sacrificing fried fish and boiled lobsters with my daughters Juanna and T'Juanna. My daughters were excited to hear that I was launching a new book project and asked eagerly about the topic of my newest endeavor. I told them *it was "Will The Real Men...Please Stand Up!, a* book for men on love , passion and romance. I described it as a sort of primer for couples who want to keep passion and romance active in their relationships.

Pat quipped: "Men who want passion? Oh so it's a fiction book!"

We all laughed because after all we knew he was just joking.

I think.

The fact remains that many people stereotype men as not wanting romance and passion, just as they stereotype women as disinterested in sex. Popular culture has portrayed men as bump and grind addicts who have no use for passion and romance.

Then again, with all this stereotyping, is it possible that you and I have bought into these roles? Is the romance and passion left to women and the sexual pursuit to men? Do men invest more time and energy into hitting golf balls than we do pleasing their mates? Could he...should he ... show a little enthusiasm when it comes to the bedroom responsibilities?

Whose responsible for the quality of sexual experience in a couple's relationship anyway? After all everyone wants to be wanted! When ever I speak to groups, they suggest that each partner should share in the quality of pleasure within a relationship. Men felt that the women they are married to expect the husband to enhance the relationship when it comes to sexual aggressiveness. But in reality men feel that the women should encourage, entice and enhance the relationship so that the husband won't seek pleasure else where. Ideally men want to be approached by their women. But in our culture the male is usually taught to be the responsible person for pleasure. He's not considered a man by many women if he doesn't take the responsibility for making sure that the partner experiences an orgasm -- preferably multiple orgasms -- by stimulation through foreplay then intercourse.

The male's responsibility to insure pleasure puts a great psychological weight on his shoulders. His performance at his job helps determine his image and self-esteem as a man, lover, or a husband. The male ego is based on the quality of how well he does his job. Make no mistake, this is not a superficial issue, it is the central aspect of the sexual experience for men of the post liberation movement of women.

Men And Their Responsibility In Sex

Many men have complained that they have tried everything in the book to please their partners sexually, but feel that nothing they do seems to work. Women state that men are selfish sexually, that all they want is one thing -- their own pleasure. When women say men don't really care about their partners pleasure, this makes a man feel inadequate as a lover. Men should understand that their partners sexual hang-ups or problems may not have anything to do with them.

Why do men feel so responsible for their partners happiness? Part of the answer is the social myths that men are suppose to have more knowledge about sex than women. Many men as well as women want to believe this myth. It works both ways. They usually have learned about sex from a friend, or they've read sex books. Once men have learned from readings or movies they brag about it as if they know it all which leads people to believe they know more than they really do. And since they are suppose to know more the female automatically lets him assume the lead role. Another reason men are said to be responsible for the sexual fulfillment and happiness of their partner is because if a woman is aggressive she is considered a lose woman or thought to lack morals. Women don't want people to look at them as a tramp or a low life.

WILL THE REAL MEN PLEASE STAND UP

Women relate sexual responsibility in one of two ways. One is to act ignorant to what is below her waist and being unaware of what her genitals are about. She plays the role of not knowing anything worthwhile about sex or sexuality and so she waits on the man to rescue her and teach what she should know. The dumber she plays the more he gives to her. She makes him feel she knows nothing, therefore he gives more thinking she's experienced. He will then teach her about sex.

If a woman is ignorant to her own sexuality she doesn't take the lead or responsibility for her sexual needs because she doesn't know what they are. The one problem that comes from the blind leading the blind is that they both get bored with one another due to their lack of knowledge.

But there is another kind of female -- the one who knows, understands and enjoys her sexuality. Either through masturbation, or her sexual experiences with other men or both men and women she knows her sexual wants, needs, and desires. She knows what makes her feel good and what will make her feel even better. Even though she may know and understand her sexuality she may still be unable to take full responsibility for her own sexual pleasures, especially if she is afraid of being looked upon as a bad girl, slut, whore, or worse. Here fears restrict her from being as free as she would like to be. She feels this could threaten her relationship.

Another reason females won't assert themselves is that they don't want their male lovers to feel inadequate sexually. If she gives direction during sex or let him know that "it's this way not the way he feels she's criticizing his sexual prowess. He might even withdraw or feel criticized at his attempt to sexually fulfill her. His ego is tampered with when he's being told how to do it. So, many women feel it's just best to say nothing and let him take the responsibility. She keeps her mouth shut and let's him take complete control sexually. If a woman results to this tactic it's usually because she feels that some sex is better than no sex at all.

Many times the male has no true sense of direction when he touches his partner from one part of her body to another. He's uncertain about what she wants sexually but he caresses, and rubs her hoping he's doing the things she likes. The female thinks he has everything under control because he appears to know what he's doing. After all he took the lead and since he's suppose to be aggressive and she's passive everything feels fine to her, at least at this time.

Finally, men avoid sex with their partner so they can reduce the frustration and boredom. When they finally do decide to have sex again, they might try one new thing, but they do that one thing so often that they finally become bored with it. They then reduce their sexual activity even more. The concept that a man is responsible for his sexuality and his partners is one of the myths that keep their relationship from becoming a more sharing experience for both partners. Here's several ways both partners can take responsibility for their sex life.

1. Learn to communicate with your mate.

Communication is the key ingredient in successful relationships. It's important for couples to talk about the big and small things in their lives. It is equally important to listen to one another in a nonjudgmental, supportive way.

2. Remember the romance.

Make sure that romance never goes out of your relationship by giving your partner little forget-me-nots. Send her flowers, send her a love notes, kiss her unexpectedly or cook her favorite meal and serve it by candlelight. All of these things say, I love you" and can keep the love light burning for years to come.

3. Don't leave sex for last.

Physical intimacy is an important part of maintaining a healthy relationship because it unites partners physically, emotionally, and spiritually. Each partner must take the initiative to communicate their sexual needs and desires. By learning to tell or show your partner what turns you on you will greatly improve your sex life.

4. Look -out for your mates best interest.

This can be really difficult in a society that constantly bombards us with the message "Look out for No. 1!" Yet in a relationship between two equals, it is not necessary to always be first. If you and your mate both make a commitment to put the others interests before your own, then ideally no one need will go unmet.

5. **Get involved in activities you both enjoy.**

The couple that plays together stays together. Having shared interests in religious activities, community service political causes and other pursuits can go a long way in strengthening a relationship. You and your mate will meet other people that you have things in common with.

6. **Spend some quiet time together.**

Easier said than done, but you must remember that quiet time doesn't just happen by itself. You have to make the effort. Turn off the television, take the telephone off the hook and turn down social invitations so that you can spend time with your special someone. By tuning out the world and tuning into your mate, you are showing that you care about your relationship as well as a new another.

7. **Learn to laugh together.**

Television shows, movies, and books are good tools for finding laughter. When problems arise with you and your mate look at the bright side. Somewhere down the road you'll look back and laugh at the situation, so why not have that laugh now.

8. **Keep your appearance up.**

It's true that beauty is in the eyes of the beholder, so it's important to maintain the same attractive appearance your mate beheld when he or she first laid eyes on you. Men don't let yourselves go. Get a shave, a new hair cut or a new outfit that you think she'll find sexy. And men loose those beer belly, get a trim and splash on some of that cologne that drives her wild.

9. **Be open to change and personal growth.**

The person you meet today, relationships experts say, is not going to be the same person

10 years from now. give your mate a chance to stumble and soar. Create an element of trust within the relationship that lets your partner know that you are there to support him or her, come what may.

10. Respect your mates private time.

Don't get so caught up in your relationship that you forget you are an individual with interests of your own. Spend time alone for reflection and rejuvenation. A renewed you will make a better you.

Sex can get a man, but sex can't keep a man
-Levon Harrington

39
REKINDLE THE PASSION

Touching that thing can cause you to become addicted to playing with it.

I know from my own experience, and from listening to others that lovers believe their time together is special and separate from the experiences of all other people of the world. It's time they savor and return to these moments of passion again and again. When I ask couples to recall and return to those first days, they describe a world transformed. People seemed nicer, colors were more vibrant, food tasted better, everything had a newness about it, just like it did when they were younger.

The biggest change was in the way they expressed their feelings for one another. Suddenly they had more energy and a healthier outlook on life. They were more wittier, playful, passionate and more optimistic. They liked the face they saw in the mirror as well. They proclaimed to be fond of their lovers affection. Some felt so good about their lives that they gave up other forms of gratification. They no longer needded to indulge in sweets, alcohol or drugs. Their lives had meaning and substance because they were in love. This intense good feeling was right in their face.

Some even said they had heightened spiritual awareness, a sense of being connected with a higher and more positive power. They saw the world as a smooth polished lens, instead of scratched and out of focus. They had passion!

The Female Erogenous Zones

When you think of passion with your partner it's easy to feel good about your partners body. Most men believe that there are only two areas of a woman's body that are sexually responsive - her breasts and her vagina. This is far from the truth. I guess you could say it's not right or wrong of them to think this way. Almost every inch of a woman's body has the ability to become fully sensitized with eroticism and no man can consider himself a great lover until he had discovered every part of her body. He has to explore and take pleasure in discovering all of his woman's sexual potential. To accomplish this, there are two techniques you must master - the use of your hands and the sensuous kiss. Sensuality exercises have helped to improve many a mans touch and sensitivity. By exploring her body with your hands and giving gentle and loving kisses all over her body you can become a skilled and more sensuous man.

Her Eyes.
Butterfly kisses are fun. Run your lips across her eyelids softly as if she were being touched lightly by butterfly wings. Is she has long eyelashes be sure not to crush them or push them towards her too far. If she has long false eyelashes be careful not to reposition or dislodge them. Let your guide be her display of interest in you continuing to kisses her eyelids.

Brush her lashes. Her lashes will probably feel very feathery and fluffy against your lips. Many women view brushing your eyelashes against hers as a form of erotica. It tickles and makes her feel good on the inside.

Her Nose.
The fresh clean smell of a new bathed man will make her feel more comfortable with you. There are subtle colognes that will make you feel sexy and turn her on at the same times. To turn her on put on more than the usual amount of good imported colognes. These are most gentle to her nose and pull her into your space.

The cheap stuff takes longer to work and many times it gives off bad odors when mixed your body chemistry. Place the cologne strategically on your face, neck, chest, abdomen and the back of your hands.

Her Ears.
Are one of the most highly sensitive areas of a woman's body. They can often times be the most erotic. Her ear lobes are especially sensitive to the flick and kiss of your tongue. The combined techniques of lobe nibbling and soft, hot breathing on her ears can

transform a cold woman to the warm blooded animal she really is. When blowing in a woman's ear, don't use force enough to stun her. Rather exhale a soft warm breathe in and around her ear while nibbling and tonguing the inner lobe section. Try your very best not to be too wet or slobber. It ruins the effect.

Her Mouth.
A woman's mouth is very soft and easy going, no matter how much talking she does. Her mouth should be the most beautiful to you. It will also be the most erotic organ you can reach while she's still dressed. It will forever hold a special place in your mind. It's the most important seduction tool. Yes! It is the main key. If the kiss is right the rest will come. Kiss her mouth as if you were kissing whip cream from the corner of her mouth. It turns her on and it prepares her body for love and lovemaking. Her lips can be sucked gently enough for her to feel a slight tug.

Her Breasts.
Men have always looked at, pointed at, measured, painted, sculptured, photographed and worshipped a woman's breast. Breast are an asset to women and men never let them forget it. Before you take a woman's breast in your hands lets discuss them.

Most women are concerned about their breast just as much as a man is about his penis. Unlike penises a females breast sensations vary. Some breast are incapable of sensations while others respond to stimuli much like clitoral orgasms. Maybe that's why so many men never truly get weaned from sucking breasts.

Men who are breast grabbers, maulers, squeezer's and torture biters have depressed women so much that they are turned off by any type of handling of their breast. The fear has become so wide spread that women fear injury. Go slowly and gently when you do breast work on a woman. The most effective means of arousing a woman is too stroke her breast in a soothing manner, brushing your hands and fingers softly and slowly over her nipples. Then cup one nipple in the palm of your hand and move your hand in a lazy, clockwise fashion with round and round motions until you began to feel nipple erection. She'll began to feel relaxed after a long sensuous foreplay.

WILL THE REAL MEN PLEASE STAND UP

Her Clitoris.

You can't consider yourself a good lover until you can wring orgasms from her clitoris with the artistry that a great violist displays in extracting exquisite music his violin.

The clitoris is the females equivalent of the penis. It comes in different sizes, becomes erect when sexually stimulated and is the seat of orgasm. Unlike the penis, however, the clitoris often retracts and even seems to disappear during the plateau and orgasmic phases (imagine, if you can, your penis reversing itself and being swallowed up by your body), it does not ejaculate, usually responds more slowly to sexual stimulation, and has a much lower pain threshold than your penis. Here are some common mistakes:

* Giving direct manipulation on the clitoris in the early stages.
* Exciting her manually (or orally) after loosing contact with the clitoris.
* Stopping the stimulation at the point of orgasm.
* Using the same tactile stimulation pattern for too long.
* Assuming she is "all through" after having just one orgasm.

Being guilty of even one of these mistakes will rob her of sexual pleasure. Women desire and need continued stimulation during orgasm, so keep those fingers busy. Many men have made the mistake of thinking he has the clitoris by it's throat only to find out he's been playing in the wrong spot. The best thing to do is stop feeling around for it and keep manipulating the mons area and clitoral shaft and she will continue to respond and will reach orgasm shortly thereafter. Retraction of a woman's clitoris is normal and failure to continue stimulating it will frustrate her.

Most women need at least three orgasms before they can testify to being completely satisfied. Don't get alarmed, after you've helped her gain the first orgasm, the others come quite quickly. Just remember to move about her clitoral area slow and sure.

Her Vagina.

The area at which men and women alike worship. Men have lost fortunes. Kings have given up their thrones. Brothers have betrayed one another and governments have toppled all because of this tiny orifice men call a vagina, cunt, pussy twat, quim, hole, and penile haven.

One of the most harmful myths that have been perpetrated on the female in the last few years is that there is only one kind of orgasm that counts - the vaginal orgasm. All female orgasms are clitoral in origin. Even though men can keep their penis in a woman's vagina for a long length of time, unless he directly or indirectly stimulates her clitoris, she isn't going to have an orgasm. That doesn't mean that her vagina isn't as important as the clitoris because it is, but it does mean that women gain orgasm from direct stimulation of the clitoris. When a man enters a woman she will began to feel possessed - a necessary ingredient to her sexual well-being.

In the beginning women often feel that her vagina is the primary source of sexual satisfaction and gratification. Maybe because it is this place that she receives the male. It is also at this place where a woman feels that a man can sexually arouse her the most. She achieves her lubrication within ten to thirty seconds after she has initiated effective sexual stimulation.

As the woman becomes more excited, the inner part of the vagina lengthens and becomes distended - ready to accept any size penis she's likely to encounter. To test for lubrication, insert one or two fingers into her vagina. If you feel that she is wet on the inside you can stimulate her further with your fingers or your penis. Pay close attention to the upper part of her vagina near her entrance so you can indirectly stimulate the clitoris as well. Now that you have her vagina completely lubricated, it is time to proceed to with what makes her feel the most aroused. If you regularly play with her clitoris with your fingers, your penis and your tongue it will bring her to new levels of pleasures.

Almost every inch of a woman's body has
the ability to become fully sensitized with eroticism.

WILL THE REAL MEN PLEASE STAND UP

40
REAL SEXUAL FEARS MEN HAVE

Mirror actions to see your true self.

Yes, the fears men have are real. Fear is a powerful force that prevents many of us from getting what we want in life. But the great news is that no one is born with complete confidence. It's all acquired and developed. And, by now you know there have been things that have held you back from feeling free of your fears. I surveyed over five hundred men on their feelings, desires, fears, and fantasies for this book. Cynically, I expected their responses to reflect the stereotypical male concerns: *getting laid; getting laid the way they want to get laid; getting laid as much as they can to get laid; and getting laid without getting entangled.*

I was in for a big surprise. The men spent long, sometimes anguished moments with me detailing their sexual feelings and fears. Their feelings astonished me. It seems men care about the same things women do: satisfying their partners and creating deep feelings. In addition, they worry about things women seldom consider major concerns: penis size; the quality of their erections; and how long foreplay, oral sex, or intercourse should last. Like women, they blame themselves when sex doesn't work. Yet, often, they don't confide their worries to the women they love. What follows are the ten most popular fears men discussed when we talked.

1. How much does a man's penis size matter to women?
"I have a small penis, and I know women are disappointed when they see it the first time. But the worst is the woman who coos, 'oh, you're so big. "Why do women do that when they have to know I know better? It hurts."

Men who are endowed with large organs also feel self-conscious. They say women immediately categorize them as studs - or even fear having sex with them. (One large man states he wishes his lover didn't "brandish the K-Y jelly so defensively.") Even women who have suffered from having small or large breasts can't fully identify. A man's sexuality, his entire manhood, is embodied in his penis. Every cultural message a man gets while growing up connects his maleness to his penis.

2. How will I know when a woman needs more stimulation?

My wife often slips her hand between our bodies to play with her clitoris during intercourse. Sometimes I do that too, but she usually pushes my hand away. Does her need for clitoral stimulation really vary that much-or am I doing something wrong when I touch her? When I ask her what she wants, she can't or won't say."

Some men fail to realize that the majority of women need direct clitoral stimulation to reach orgasm. Beyond that, men are often confused. They ask, for instance, if direct means stroking the clitoris or merely the area surrounding it. And is clitoral stimulation prior to intercourse sufficient-or should it be continued during intercourse? The tiny clitoris is still the mystery organ to men.

Motivate her to direct you, but make it as nonverbal as possible. Instead of stimulating her during intercourse, take her hand and let her guide yours in the movements that pleases her. Many times you can avoid hurting her feelings when you express yourself nonverbally.

3. How important is it for me to stay hard during our lovemaking?

"Now that I'm approaching forty, the quality of my erections varies. I'm not always rock hard, but I can still perform. My girlfriend, who is several years younger, doesn't seem to enjoy sex as much when I'm not as hard. Is there anything I can do to make it better for her?"

As soon as the average man passes age 30, he begins worrying about the quality of his erections. Some men worry even in their 20s because they never get as hard as they believe they should. Most men model their image of what an erect penis should look like on the pornographic ideal of a steel like rod. When he doesn't get that hard and she doesn't don't respond as enthusiastically to lovemaking as usual, he misinterprets her response. He assumes the blame for not exciting her, rather than blaming her for not exciting him.

Many women ardently perform fellatio on his penis that seems too soft; but that often fails to help because he feels under so much pressure to respond. Try to please her instead; guide her hands or mouth to where you would like them to go. At this point, your passionate response is more likely to stimulate her than all your best efforts to arouse her.

4. Why do some women "fake it"?

"Shortly after we got married, my wife told me she sometimes fakes orgasms. I was mad. Why in the hell would she fake? Now I'm not sure when she's faking and when she's really having an orgasm. Is there a fool proof way to tell?"

Believe it when she says your orgasm is as important to her it really is. If you didn't have an orgasm, she thinks, you didn't enjoy sex. It follows: If you don't enjoy sex, she isn't a good lover to you. Despite feminism, many women sometimes fake it, simply to relieve the pressure put on them when men are trying to help them climax. Unfortunately, she's hurt anyway if she guesses, or later hears, the truth from you. She's also more determined to "make" you come-and "be sure" you did-which only increases the pressure she feels.

5. Should I perform oral sex to please my partner?

"My girlfriend seems to enjoy cunnilingus, but she's never had an orgasm this way. Am I stopping too soon? Or not giving her exactly what she needs to come? My last girlfriend didn't come this way either."

The men who love cunnilingus have usually had partners who were very responsive to their oral administrations. They feel good about their ability to please women this way and are eager to do so. A few unresponsive women in his past, on the other hand, convince a man he doesn't have the touch. If you're hesitant about performing cunnilingus, don't assume it's distasteful.

This is one of the few areas where verbal instruction is helpful. Because women all are so different from one another in the type of clitoral stimulation they desire, they have to spell it out. Even if you were a perfect lover for a prior girlfriend, what worked for her may not work for the new woman. You will have to learn what makes her tick.

6. What can I do to help her enjoy performing oral sex?

"My wife will perform fellatio occasionally to please me, but she makes it clear she doesn't like doing it. I would love to have more of this-and with her enjoying it, not suffering through it. Don't some women enjoy fellatio? How can I make it enjoyable for my wife. I don't expect her to swallow or anything.

Number one on the average man's sexual wish list is more fellatio. They love the physical sensations, the complete attention erotically under your penis, and even the feeling of being erotically under a woman's power. Yes, they want more fellatio, but they also want their woman to get pleasure from performing it, but not from a woman who is secretly thinking, Oh, yuck, as she does it.

Men don't understand the major problems women have with fellatio: performance anxiety and reluctance to take the penis deep into their throats or swallow the semen, which many women find objectionable (especially in the age of AIDS) and incorrectly believe is necessary to the act. Men aren't kidding when they say you almost can't do it wrong, so they have trouble comprehending why a woman would hold back for fear of being inept. The majority of men also don't expect you to deep-throat or swallow. Men are delighted when she fellates him, even briefly, as a regular part of foreplay.

7. Why does my desire to watch her touch herself embarrass her?

"My girlfriend is a beautiful and sensual woman. Watching her undress excites me. Sometimes, in the height of passion, she touches herself, and watching her makes me even hotter. I've asked her to masturbate for me, but she thinks that is 'kinky, sick, and weird.' Is it?"

Men have been given social permission to enjoy graphic sexual images; and women, for the most part, have not. From the biological perspective, men need those images more than women do, because sexual intercourse depends on their full arousal-not a woman's. When a man asks his woman to masturbate for him, he is asking her to star in his private erotic fantasy, to participate in what he sees as an ultimate act of intimacy.

He is also asking her to share something that she may regard as private rather than intimate. Some women masturbate in front of their partners naturally, as part of lovemaking. Certainly a man will learn how you like to be touched by watching you touch yourself!

8. How can I help her become multi-orgasmic?

"My wife has one orgasm. Sometimes it takes a lot for her to have one. What can I do to take her on to more orgasms? Shouldn't the second and the third be easy to have once she has had the first?"

The myth of the multiple orgasm tyrannizes men as well as women. As comfortable as women may be with one orgasm, many men aren't satisfied with that. It is difficult convincing men they aren't totally responsible for all orgasms, theirs and hers.

If you want to her achieve more than one orgasm, tell her so. However, if she's the one interested in intensifying, prolonging, or multiplying her climax you will probably have no trouble enlisting her aid. I recommend the books *The New Our Bodies, Ourselves* by the Boston Women's Health Book Collective and *For Yourself* by Lonnie Barbach, Ph.D. Read them together so the both of you can see how to help, and learn as much is really yours to do for yourself.

9. How long should lovemaking last?

"I feel like I'm cheating the woman I love if I ever give her less than fifteen or twenty minutes of foreplay. Afterward, I enjoy concentrating on her as long as she still wants to have orgasms. I overheard one of her girlfriends complaining about a 'man who couldn't last five minutes,' meaning actual intercourse time. Have I been focusing on before and after too much?"

This habit men seem to have with numbers about orgasms, or the length of foreplay and intercourse, can put emotional distance between couples, unless they understand why they're so concerned. In part, as you may suspect, they are always competing mentally with other men. That competition is apparently set up as soon as they're old enough to notice one another's anatomies in the boys' room.

Tell me you've never seen a woman hold her thumb and forefinger an inch apart in reference to some man's penis-or call him a "Five minute wonder in the sack." If you want foreplay or intercourse to last longer, ask for more of it don't say, "I wish foreplay could last more than two minutes:" say, "I'd really enjoy more foreplay." Maybe we all would have more fun in bed if we turned the bedroom clock toward the wall while we made love.

10.   How can I get her to help me spice up our sex life?
"One of the things that soured my first marriage was sex. My wife wouldn't do anything that didn't involve one of us lying beneath the other. Now I'm living with a woman who was wonderfully wild and inventive until we'd been living together for six months. Why do women equate commitment with sexual conservatism?"

Sexual variety is number two on the wish list. Again, strictly from a biological standpoint, men may need the varied routine more than a woman. Dullness is death to the erection. Some men also like to see themselves as sexually adventurous. And many men still believe they're as responsible for sexual entertainment as they are for picking up the dinner check. When a woman is asked to make love on the balcony or on the dining room table, her partner is thinking of how he can make sex hotter-not about how to embarrass or discomfort her.

Spend a lot of free time with the opposite sex, you never know whom you'll meet through them.

41
HELPFUL SEX TIPS

Treat others the way you wish to be treated.

Are you frustrated by the endless stream of suggestions for magically improving your love life-like having sex in strange places or going to motels with no luggage? Are you tired of trying all the gimmicks that make you feel foolish, like Saran Wrap surprises, wearing no underwear, or talking dirty on the phone? Are you discouraged by seeing that these tricks don't seem to work the way you hope they will-or that they work only temporarily and then you're right back where you started?

If you've ever felt doomed to a life of struggling to keep a good relationship, don't give up. You can have a lasting one. And it doesn't require miracles. Deep down, you know everything you need to know about making love last; you just forgot. What you need to do is calmly reflect on what you already know-and then act on it.

Bedroom Skills For Passionate Sex

He wants sex. She wants romance. They both want passion. Sometimes it seems as if men and women are from different world when it comes to making love with one another. In the bedroom men and women work very hard to be in the same place, but it's obvious they aren't there all the time. We may not realize how different we are from one another until we get to the bedroom. Through understanding and accepting the obvious and not so clear that we can achieve true intimacy and great sex.

We are all aware that romance and passion are the way to a woman's heart and sex is the way to man's, but we don't always understand why. When we fail to understand this fundamental difference we underestimate the importance of sex for men and many times judge them as superficial for wanting only one thing.

WILL THE REAL MEN PLEASE STAND UP

Here are some tips on how to get back in touch with what you instinctively know about enriching your sex life. Good-bye, Saran Wrap; hello, lasting love and pleasure.

1. Sexual enjoyment can be increased simply by paying attention.

Our modern life-style, with its focus on accumulating things and experiences, has dulled our ability to listen and respond to the subtle stream of messages from our bodies. Many of these messages are sexual, but they are competing with many other stimuli.

Make a commitment to monitor your own sexual needs more carefully-first, by simply paying attention, and second, by acting on what you notice. Be patient with yourself. This sounds simple, but it isn't always easy.

2. Use your brain to create the sex life you want.

Planning ahead is probably the surest way to eliminate the not-in-the-mood response you often get when you surprise your partner with a sexual invitation. Don't wait for your partner to prompt you to think about sex. Put it on your own agenda. And don't count on her always being able to shift mental gears whenever you get the urge. Tell her about your plan ahead of time. Choose a time and place for your next sexual encounter with your partner. Imagine in graphic detail how it will go. Tell her about it. The biggest risk is that you'll get her so excited, she wont be able to control herself.

3. Accept that nothing-not even your lovemaking-is perfect.

Try to make your lovemaking as good as possible, but don't expect perfection. It won't happen. Sometimes your best efforts to produce pleasurable feeling in your woman will not succeed. Sometimes carefully crafted plans to create a time and place for lovemaking simply won't work out. Give yourself credit for having had good intentions. Just beginning the process will be a step in the right direction.

4. Appreciate you body and that of your partner as sexy and attractive.

The emphasis on the perfect figure in our society has made it very difficult to feel good about our bodies. You may not feel sexy if you don't think you look sexy. But this is getting things backward. In fact, you will look sexy when you feel sexy. So your focus needs to be on getting in touch with your sexual feelings. A body that feels sensual is as sexy as it feels and acts, especially when it comes to engaging in loving sex with your partner.

5.   Don't be preoccupied with performance or someone else's definition of it.
Having an orgasm is usually the primary goal of sex, but it needn't be the only one or even the most important one. Too much focus on performance can keep you from responding naturally and spontaneously in the moment. When you're thinking too much about sex, you're not completely present. Thinking about what should happen (or how often it should happen) is a distraction from being in touch with what is happening.

Remember that what matters is *not* how your sex life compares to some ideal but how satisfying it is to you and your partner. Go with the feeling. Genuinely expressing your love and knowing that it will not always result in the same outcome can be the best performance of all.

6.   Always remember: The best sex is based on teamwork.
In any team situation, it's best to start with people who are individually talented, but that's no assurance that the team will perform well. You must also cooperate to reach your full potential. The same is true of sex. You can get some sexual satisfaction without the full cooperation of your partner, but if you want to achieve the best of what's possible, you'd better learn to work as a team. You need to be vary clear about what you're trying to do together and stay sensitive to each other a you proceed. It means sometimes leading and sometimes following-but always cooperating, because good sex is a team sport.

7.   Use all your senses to enjoy and appreciate sex.
The human anatomy is a thing of beauty. Appreciate the appearance of your unique bodies. Look without embarrassment as long as you like. Taste and smell are probably the most delicate subjects for lovers to talk about, but in some cases are most important if you enjoy oral sex. The odors you generate during sexual arousal are different. Whether

you enjoy them will depend as much on your attitude as on the odors themselves. Notice your partner's response to your touch. Be explicit about how and where you like to be touched. Revel in the sounds you make. Sounds often provide important clues to what's going on. For instance, noticing the changes in her breathing can be a good indicator of when she's nearing orgasm. Tuning in to each other during sex can make the sexual experience better for both of you.

8.   Be honest about what you like and don't like-what you want and don't want.
Remaining open to sharing your fantasies and desires is probably the best way to keep sex fresh and exciting. Too often we think that sex can be great only when a relationship is new. Wrong! By communicating honestly about sex and other feelings, you can keep your sex life exciting. It's the distance that's created when you hold back that contributes to a loss of sexual excitement.

9.   Broaden your view of what's appropriate sex.
While a leisurely sexual encounter with full expression of your loving feelings is great, it's not the only appropriate way to have sex. A quickie can be fun and satisfying too. It's nice when you and your partner desires sex at the same time, but you can be sure there will be times when one of you aren't in the mood. Going along with your partner's desire for sex can have a very positive effect on your relationship. While your own satisfaction is important, you can also find a lot of pleasure in contributing to your partner's satisfaction.   Be flexible. Keep experimenting. Enjoy it.

10.   Don't try to exercise too much control during sex.
Some things do need to be controlled during sex. Locking the door makes sense if there are young children who might walk in unannounced, Turning off the radio makes sense if it distracts you. Playing romantic music is fine if it makes you more comfortable or masks some of your lovemaking sounds which others might hear. At the same time, realize that the best sex can happen only when you let yourself go.

WILL THE REAL MEN PLEASE STAND UP

11. Continue to explore new ways of expressing your love sexually.

Regardless of how sexually experience you may be, there is always more to learn. Sometimes we're unaware of sexual possibilities that can bring newness and variety to our lovemaking, and we settle for repeating what ever worked in the past. Even the best routines get boring if nothing new is ever introduced.

12. Don't neglect sex, ever!

Which is the best kind of sex, spontaneous or planned? The answer is both. The idea that sex should always be spontaneous and never planed is silly. After all, when you were starting your relationship, you planned when and how to make sex possible. Planning for sex doesn't diminish pleasure- and may, in fact, increase it because of the anticipation. The afterglow of good sex is likely to remain for several days, and there's a chance that you and your partner will be inclined spontaneously to have sex soon again. However, other demands sometimes interfere with acting on that urge, and those feeling just slip away. If you let a lot of time go by (waiting for it to just happen), the less likelihood there is that it will happen spontaneously. At such times, it's important to plan for sex.

He wants sex. She wants romance. They both want passion.

42

HAVE CONDOM SENSE

Safer sex extends beyond simply using condoms.

Now that most people have agreed that condom-wearing is a highly recommended activity for new partners, let's take a stroll through the mind of a guy who needs to put one on, use it, then dispose of it.

In the dim blue light of the wee hours of a recent evening, my friend and Rosa are locked in a fierce and lovely horizontal position engaged in affection and hand-to-hand romance. I suggest it might be time for sex. Happily, she agrees, and I wonder to myself: Now that I've received her blessing, do I make a beeline for the condom? Or is that crass? Should I take my time about putting it on, be cool, show that I knew all along she'd say yes or would waiting signify classic passive aggression?

I split the difference. After 30 seconds more of kissing and advanced-level foreplay, I excuse myself to go hunting for my condom. In crawling forward and scrambling to find where I believe my jeans were abandoned, I nearly break my head on a low bookshelf. Perhaps I should have prepared and had the package nearby. On the other hand, that might have been somewhat presumptuous and indelicate, a mood-killer and hardly spontaneous. I didn't want her to feel that I was the type who indulged in spontaneous sex either.

I continue to look for my condoms and finally, my hand finds my pants pocket. It so happens I brought with me a little variety, since I was unsure which would feel better for her--ribbed or unribbed? With tip of without? Extra-large or monstrous?

Actually, I bought three with me. What guy really ever knows what's the right amount? One? A box of 36? In today's climate, maybe she'll ask me to wear two at once.

WILL THE REAL MEN PLEASE STAND UP

Enough of this kind of thinking. I'm starting to miss her while down here near the foot of the bed. I grab the first square package I find. I return, and tear open the condom package, gingerly. I fear ripping the damn thing in the dark.

I want you (and my friend) to know that, despite this microanalysis, my attention never wavers from her. While the condom has gotten considerable bad press, it really isn't that much of a nuisance.

"And anyway, unless I can readily produce a doctor's certificate saying I am HIV-free, have no other communicable diseases, am incapable of impregnating anyone, get straight A's in school and never forget my mother's birthday, I must acknowledge the wisdom of using it." "Plus, as everybody knows, it takes no time to put on."

I remove the squishy ring from this package. Wordlessly, the question of who will put it on arises, or maybe I just imagine this. I hesitate only briefly. Not to worry; so let me take the liberty here.

"Which way does the damn thing go?" I ask, after many seconds of frustration.

"Am I unrolling it or rolling it back up? Must it be so lubricated? Should I maybe have worn it to dinner to save myself this present embarrassment?"

Dim though the light may be, I see that my friend is amused by my difficulties. I thought putting on a condom was like riding a bike: do it once, you never forget. Then again, I never could figure out how to make cloth napkins stand up at a place setting. Expertly leaving the little space at the tip. I finally get the thing on. Had it taken any longer, I might have needed to return to the battle front for substenance.

Now that you're in protective custody, I think, *do I put it right in? Or is that brutish? You've obviously put it on for a reason, not for the aesthetics; on the other ...hand, you don't want developments to be dictated now by anything but the natural rhythm of mutual desire.*

Things progress.

How does it feel? She feels wonderful. I feel wonderful. We feel wonderful! Yet wearing this latex supramembrane, I also feel a vagueness, as if I'm having an out-of-body experience. *Does she think I'm being distant because I'm one half of an inch from true contact with her?*

We make love.

Afterward, I must do away with the offending article. *Where's the garbage can? Should you be thinking recycling?* I neatly tie a knot in the limp sucker, something I learned from a previous lover and one of the two most efficient ideas I ever appropriated from friends.

It is so quiet. We hold each other. We purr. I'm thinking, *You and she felt a profound connection tonight, didn't you?"* (the condom that is)

In fact, condom or not, the night was down right magical. Don't believe me? Ask my friend. What does she think?

"Was it a magical night, Sweetheart?"

"Uh-huh."

See? This condom business isn't so awful. I can deal with it, the fumbling fingers, even the slightly desensitized feeling. I like being mature and responsible. I think condom-wearing might work out just fine.

I really can talk myself into just about anything, can't I?

BEYOND CONDOMS: Latex For Every Occasion

Safer sex extends beyond simply using condoms. For virtually every kind of sex act, a corresponding form of latex exists to protect you against AIDS and other viruses transmitted through bodily fluids.

Lube and latex go hand in hand. Lube creates a deliciously slick, wet feel with your latex and reduces friction, which can cause condoms to break. Use water-based lubricants only, and store your latex in a cool, dark place. Remember, latex is disposable. It's designed to be used only once. (That means one sex act, one session, one condom.)

Condoms are the most common latex barrier, and if you're sharing sex toys, the toys need to wear them too. Aside from condoms, the safer-sex products mentioned here are rarely found in drug stores. Your best bet is a condom store, a specialty sex shop or mail-order company.

Latex Gloves

You may associate latex gloves with your doctor's office, not your bedroom, but once you add a latex glove to your foreplay, that characteristic snap of the glove may develop a new sensuous response to you. Gloves prevent viruses from entering your bloodstream through any cuts on your hands. They also smooth sharp fingernails, which is important when encountering delicate tissue. Latex gloves come in a variety of sizes and colors. For special occasions, try some black elbow-length latex gloves. These are thicker and reusable, not to mention very fashionable. Gloves usually come dusted with talc, which can cause irritation. Vinyl and hypoallergenic gloves, though thicker and less flexible, provide an alternative for those with latex sensitivities.

Finger Cots

Finger cots look like miniature condoms and can be rolled onto your finger like a condom. Use finger cots for preventive sex if you are using one or two fingers and don't want to bother with a glove. If your fingers are small, latch your thumb over the base of the cot to prevent it from slipping off into parts unknown. Cots work well to sheathe small sex toys, too.

Dental Dams

Dental dams, originally created for use during dental procedures, are thin, flat squares of latex that you place between your tongue and your partner's vagina (for cunnilingus) or anus (for rimming). They come in a variety of colors and flavors. Glyde Dams (Lollyes) are the largest and thinnest. Latex Dams are also quite thin and come in strawberry and vanilla flavors. You can make your own dam by cutting the end off of a condom, then cutting the length so it lays in a flat square. Ordinary kitchen plastic wrap is a cheap and easy alternative to dental dams. The disadvantages are that it isn't stretchy, and as you know from the kitchen, it clings to itself.

To use a dam, dab a little lube on your partner's vagina before placing the sheet of latex over her. This will create a nice slippery feeling. Hold the dam firmly in place with both hands; this can be a little awkward at first. You may want to get a Dam Garter, a black elastic device similar to a garter belt, which holds a dam in place. (It's sexy and practical.) Stretching the dam allows for closer contact, but the dams are thin so get carried away and perforate it.

Female Condom

Another innovative barrier is the Reality female condom. Reality is made of polyurethane rather than latex. It consists of two flexible rings inside a condom-shaped bag. The larger ring is attached around the opening, and the smaller ring is designed to fit over the cervix - is loose inside the bag.

Female condoms tend to be rather noisy (imagine rubbing a wet baggy), awkward to insert, expensive and just plain too obtrusive for some people. They are good is your partner does not like condoms, though, or if either of you has latex sensitivities. Use a lot of lube and be careful that the penetrating partner is actually inside the bag and not between the ring and your orifice of choice.

Latex Face Masks

There is also a latex face mask on the market, called Oradam. Designed for oral sex, the Oradam is a molded latex band that covers the lower half of your face (breathing tubes are thoughtfully included) and wraps around your head. Unless you are bald, getting it off and on can be a bit tricky. It also doesn't look attractive unless gas masks are your fetish. The advantage is it leaves you hands free.

There are still a lot of unknowns regarding disease transmission, so it's best to educate yourself and get tested for AIDS. Don't limit your sexuality, but play it safe. Get some latex, cover your bases and your partners and then have some real fun.

Condoms are the best protection for enjoying sexual intercourse. Condoms help make sex last longer and can prevent premature ejaculation.

WILL THE REAL MEN PLEASE STAND UP

Unprotected Intercourse and Oral Sex

If you have unprotected intercourse you are at high risk for

* Trichomoniasis   * Bacterial vaginosis   * Gonorrhea   * Clamydia
* Syphillis   * Chancoid   * Pubic lice   * Scabies
* Hepatitis B virus (HBV)   * Cytomegalovirus (CMV)
* Human immunodeficiency virus (HIV), which can cause AIDS
* Human paplioma viruses (HPV's) which can cause genital warts
* Herpes simplex virus (HSV) which can cause genital herpes
* Pelvic inflammatory disease (PID) which can cause sterility

Sex Play

If you have sex play without sexual intercourse you are at risks for
* HSV   * CMV   * HPV   * Pubic lice   * Scabies

Lots of other diseases from the flu to mononucleosis, can also be transmitted sexually.

There are twenty three states that view oral-genital contact between consenting adults as illegal, including the District of Columbia and the U.S. Military. They are:

Alabama	Arizona	Arkansas	Florida	Georgia
Idaho	Kansas	Louisiana	Maryland	Massachusetts
Minnesota	Mississippi	Missouri	Montana	Nevada
N.Carolina	Oklahoma	Rhode Island	S. Carolina	Tennessee
Texas	Utah	Virginia	including...	

District of Columbia   US Air Force   US Army   US Coast Guard
US Marines   US Navy

One sex act, one session, one condom.

After Thought: Celebrate Your Relationships

This book is a celebration of love, life and relationships. The rich rewarding love life we have all dreamed of really can be yours, and you deserve to have it. For years -- like you perhaps -- I thought a great relationship was something other people had or something that didn't exist at all. If anyone I knew had a great relationship I reasoned that they were just plain old lucky. I felt they were luckier than me, more lovable and less needy.

My husband and I have made a lot of mistakes in our relationship and it surprises me that we've been married now for more than twenty years and still love one another. I always felt like I was a rescuer of others and at times have expected my husband to read my mind and he has expected me to understand exactly what he wanted and needed. We both have sometimes taken each other for granted and almost let the passion die. By some strange miracle we became aware of the mistakes we've made and we have discussed our problems until we were not discussing, we were shouting through them.

The warm, intimate, exciting, loving and respectful relationship we have today took work to get where it is. It did not evolve out of either one of us being smarter than the other or one being more right than the other. The only thing I know is that when we first met we fell for one another because we saw something we liked about each other and we knew we wanted to spend the rest of our lives together. Our relationship has had it's problems and we've fought like hell sometimes, but our longevity comes through our determination to make it work and never give up on each other.

Couples aren't as bad as they think they are if they stand up *for* one another instead of standing up *against* one another. Couples now, more than ever before are celebrating their relationships.

A good relationship is a gift from God; it's one of life's greatest pleasures. However our relationships must be treated special. It is a living, growing intity that must be nurtured and protected if you expect it to survive the challenges and changes ahead. When you strive for balance, when you feel free to compromise, and commit to emotional honesty, the bond grows deeper and stronger. Your problems can often create doors for greater and real intimacy instead of barriers between you.

We do have our differences and relationships can be difficult, but -- men and women alike need love, support and respect, and a healthy relationship can provide these ingredients in a way that nothing else can.

In order to attract and maintain healthy relationships with our mates we must first be able to love ourselves. Opening and exploring new ideas and changing old habits to new and more rewarding habits can become increasingly more appealing.

Our relationships can remain rich by surrounding ourselves with family and a close circle of friends. Learn to accept others for who they are and not for who we want them to be. Accept that if we cannot change the world at least we can work to change ourselves. Understand why forgiveness frees us from anger and opens the doors of heaven for God to shield and protect us. Keep smiling because when we smile God has got our back.

Couples who build and maintain happy fulfilling relationships don't follow rules and recipes -- they write their own - they are smart enough to know that their relationship is different from anyone else's. They know that their taste is different from everyone else's. They also know that they will probably have to alter or change the recipe in their relationship from time to time as well, to keep it fresh and interesting. They know that they must protect and nurture something as precious as a healthy, stable and supportive relationship.

To be loved and cherished is everyone's heartfelt desire. This book is written to restore hope and to provide principles that will help even the most successful relationships grow. I wish you lots of romance and passion, peace, love and much happiness in all of your relationships.

By keeping the romance alive and practicing the skills in each chapter, you can and will continue to enjoy great romance and passion. You deserve it.

-Ella Patterson

Will The Real Men...Please Stand Up Discussion Topics

Here's a wonderful way to have some fun and excitement as you establish better communication skills with your partner. Have a *Real Men* discussion night. Get your book club, fraternity, church group, or social groups together and prepare a series of topics to be discussed from this book. It's very important to have as many men and women at the discussion as you can. The more the merrier is wise in this case. This helps bring diversity to the forefront. Make sure there are just as many men there as women. Invite me too, if I'm in your city I would love to sit in on your discussion, and maybe I can participate also.

As a former high school teacher I've found that one of the following formats are best because they help make the discussions entertaining, motivations and inspirational.

* A round table discussion with freedom to talk openly and honestly. Call it a tell it a Real Men discussion.
* Have a panel of experts that are down to earth and able to take constructive criticisms.
* Be sure to plan it with plenty of time to effective communicate and learn from one another. Most groups tell me at least 2 to 4 hours is great.
* Use the talk show style with a moderator to lead the discussion and keep the flow going smoothly.
* Try the mixer method. This allows the moderator to read a controversial chapter from my book and each participants writes his thoughts, comments or questions on a piece of paper or an index card. The moderator collects the cards or sheets of paper mixes them in a bowl and randomly collects a piece of paper from the bowl. The moderator precedes to read from the piece of paper to the audience. If the question is about men, the moderator selects a man from the audience to answer. If it is about women a woman is selected to answer. Each sex has rebuttal time given. A time limit is appropriate in order to move along smoothly.

WILL THE REAL MEN PLEASE STAND UP

*   Each topic in this book can be used for discussion but I have listed some that may help you get started. You can refer to the end of each chapter "Things to remember" if you need more reference to questions.

TOPICS FOR DISCUSSION

1. Do men expect sex too soon from women in relationships?
2. What factors are important to you in order to have a lasting relationship?
3. Is more important for the woman to keep the relationship monogamous?
4. Why do men feel having more than one woman makes him a real man/
5. What is the best way to make a love connection?
6. Why do men feel they have to be so macho.
7. Why are short men so self-conscious and have to prove themselves ore than 8. average height men or taller men?
8. Why do men come on to women in negative ways.
9. Why do men have to call women bitches just because she's not interested in him?
10. Why does married men feel that having an extra-marital affair is so beneficial to their ego?
11. What do men really want from women?
12. Why don't men like taking baths?
13. Men and pregnant women.
14. Why does people find it difficult for women and men to only be friends?
15. Who are your male role models?
16. Who are your female role models?
17. What does the word friend mean when referring to the opposite sex by married/committed people?
18. How do you introduce a new partner to your children?
19. When should parents began to talk about sex with their children?
20. Why do women cheat?
21. Who should pay for the dates?

WILL THE REAL MEN PLEASE STAND UP

22. Is light skin and dark skin still issues in relationships?
23. How can I help my friend to let go? The relationship is over?
24. How do I find the strength to move on after breaking up.
25. How do I find positive ways to feel single and complete?
26. Why do men run from relationships that make them feel as though they may fall in love?
27. How good is the advice men give women about other men?
28. How good is the advice women give men about other women?
29. What are some of the things that really irritate men about women?
30. What are some of the things that really irritate women about men?
31. Why are younger women finding reasons to date older men these days.
32. Why are older men obsessed with dating younger women?
33. Why are so many young girls turning into strippers?
34. Why are married men hanging out and even spending the majority of their moneys in strip clubs.
35. How do I help keep my man's ego at a positive level?
36. Why is so hard for men to be honest?
37. Why is so difficult for women to tell men what they want to know?
38. Why are committed women starting to have sex with so many men?
39. How does a single man meet upstanding, women?
40. Why are men so caught up in porn?
41. Why do women want men to pursue them?
42. How do I get rid of the date from hell?
43. Why do men ask for your phone number or give you theirs and don't call or take your calls?
44. What makes men cry?
45. Why do women work to scare men away?
46. How can I be more open about my sexual preference?

WILL THE REAL MEN PLEASE STAND UP

ARE YOU TOO WEAK FOR WOMEN?

We all have our weaknesses, but many times men allow themselves to get pass the stage of being weak for a woman and they enter the twilight zone of just being an outright fool for a her. If you have let it get out of control, here are sure signs to tell you if you have.

1. You do things that are against the law just to prove to your mate you are going to stick with her no matter what.
2. You meet woman and on the first date she starts telling her how broke she is, so you loan her money to help her out.
3. You believe her when she says she's going to leave her husband for you. Better yet you believe her when she says she's not sleeping with your friend.
4. She has an affair with your best friend and you forgive her, even though she asked him to move in with the two of you.
5. She continuously tells you she's been faithful, but your doctor tells you for the third time you have contracted a sexually transmitted disease.
6. She lets you drive her car, but insist you pay her for using it.
7. She always forgets her wallet when it's time to pay for her items.
8. She gives you jewelry, but she gets it from the pawn shop.
9. She refuses to accept money or gifts from you because she's afraid she might have to do the same for you.
10. When she takes you out, she insist that you bring your best friend along.

MAKING LOVE CONNECTIONS DISCUSSION POINTS

Share ideas with these topics:

Singles clubs, classified ads, churches, internet, nightclubs, volunteer activities.

Pressures on men, male attitudes, pressures on women, female attitudes, men therapy, getting in touch with emotions.

Media images of men, stereotyping,.

Multi-cultural relationships, compatibility, raising children in mixed marriages.

WILL THE REAL MEN PLEASE STAND UP

Relationships that drain your energy, men who are unfaithful, loving yourself, letting go of an abusive relationship, starting over.

Common complaints men have about women. How can men and women work together to improve relationships.

Myths about romance and passion, myths men Tell other men about women, myths women tell other women about men.

How can men better connect with their feelings, how can women help men connect with them, fear men have going into a new relationship.

Family and social pressures that ruin relationships. Single stereotypes placed on people. Being single and complete.

CRAVING COMPLETION DISCUSSION TOPICS

1. What do you make of the idea that it is only when we no longer compulsively need someone that we can ever attempt to build a healthy relationship with them?
2. Of the two topics, which do we encounter more often: (1) I need this person to be complete; or (2) If this person needs me I'll be complete?
3. How willing and comfortable are you to disclose yourself to others and let yourself be known by others? What social masks do you sometimes wear that guard you against being vulnerable? When are you most likely to wear them?
4. On a scale of one to ten, how would you rate your current tendency to delay immediate gratification? If you do this well, what's your secret? If you are striving to do this better how can you improve?

ENDURING FRIENDSHIPS DISCUSSION TOPICS

1. It's been said that we audition to be a friend, but only a few of us make the cut. What is it about your friends that cause them to play the part? Did it have more to do with personal qualities or the circumstances.
2. The medical benefits of having friends is quite remarkable. What benefits do you receive from having friends? What fruits of friendships do you enjoy most?

3. Do you agree that friends come in two forms: as friends of the road and as friends of the heart.
4. What friendship have you had that did not last and why? What purpose did this friendship serve in your life?
5. Forgiveness can be one of the most challenging struggles for any relationship. When was the last time you were on the receiving end of friendship? When was the last time you were on the giving end?
6. There are four qualities of friendship -- loyalty, forgiveness, honesty and dedication -- which is the most important to you and why? What other qualities would you add to the list.

FAILED FRIENDSHIP DISCUSSION TOPICS

1. As you consider friendships that you have lost along the way, are there some that are more important to you than others? If so, why? What makes them valuable to you, and how do you feel about building a connection to them?
2. How can you personally, determine whether a broken relationship should be repaired or not? In other words, how do you decide if your differences are truly irreconcilable or not?
3. When it comes to the practical side of mending a broken relationship with a friend, which of the five steps suggested in this chapter (count the cost, make contact, forgive, diagnose the problem, and rebuild respect) would be the most difficult for you to take and why? What could you do to make taking this step a bit easier?

FALLING IN LOVE DISCUSSION TOPICS

1. In specific terms how would you describe the emotions surrounding infatuation and falling in love? Are they the same thing?

WILL THE REAL MEN PLEASE STAND UP

2. Do you agree that detecting your partner's value can be one of the smartest moves you make while dating? Why or why not? If you believe it is important, how do you go about discovering them?

3. How have you tried to change another person to please you more? And how have you tried to change yourself in dating other people? Do you need to communicate them to the person you are dating? If so how do you do this?

4. Do you know exactly what you are willing to deal with in a dating relationship? Have you determined what you will absolutely not put up with?

WILL THE REAL MEN PLEASE STAND UP

PURPOSE

Knowledge Concepts International Systems, Inc.

Knowledge Concepts International Systems, Inc. as an Educational System is growing and continually bringing people into leadership. The effectiveness of KCES' will, to a large extent, determine your organization's future. Our company is destined to become a premier leader in the programs of unlimited success and personal development. We will give care, attention and professional training and motivation to all people.

Because our company speaks to people from all walks of life, we offer consultations, lectures, seminars and workshops ranging from essential life and personal skills to topics on careers, business and financial management. Workshop topics fall in the following categories:

Motivational/Inspirational	Taking Charge/of Your Life
Goal Setting/Self-Esteem	Career Development Issues
Health and Fitness	Personal Development
Business Development	Educating/Empowering Children
Family/Love Relationships	Stress Management
Leadership Skills	

After deciding to began my businesses, I researched companies that are generally considered to be the best managed companies in our country. I was surprised to find that few companies have developed a handbook explaining their programs for obtaining unlimited success. This manual represents a major effort by Knowledge Concepts International Systems, Inc. to improve standards of personal, professional and social values on all levels to all employees and all companies.

As people and companies grow there are choices. My effort is simple. It is to:
* Empower people and companies through understanding and living principle centered lives.
* Improve and develop new, strong and capable self-motivated employees.
* Help women prepare and make decisions that fit each situation.
* Increase creative leadership abilities and styles in employees.
* Improve leadership skills in supervisory, managerial and employees.
* Stimulate individual and organizational initiative through personal and professional performance.
* Significantly increase the height of personal and professional capabilities in all women.
* Build a positive self-image in all employees, no matter what the problem.
* Help employees realize that there is enough faith within to move mountains if the desire is there.

WILL THE REAL MEN PLEASE STAND UP

I have spent a great deal of time developing a program that would be highly beneficial to companies and their employees. The KCES manual marks the beginning for a companies desired improvement.

If you train and develop well, you help assure a bright future for yourself personally and professionally. With positive self-esteem in companies at every level, in life employees will remain productive encouraged, and excited about every facet of life: professionally and personally.

Since developing this business, employees from all walks of life, and the general public, alike have enjoyed the warmth, humor, and dynamic presentation, style and informative nature of Ella's professional empowerment, and personal development seminars.

About Ella Patterson Companies

Knowledge Concepts Educational Systems (KCES) is dedicated to constantly improving the quality of life for individuals and organizations who truly desire it. KCES, empowers individuals to recognize and utilize unlimited choices. Listed below are just some of the useful resources KCES offers you or your organization. For more information and a complete list of available services and products, please call KCES 1-214-223-1558 or write

Knowledge Concepts Educational Systems, Inc.
P. O. Box 973   Cedar Hill, Texas   75104-0973
Fax: 972-223-1609
EMAIL msreal @big planet.com
Website www.msreal1.com   Website www.ellap .com

TO PLACE AN ORDER CONTACT:

Hervey's Booklink & Cookbook Warehouse
John Hervey, President   214 - 221 - 2711
P. O. Box 831878   Richardson, Texas 75083
www.hervey's.com   hervey's booklink @ AOL.com

WILL THE REAL MEN PLEASE STAND UP

ABOUT THE AUTHOR

Ella Patterson is a pioneer and leader in the field of women's issues, women's studies, and innovative management. She is also known across the world as a motivator, sex-educator and one of the most knowledgeable teachers in the area of personal success and empowerment. She has conducted leadership seminars nationally and internationally, and is the President and CEO of Knowledge Concepts Educational Systems, a leadership development company for all people and companies.

Books, cassettes are available for the training of all employees. She is the author of three other published books. (Will The Real Women Please Stand Up!, 1001 Reasons To Think Positive and Write-To-Publish: A Step By Step Guide To Writing Your Own Book.

Ella Patterson has become recognized for her straight-forward and down-to-earth style on how to develop, and maintain high levels of quality, and personal innovation. She is one of the most informed women on women's issues and motivational techniques for groups of all ages. If you would like to inquire about utilizing Ella Patterson as a consultant, speaker or author appearance for your company, business or group please feel free to contact: Knowledge Concepts Educational Systems at 1-214-223-1558, or by writing to KCES, PO Box 973 Cedar Hill, Texas 75104

Ella Patterson, author, mother, spouse, teacher, coach and motivational speaker present an empowering guide to taking action, taking charge and taking responsibility for your life and your overall success in life. Live a happier and healthier life. Don't wait until you're convinced it's time to live. Become a witness to your own life. Practical and positive thinking, relaxation and distressing is the key. Meditation helps to make your life better. Deal with change. Take action. Take Charge. Take Responsibility. Take Control of your life. Understand Your Life. Honor Your Body. Change the way you think and you'll change the way you feel. Change yourself and your future will change.

INDEX

—A—

Absence, 170
Absentmindedness., 130
Acceptance, 144
Adult education classes, 51
Advice, 122
Affection in public, 126
Afraid to commit, 23
After thought, 265
Age, 8, 149
Agreeable, 65
Alcoholic, 140
Ambiance, 79
American couples, 27
American Couples study, 24, 26
American Society of Plastic and Reconstructive Surgeons., 25
Anger., 144
Animal magnetism magnetism, 50
Appearance, 241
Appreciate her., 123
Appreciate sex, 256
Aromatic Herb's., 227
Art of kissing, 214
Art of touching, 211
Attention., 70
Autonomy, 171

—B—

Background, 135
Bacterial vaginosis, 264
Bargaining., 144
Bath oils., 226
Bath pleasures, 223
bathhouses, 223
Bedroom skills, 254
Being a Bitch, 99
Best Self, 36
betrayal of a relationship, 24
Beyond condoms, 261
Body, 38
Body Images, 198
body massage, 125
Botanical Baths., 226
Boundaries, 44
Brave, 63
Breakfast in bed, 126
Breaking up, 142
Breakups, 25
Breast-obsessed, 24
Bubble baths, 226
Business card strategies, 74
Business development, 274

—C—

Candlelight bath, 225
Carbohydrates, 202
Career crisis., 98
Career development issues, 274
Ceremonial meal, 161
Chancoid, 264
Change, 7
Change your routine, 48
Choosing partners, 117
Circle of friends, 52
Cleanse your mind, 233
Clitoris, 249
Clubs, 73
Co-host, 80
Commit, 23
Commitment, 170
Communicate, 240
Communicating, 42
Communication, 126, 179
Communication problems, 141
Competitiveness., 129
Complete Herbal Guide To Natural Health & Beauty Book By Diann Dancing Buchman, 226
Concentrate, 63
Condom sense, 259
Condoms, 261
Confidence, 124
Conflicts, 170
Control freak, 141
Conversation., 67, 71
Cook, 49
Craziness, 97
Crush., 173
Cutting down on fats, 201
Cytomegalovirus, 264

—D—

Dance, 160
Date for food., 70
Deep tissue massage, 213
Delegate!, 109
Demand, 18
Demonstrate your affection, 171
Dental Dams, 262
Depression, 144
Desert, 51
Desirable., 97
Desperate, 163
Detoxifies, 226

Differences, 136
Disagreement, 44
Disappointments., 170
Discussion topics
Discussions, 43
Distance, 184
Divorce, 25
Dog and pony show, 68
Domination complex., 129
Doormat, 65
Dress appropriate, 64
Drinks, 79, 80
Drug addict, 140
Dysfunctional, 129

—E—

Economic benefits, 86
Effectiveness, 274
Effects of the past., 169
Ella Patterson, 276
Ella Patterson Companies, 275
Embarrass her, 251
Embellish, 39
Emil Ludwig, 215
Emotional baggage, 139
Emotional disputes., 44
Entourage, 76
Equal relationships, 117
Erections, 248
Ex-boyfriends., 98
Exercise, 203, 257
Exercise goals, 205
Exercise, 208
Expectations, 9, 177
Explore, 258
Eyes, 61

—F—

Fake it, 250
Fake orgasm, 28
False chemistry, 177
Family craziness., 99
Family/Love Relationships, 274
Fantasies., 86
Fantasy, 89
Fear, 144
Fears men have, 248
Fellatio, 251
Female Condom, 263
Fillers, 38
Find out more about her, 69
Finger Cots, 262
Fireworks., 176
First move, 59
Fitness, 204
Forbidden Topics., 98
Foreplay, 28, 248

Frank Discussions, 19
Frank Sinatra's, 105
Freak out, 17
Fried Green Tomatoes, 85
Fulfillment, 65
Fun, 209

—G—

Game playing, 89
Gasses, 186
Genital warts, 264
Getting organized., 73
Getting your way, 105, 108
Go out alone, 49
Go slowly, 122
God, 234
Gold digger, 141
Gonorrhea, 264
Good love, 166
Good times, 79
Grateful, 235
Grieving, 144
Guessing game, 78
Guilt, 117

—H—

Hard to get, 65
Healing, 229
Health and fitness, 274
Health priorities, 208
Healthy eating, 199
Healthy love, 181
Heated phone conversations, 125
Hectic schedules, 139
Helpful sex tips, 254
Hepatitis B virus, 264
Herpes simplex virus, 264
Hoard, 39
Hobbies, 40, 73
Hope, 144
Horniness., 172
Hugs, 186
Human immunodeficiency virus, 264
Human paplioma viruses, 264

—I—

Ideal women, 31
Images of a woman, 83
Images of a man, 22
Incompatibility, 139
Independence, 184
Independence., 127
Infatuation, 173
Insecurities, 19
Insensitivity., 130
Intercourse, 27

Interesting, 16
Intermission, 50
Interrogate, 68
Interview, 70
Introduction, 1

—J—

Jealousy, 139
Jitters, 67

—K—

Keeping a job, 141
Kisses, 186
Knowledge Concepts International Systems, Inc, 274
K-Y jelly, 249

—L—

Lack of desire, 28
Lack of intuition., 129
Large breasts, 249
Latex face masks, 263
Latex gloves, 262
Laugh, 241
Leadership skills, 274
Leave him, 71
Life has value, 17
Listener, 64
Locker room, 30
Lonely, 26
Look your best, 64, 77
Louisiana State University Medical Center, 24
Love connections, 270
Love madness, 174
Love signal, 184
Lovemaking, 252, 255
Loyalty, 77

—M—

Make yourself unavailable, 16
Making friends, 6
Making healthier choices, 115
Male tailored activity, 48
Marriage retreat, 169
Master's degrees, 30
Meeting women., how to 46
Men and sexual responsibility, 238
Men only, 77
Mental attitude, 204
Milk baths, 226
Mirror exercise, 125
Mixer method, 267
Money, 49
Money matter, 137
Monogamy, 24
Motivational/Inspirational, 274

Mouth, 62
Move at her pace, 18
Ms. Flirt., 140
Ms. Tease, 140
Ms. Wrong, 138
Multi-orgasmic, 252
Mutual respect, 20
Mystery, 163
Myths about men, 23

—N—

Nasal whine, 38
Neglect 258
   neglect sex, 258
Nervous, 63
Next person, 79
Numbers game, 77

—O—

Obsession., 173
Open Up, 69, 97
Opening lines, 62
Opportunities, 53
Opposite sex, 46
Oral sex, 248
Outlaw spirit, 91
   men, 91
   women, 91
Outrageous acts, 78

—P—

Pace yourself, 17
Pain, 144
Participate, 40
Party, 76
Passionate sex, 254
Pay attention, 68
Pelvic inflammatory disease, 264
Penis size, 248
Perform oral sex, 250
Personal development, 274
Personal growth, 241
Personal Insults, 44
Personal power, 108
Personality, 65
Photographer, 78
Physical attraction, 174
Physical intimacy, 240
Pickup lines, 62
Playboy Report on American Men, 26
Pleasure in bed, 29
Point of view, 45, 66
Poor body image, 199
Poor eyesight., 129
Pornography, 28
Positive change, 7

WILL THE REAL MEN PLEASE STAND UP

Post cards, 114
Prayer, 229
Preoccupied, 256
Presence, 170
Pretend, 18
Priority distortion, 129
Productivity, 7
Professional clubs., 52
Props, 63
Proteins, 202
Provide independence, 16
Psychology Today, 25
Pubic lice, 264
Purpose of KCES, 274
Pursuing men, 85

—Q—

Quality, 90
Quantity., 90
Questions, 66
Quiet time, 241
Quiz, 21

—R—

Read The Papers, 73
Reality, 89
Rebelling, 136
Rebuilding., 144
Relationship Boosters, 122
Relationships, 112
Relaxing baths, 223
Religious organization, 52
Remain neutral, 69
Researcher Shere Hite, 24
Resuming intimacy, 161
Romance, 240
Romance., 16

—S—

Sadness, 144
Salt, 202
Sanctuary., 227
Say hello to women, 48
Scare men off, 87
Secret notes, 125
Security, 170
Selective incompetence, 130
Self-centeredness, 128
Self-delusion., 130
Self-dramatization, 129
Self-improvement, 7
Self-obsession, 129
Self-sufficient, 64
Senses, 225
Sensitive, 27
Serious like., 173

Set your priorities, 208
Sex life, 253, 255
Sex play, 264
Sex with lots of men, 100
Sexual enjoyment, 255
Sexual partners, 88
Sexually confident women, 29
Shame, 117
Share, 19, 136
Shiatsu, 213
Shut up, 67
Shyness, 62
Silence., 130
Simon-Schuster, 276
Sit down dinner, 81
Sleep, 206
Sleep., 208
Small penis, 248
Snacks, 81
Snap decisions, 44
Snuggles, 186
Social gatherings, 76
Soothing bath., 125
Sources, 72
Sovereignty, 171
Speak, 38
Special place, 43
Special time, 43
Spontaneity, 17
Sport, 51
Sports massage, 213
Stamps, 114
Staring, 48
Stationary,, 114
Stay alert, 63
Stay hard, 249
Stimulation, 249
Stress management, 274
Swallow the semen, 251
Swedish, 213
Syphilis, 264

—T—

Table of contents, 73
Taking charge/of your life, 274
Teamwork., 256
Telephone number, 139
Testing your dates, 97
Things that drive men crazy, 130
Things that drive women crazy, 130
Time together, 43
Topics, 268
Tourist, 49
Trade shows, 50
Travel, 53
Trytophan, 207

—U—

Unprotected intercourse, 264
Unusual places, 78
USA Today, 26
Use your resources, 72

—V—

Valentines, 2
Values, 139
View, 257
Violent behavior, 139
Virginia Slims American Women's Opinion Poll, 24
Volunteer, 51

—W—

Walking, 204
Water and Exercise, 201
Weak, 270
Weaknesses, 270
Website, 275
Weekend of romance, 157
What men really want, 248
Will The Real Men...Please Stand Up, 1
Will The Real Women Please Stand Up, 30
William Becker, a professor of religion at Bucknell University, 25
Women who don't call., 93
Women who talk too much, 97
Work a room, 81
Work, 208

—Y—

Yellow pages, 73
Your medical profile., 98

SHOWER COLLECTIONS

You can delight the mother-to-be or the bridal couple and your guests with a collection of favorite recipes, memories and advice for the bride and groom with a Knowledge Concepts Shower Book or Cookbook.

By simply enclosing our collection form and following the step by step process, you can involve everyone in the fun of publishing a favorite book.

Our shower books or cookbooks feature a beautiful shower sentiment in soft colors on a personalized cover. Your book can feature not only recipes but also your guests' special greetings and memories of the couple.

Your party will live on for years with your guests being able to enjoy a collection of everyone's best recipes.

"Marriage is a promise to share on life together"

FAMILY COOKBOOKS

You can easily compile a unique Family Cookbook keepsake with Knowledge Concepts Publishing System. Imagine the value and memories to your children and grandchildren of having a collection of special recipes that were family favorites of past generations.

Your cookbook can be a distinctively personal keepsake with the addition of personal stories, anecdotes or children artwork.

Knowledge Concepts Publishing offers beautiful family cover selections or you can produce your own design to be personalized, bound and laminated on your books.

Family Cookbooks are a perfect family reunion project or a wonderful surprise gift for your family or friend on any special occasion. We guarantee everyone you share your cookbook with will be delighted with your recipe collection.

REUNION DIRECTORY

Allow Knowledge Concepts Publishing to ease the burden from your reunion committee by professionally producing a Knowledge Concepts Customized Directory for your group or reunion.

By including our collection form with your reunion invitation, we can help you compile a directory of your groups names, addresses, memories, and accomplishments.

You may add statistics, trivia, and news events to create a lasting memento of the event.

These projects often fund themselves by offering your participants advertising in your program. Save your efforts for planning and enjoying this event.

CUSTOM PROJECTS

Your group, office, or club will enjoy the team process of publishing a collection of best recipes, poems, or favorite short stories. You may wish to sell your books as a fund raiser or enjoy them as a personal keepsake.

ORDER FORM

Telephone Orders: Call Toll Free 1-(800)-269-6228

Postal Orders: Make check or money order payable to:
Knowledge Concepts Educational Systems
P. O. Box 973 • Cedar Hill, Texas 75104-0973

Please send the following books.

_____ 1. 1000 Reasons To Think $14.95

_____ 2. Will The Real Women Please Stand Up $14.95

_____ 3. For Women Who Live Alone $19.95

_____ 4. Teenage Etiquette Guide $10.95

_____ 5. Basic Hygiene... Do It For Yourself .... $ 9.95

_____ 6. Easy Alternatives For Healthy Eating $12.99

Please rush me copies of the following book(s). I have enclosed the price of each book plus $3.00 per book for shipping and handling cost. I understand that if I am not completely satisfied, I may return the book(s) within 10 days for a full refund. All books must be unblemished to qualify for a full refund. Covers not torn, interior like new. If books are damaged in return process it is the buyers business to collect from the shipper. Please add my name to your mailing lists too, so that I may receive more information on any new books that you have written.

Name:_____

Address:_____

City:_____

State:_____ Zip: _____

Sales tax: *(per order)*
Please add 8.25% for books shipped to Texas addresses.

Shipping Fees:
Book Rate: $3.00 for the first book and $2.00 for each additional book.
(Surface shipping may take three to four weeks)

Air Mail Fees: $4.00 per book

Payment Options:
Check, Cashier's Check or Money Order's please.

Total Amount Enclosed $_____

Your Signature_____

Request for Publishing Information

Please send me a Publishing Planning Package for the following project
- Family Cookbook
- Baby Shower Collection
- Bridal Shower Collection
- Reunion Directory
- Custom Project (Describe below)

_____
_____
_____
_____
_____

Send Materials To:

Name_____

Address_____

City/State_____ Zip_____

Home Phone (_____)_____

I tentatively plan to complete my project by the following date:
_____

Mail To: Knowledge Concepts Publishing
P. O. Box 973
Cedar Hill, Texas 75104-0973
1-800-269-6228